Selling the Kimono

Based on twelve months of in-depth ethnographic research in Japan with retailers, customers, wholesalers, writers and craftspeople, *Selling the Kimono* is a journey behind the scenes of a struggle to adapt to difficult economic conditions and declining demand for the kimono.

The kimono is an iconic piece of clothing, instantly recognised as a symbol of traditional Japanese culture. Yet, little is known about the industry that makes and sells the kimono, in particular the crisis this industry is currently facing. Since the 1970s, kimono sales have dropped dramatically, craftspeople are struggling to find apprentices, and some retailers have closed up shop.

Illuminating recent academic investigations into the lived experience of economic crisis, this volume presents a story of an industry in crisis, and the narratives of hope, creativity and resilience that have emerged in response. The ethnographic depth and theoretical contribution to understanding the effects of economic crisis and the transformation of traditional culture will be of broad interest to students, academics and the general public.

Julie Valk is a Postdoctoral Research Associate at King's College London. She is a social anthropologist who has produced a substantial body of work on the Japanese kimono industry and contemporary kimono culture. Her work has appeared in *HAU: the Journal of Ethnographic Theory* (2020), the *Journal of Material Culture* (2020) and *Fashion Theory* (2018). She has research interests in economic anthropology, the sociology of expertise, financial systems, Japanese society and culture, as well as clothing and fashion.

Routledge Advances in Ethnography
Edited by Dick Hobbs, University of Essex and Les Back, Goldsmiths, University of London

Ethnography is a celebrated, if contested, research methodology that offers unprecedented access to people's intimate lives, their often hidden social worlds and the meanings they attach to these. The intensity of ethnographic fieldwork often makes considerable personal and emotional demands on the researcher, while the final product is a vivid human document with personal resonance impossible to recreate by the application of any other social science methodology. This series aims to highlight the best, most innovative ethnographic work available from both new and established scholars.

21 **Migrant City**
   Les Back and Shamser Sinha

22 **The Logic of Violence**
   An Ethnography of Dublin's Illegal Drug Trade
   Brendan Marsh

23 **Black Men in Britain**
   An Ethnographic Portrait of the Post-Windrush Generation
   Kenny Monrose

24 **Moving Difference**
   Brazilians in London
   Angelo Martins Junior

25 **Selling the Kimono**
   An Ethnography of Crisis, Creativity and Hope
   Julie Valk

For more information about series page, please visit https://www.routledge.com/Routledge-Advances-in-Ethnography/book-series/RETH

Selling the Kimono

An Ethnography of Crisis, Creativity and Hope

Julie Valk

LONDON AND NEW YORK

First published 2021
by Routledge
2 Park Square, Milton Park, Abingdon, Oxon OX14 4RN

and by Routledge
605 Third Avenue, New York, NY 10158

Routledge is an imprint of the Taylor & Francis Group, an informa business

© 2021 Julie Valk

The right of Julie Valk to be identified as author of this work has been asserted by her in accordance with sections 77 and 78 of the Copyright, Designs and Patents Act 1988.

All rights reserved. No part of this book may be reprinted or reproduced or utilised in any form or by any electronic, mechanical, or other means, now known or hereafter invented, including photocopying and recording, or in any information storage or retrieval system, without permission in writing from the publishers.

Trademark notice: Product or corporate names may be trademarks or registered trademarks, and are used only for identification and explanation without intent to infringe.

British Library Cataloguing-in-Publication Data
A catalogue record for this book is available from the British Library

Library of Congress Cataloging-in-Publication Data
A catalog record has been requested for this book

ISBN: 978-0-367-48213-8 (hbk)
ISBN: 978-0-367-49498-8 (pbk)
ISBN: 978-1-003-03869-6 (ebk)

Typeset in Times New Roman
by Newgen Publishing UK

This book is dedicated to my wonderful mother,
Jennifer Griffith, for all her love and support.

Contents

List of figures	viii
Preface	ix
Acknowledgements	xii
A note on Japanese orthography and names	xiv
A note on website links and currency conversions	xv

1	Kimono in crisis? The paradox of contemporary kimono culture	1
2	The kimono and the kimono industry	22
3	The rise of the formal kimono in the post-war years: selling status and commercialising knowledge	48
4	The path of resilience: weathering the economic crisis and managing public perceptions	70
5	Azumaya: the 'nail that stuck up so far that no one could hammer it down'	88
6	The kimono as fashion: lifestyle, taste and individuated consumption	111
7	New directions: second-hand retail and new business models	135
8	Crisis and hope interwoven: the future of the kimono industry	158

Glossary of Japanese terms	173
Index	178

Figures

1.1	The Gotō family's second-hand shop in a shopping mall, one of four owned by the family	3
1.2	Main field sites	14
2.1	Kyoko's kimono and obi (front)	26
2.2	Kyoko's kimono and obi (back)	27
2.3	Differences between women's and men's kimono	29
2.4	Kimono structure	31
2.5	Distribution in the kimono industry	43
3.1	Kaga Yūzen hōmongi (formal kimono)	50
3.2	Detail from a *kurotomesode* (formal kimono usually reserved for the mother of the bride or groom at a wedding)	51
3.3	Kaga Yūzen panel depicting plum, bamboo and pine, a traditional trio of auspicious plants on a sliding door in a guest house run by the accommodation manager Comingle Co.	53
4.1	*Ōshima tsumugi* specialist Tetsuya Ueda showing *tanmono* ('bolts') of the fabric which is particularly prized for its lengthy and labour-intensive production process	81
5.1	Azumaya shop front in early summer	89
5.2	Shibakawa-san's father, Kazuyoshi Shibakawa, in the process of cutting and preparing a cotton bolt for the seamstress	100
5.3	Shibakawa-san replaces the *hanao* (straps) on a pair of *zori* shoes	101
5.4	Azumaya shop front viewed from inside the shop	104
5.5	The Shibakawa family at work	105
6.1	Tetsuya Ueda in the headquarters of Masugi	114
6.2	Writer, designer and stylist Ima Kikuchi	118
6.3	Fujii Shibori wares	120
6.4	Takashi dressed in a kimono with a long *haori* (kimono overcoat)	131
7.1	A Tansu-ya shop front	136
7.2	Craftspeople at work in Some Kōbō Yu	147
7.3	The central pink honeysuckle pattern on the obi made for me by Some Kōbō Yu	150
7.4	Chiesu brand *hanhaba* (half-width) obi	152
7.5	Chiesu brand kimono and obi	153

All photos, maps and diagrams are the work of the author unless otherwise stated.

Preface

The simplest way to address the question of where this idea for this book came from would be to say that it is based on my doctoral fieldwork, conducted over the course of twelve months in 2015 and 2016, and my thesis. But this book is, in fact, the product of a long process of reformulation of that original fieldwork. Above all else, this book is the result of long-lasting collaborative relationships with a wide range of retailers, designers, producers, wholesalers and customers in the Japanese kimono industry.

My first experience of wearing a kimono was in 2008. In my very early 20s at the time, I was studying Japanese at Nanzan University, and I was living with my host family in Toyota – the same family who would welcome me back to live with them during my doctoral research seven years later. My host mother, Sachiko, had welcomed countless foreign female students from Nanzan, and she dressed each one in a kimono. A lifelong tea ceremony practitioner and kimono aficionado, this was one of her favourite ways of having her guest experience Japanese culture. For me, however, this was a formative moment. Never had I experienced a form of dress so complex and time-consuming, and so different from what I was used to. It would be some years before I was to undertake serious research into the kimono, but that moment stayed with me.

I first stepped into a kimono shop in 2012, when I returned to Japan and worked in Kanazawa for two years. From my initial fascination with the kimono itself, I became curious about the industry. Who makes the kimono? Who sells the kimono? How well is the industry doing? Kimono retail appeared to be a world that was both part of Japan's capitalist economy and, at the same time, one step removed from it, with its own conventions, structure and rules. It is a world largely unknown, especially outside of Japan, but even within the archipelago, where relatively few people get to see the inner workings of the industry. And it is an industry facing significant difficulties: deeply impacted by the economic crisis of the 1990s, it has been facing a steady decline in sales and revenue.

As this book explores in detail, by the late 20th century the formal kimono had become the standard form for Japan's national dress. However, at the same time, demand for it was falling as Western clothing became more and more accepted for ceremonial and ritual occasions such as weddings, funerals and graduation ceremonies. As a result, the business model of the industry based on formal kimono was therefore less and less lucrative. And yet, what really struck me and ultimately motivated me to write this book was the resilience and creativity of those in the industry, and their capacity to hope in the face of crisis. My doctoral thesis focused, for the most part, on the transition from formal kimono to fashion kimono in the late 20th and early 21st century, exploring the socio-economic and cultural reasons for this shift: the 1990s economic crisis significantly impacted disposable incomes and spending practices, just as attitudes changed towards ritual life in Japan and the appropriate attire for ritual life. But in the two years following the completion of my thesis, and in my continued conversations with my research participants, I reflected more deeply on the mechanisms behind these changes, beyond their immediate socio-economic and cultural causes. It appeared to me that there was an apparently paradoxical relationship between economic crisis and hope, and that this complicated relationship has spurred the creativity with which a section of the kimono industry has reinvented its business model and carved out new markets.

Because crisis has the ability to force people to do things differently or look for new avenues to explore, for kimono makers and sellers, this has been expressed in new ways of making and selling the kimono. In doing so, the act of adapting to economic conditions has profound and transformative effects on the nature of traditional Japanese culture itself, potentially re-inventing the role of the kimono in Japanese society. Traditional culture, exemplified in artefacts such as the kimono, is often thought of as immutable or at least slow to change and evolve, but in fact this is not always the case. By situating traditional culture within the economic conditions of its production, we can develop a more nuanced understanding of the ways in which traditional culture changes and evolves to adapt to periods of crisis, but also to broader socio-economic and cultural change.

This book is a testimony to the ways in which the negative forces of crisis, with all their destructive potential, can have a complex relationship with hope and creativity. Little did I know, however, as I began the process of writing this book in late 2019, that a new and different crisis was on the horizon. As I completed my first draft in early March 2020, the extent to which Covid-19 was going to affect our world was only just becoming apparent. Even now, as the book goes into production in March 2021, the world is only at the initial stages of assessing what the long-term effects of the Covid-19 pandemic will be. For the writing of this book, the crisis of Covid-19 certainly pushed the limits of my creativity and resourcefulness. A planned trip to Japan in April 2020 for a long-awaited reunion with research participants to obtain updated data on their situation naturally was first postponed, then cancelled altogether. I feared for the health and safety of my participants, as they feared for mine. To collaborate on the completion of this book, we improvised meetings online and over the phone, and in some cases through letters. My participants reacted with the wonderful creativity and adaptability that I witnessed them use in their businesses. They recounted the travails of Covid-19 through video, wrote pages of updates to their business via email, and discussed details of the book over the phone. While my preference, and theirs, I think, would have been to see each other in person, I have never been so thankful for technology. This book, in its own modest way, is itself a story of creativity in the face of crisis, or at least the ways in which difficulty prompts creative problem-solving. I could see the same resilience, creativity and hope that is the subject of this book in the way that my participants responded to Covid-19, but there is, at this stage, little doubt that Covid-19 will impact the Japanese economy, including the kimono industry, further deepening the slump in sales. Some of my participants have stepped up their online sales to cope with the absence of in-person customers, and in this way weathered the worst of the crisis in the spring of 2020. For others, the financial blow has been more severe.

Covid-19, then, is a spectre that hangs over this book, much as it does over our day-to-day lives at the beginning of 2021. As I recount the ways in which the kimono industry has adapted to a past economic crisis, focusing on narratives of creativity, hope and resilience, I am keenly aware of the unfolding crisis and the effects that it will have on my participants. While I have already been privy to some stories of how my participants approached this crisis, and I allude to these stories in parts of this book, I have kept my focus on how they survived the economic crisis of the 1990s and were continuing to adapt their business models to falling sales at the time of my fieldwork. It is too early to gauge what the longer-term effects of the pandemic on the kimono industry will be. I can only imagine that this new, challenging crisis will bring about significant difficulties – but nonetheless I am hopeful. As this book details, hope and crisis are old friends for the kimono industry, and my academic hypothesis, as well as my own personal hope, is that the same resilience, hope and creativity that I describe in this book will serve the kimono industry as well in the challenges ahead.

And, perhaps, once the storm is weathered, kimono culture will be transformed once again.

Acknowledgements

This book is the culmination of a six-year process in which, certainly, I was the researcher and the writer, but many hands and many voices have shaped the final result, and there are countless people whom I would like to thank for their time, input and generosity.

The first person I would like to acknowledge is my father, William Valk. My father never got to see my doctoral thesis on which this book is based, as he died in September 2014, not long before I was due to start my research. He gave me his blessing before he passed away, and I have carried it with me since. I used his camera and his voice recorder during my fieldwork, and with his blessing in my heart and the devices he owned in my hands, he was very much a part of my research.

I would also like to thank my mother, Jennifer Griffith, for her unfailing love and support throughout this project, and for being a truly outstanding proofreader. My mother was present during parts of my research in Japan and, having met some of my research participants, she is also very much a part of this project. My brother, Max Valk, came to Japan as well and met my research participants, and for his staunch support of my work I am also grateful. For my partner Nawar Noori's love, support and willingness to read over my drafts I am also thankful.

Many academics have had a hand in helping me shape this book. As it is based on my doctoral thesis, I would like to thank my supervisor Dr Inge Daniels for the many hours she spent reading drafts of my thesis and advising me on how to improve my work; Dr Daniels remains an inspiration for me as an academic. I would also like to thank Professor Roger Goodman for his long-standing support of my work and his excellent input together with that of Dr Joanne Entwistle as my thesis examiners. Their feedback provided the critical input necessary for its transformation into a fully fledged academic monograph. Professor Rebecca Empson also gave me helpful advice in the initial stages of writing my book which proved essential in shaping my theoretical contribution to discussions of crisis, hope and creativity. I would also like to thank Professor Susanne Kuechler for her support as my mentor during my post-doctorate at University College London. For always having a kind word of encouragement at the ready and the best advice, I am also thankful to Dr Maria Șalaru.

I am deeply grateful to all my research participants for their willingness to share their lives and their stories with me, for allowing me into their homes and places of business, and for taking the time to give me a flavour of what it is like to make and sell the kimono in 21st century Japan. There are too many to name them all here, but I hope to have done justice to them all in this book. In particular, I would like to thank Sachiko for being a generous host during my year of fieldwork in Japan, and for the kindness and generosity she has shown me for over a decade. Kyoko and Takashi, also featured in this book, became wonderful friends to me during my fieldwork, and without them I would not have accessed a great many field sites and research participants; for their enthusiasm and their friendship I am deeply grateful. The Gotō family, appropriately featured at the start of this book, were the first kimono shop owners to speak to me about the industry, and were happy to do so even though I simply walked into their shop with no introduction: I owe them many thanks. I am very grateful, too, to the Shibakawa family for always making time for me during their busy working hours, and always letting me do some 'deep hanging out' at their shop, Azumaya (see Chapter 5). Also featured in this book are the Kanamaru family, the Yamada family, Kenichi Nakamura and Nakasaka-san whom I thank profusely for their generosity, time and kindness. I would also like to thank Professor Akira Gotō (no relation to the Gotō family) and the Anthropological Institute at Nanzan University for hosting me as a visiting scholar during my year of fieldwork.

Finally, the research and writing of this book was generously supported by different funding bodies at different stages. The funding provided by the Clarendon Fund and the Economic and Social Research Council made it possible for me to undertake a DPhil at the University of Oxford. The Japan Society for the Promotion of Science supported my 12 months of fieldwork in Japan, and the Great Britain Sasakawa Foundation has supported my research on several occasions, including my fieldwork, supporting the invitation of my research participant and kimono shop owner Yoshihide Shibakawa to give a talk in the University of Oxford in November 2017, and finally for the research visit to Japan that in the end was cancelled due to the Covid-19 pandemic. Lastly, I am thankful for the support of the Economic and Social Research Council, in funding the postdoctoral Fellowship during which much of the writing of this book was completed.

A note on Japanese orthography and names

In this book, I have used the Hepburn romanisation system to render Japanese words into English. Japanese words which are not in common usage in English are in italics. As there is no plural form in Japanese words, all Japanese words are in the singular, even when there is more than one (for example, 'there are many kimono'). Macrons are used to indicate long vowels.

With regard to names, it is an accepted convention in books written in English about Japanese people to adopt the Japanese convention of writing last name + first name. After some consideration, I have chosen to write Japanese names as first name + last name. This is due to several factors. Firstly, to ensure consistency when citing both Japanese and non-Japanese authors: both are always introduced as first name + last name, and thereafter by last name only, as is most widely accepted. Secondly, some of the people featured in this book are public figures, and they have themselves chosen to render their names publicly as first name + last name, so for consistency purposes I have kept this convention throughout the book. Once introduced, most of the people in this book are referred to as last name + san, as would be typical in Japanese, but there are some exceptions, which I have made efforts to point out and explain when they appear. The result is, I hope, not too confusing. As anthropologists are quick to note, systems of language and naming conventions are patterned onto our wonderfully complex modes of interaction, and I have attempted to be as faithful to the ethnographic reality of my research as possible – inconsistencies and all.

A note on website links and currency conversions

All website links functioned correctly at the time of publication.

Currency conversions are provided for the sole purpose of giving the reader a sense of monetary value. Conversions from Japanese yen to British pounds are estimates and will be subject to variation along with the fluctuation of the market.

Chapter 1

Kimono in crisis?
The paradox of contemporary kimono culture

A morning in April

The house is beautiful. Certainly among the grandest I have seen in Japan.

Gotō-san is decked out immaculately in a kimono as she welcomes us on the doorstep, this time a subtle shade of sea green that suits her complexion. As always with Gotō-san, wearing a kimono looks effortless.

Gotō-san puts on a royal welcome. She conducts an impromptu tea ceremony, speaks knowledgeably of every plant and flower in the garden and shows us exquisite rooms in the house. For some time, she had promised to show me their house and old kimono shop in Gifu prefecture, but she is even more eager to do so as my mother is with me, visiting Japan.

I had first met Gotō-san some five months earlier in one of the second-hand kimono shops belonging to her family in the centre of Toyota city, where I lived for twelve months in 2015–2016. With many years of experience in kimono retail, at that time she was still working in the shop with her son. I quickly learned that the shop did more than sell second-hand kimono: it was also a source of advice on kimono cleaning, re-dyeing, re-stitching, outfit coordination, sewing, and many other things – in other words, the same services a regular kimono shop would provide. Most customers came specifically to seek her advice, or that of her son, who had spent many years working in a company in Kyoto specialising in dyed kimono. Their combined knowledge of the kimono was detailed and delivered with enthusiasm, something appreciated by their customers. As a result, a notice board on the wall announced the times she and her son would be in the shop, so people knew when to come to get the advice that they needed.

Her son, whom I met first, had allowed me to work in their shop once a week on Saturdays, where I helped with small tasks such as folding kimono and obi (sashes which are wrapped around the body), and interacting with customers. In the course of the three months or so that I spent there, I learned that the Gotō family had not always worked in the second-hand business – they had an established kimono shop that had been in the family for 120 years in the neighbouring prefecture of Gifu. The family head was Gotō-san's husband, but at the time when I got to know the family, she and her son ran the business.

2 The paradox of contemporary kimono culture

Kimono are most often bespoke. In a standard kimono shop, the customer usually first purchases a bolt of cloth, known as *tanmono* in Japanese, which is then tailored to fit the customer. Kimono shops – *gofukuya* – are more like cloth shops than clothes shops in that respect. Because bolts are constantly unravelled, held up against the customer for them to get a sense of what the flowing fabric would look like as a kimono, and then rolled up again, the skill to unravel and roll up a bolt quickly and efficiently is indispensable.

Gotō-san explains to my mother and myself that, for most of her working life, much of the purchase of stock with wholesalers and interaction with customers has been left to her, and indeed she appears every inch the queen of her domain in the family home.

'I know everything,' she says, and it doesn't come off as boastful. 'Every bolt of cloth, every taste or distaste that the client has. All the prices, all the colours, all the types. I know it all.'

She opens a large sliding door to reveal an in-built storage wall filled with bolts of kimono cloth. Her fingers hover for a moment before she chooses the one she wants to show us. She picks a fine-woven, yellow silk bolt. The pattern is simple and subtle, but the bolt itself is expensive. Many established regional weaving and dyeing techniques in Japan produce items that are relatively plain in appearance, but the complexity and time-consuming nature of their production push up the price.

Pieces made by craftspeople designated as *dentō kōgeishi* ('masters of traditional craft') by the Ministry of Economy, Trade and Industry can cost several thousand pounds, although this varies widely. Formal kimono worn for ceremonial occasions, and statement pieces made using special regional craft, made the fortunes of kimono shops in the 1970s and 80s. But nowadays, these bolts are not sought after as avidly as they were.

Gotō-san smiles as she lays an obi sash across the kimono cloth to see the effect of colours and patterns combined. Pairing the right kimono with the right obi is one of the essential facets of kimono styling and wearing, and something that Gotō-san is skilled at. More than that, she enjoys it.

The shop itself is attached to the big, beautiful house, which is listed on the town's webpage as a site of cultural interest. As with many kimono shops, fewer customers come through its doors these days.

'We had three generations of customers, but it's hard to sell now. Our customers tell us that they have too many kimono, that they are spilling out of their *tansu*![1] That's why we started opening second-hand shops in 2008.'

The Gotō family had carefully nurtured their customers over the years, establishing relationships with local families that spanned generations. But the Gotō family were realists: they looked at the sharply declining kimono market and recognised that formal kimono with their expensive price tags were simply not selling as they used to. Gotō-san's husband had a keen interest in economics, which he discussed with me on a couple of occasions over a coffee. Informed by their understanding of the broader economic context, the family

Figure 1.1 The Gotō family's second-hand shop in a shopping mall, one of four owned by the family.

had sought alternatives that would utilise the family's expertise, connections in the industry and the know-how built over the decades.

So the family opened four second-hand kimono shops, inviting locations peppered with friendly, hand-written notes (see Figure 1.1). But business has remained difficult, as it is for many kimono retailers: attracting and keeping customers is challenging, and with fewer people buying kimono in Japan the market continues to shrink. As with many shops that invite customers to browse, footfall may increase but while this may mean that people pop in to take a look, they do not necessarily buy anything.

In the years since 2016, the family has continued to show resilience in the face of difficulty. Even though the family head, Gotō-san's husband, has sadly passed away and Gotō-san herself no longer comes to work in the second-hand shops, her son runs the business and his wife populates their new Instagram feed with outfits put together from items in the shops. The family faces the anxiety of belonging to an industry in crisis with quiet dignity. Their outlook is summed up in the words of the late Gotō senior, who once said to me with a wry smile: 'We grit our teeth and carry on'.

An afternoon in March

It is unseasonably warm for March. The morning's torrential rain would seem like a dream had it not left its signature humidity as proof of its passage through Aichi prefecture.

People with a very particular hobby are converging on the Nagoya Agricultural Centre. This is today's chosen venue for a gathering of the Aichi division of Kimono de Jack[2] (hereafter KdJ for short). They are from different walks of life, but they all have the same aim in mind: to wear a kimono, and to wear it with style. Two of these people are a married couple, Kyoko and Takashi,[3] with whom I am attending the event. Kyoko was introduced to me through a friend in Toyota, where I lived, and she works part-time in the kimono shop Azumaya (see Chapter 5 and 6). Kyoko and her husband both dress in kimono for KdJ outings, but also for social and cultural events. In Japan today, the kimono is typically worn for formal events – coming of age ceremonies at age 20, weddings, graduation ceremonies, tea ceremonies, funerals, and so on. As a result, kimono are classified according to levels of formality and appropriateness for ceremonies. The objective of the people coming to KdJ is different. Like Kyoko and Takashi, they dress to impress. Outfits are planned, carefully, sometimes over the course of years, with accessories such as obi sashes, obi decoration, inner collars (*haneri*) and *tabi* socks acquired meticulously to put together a finished outfit. As I was later to learn, this is a hobby that requires thought, planning and financial investments.

Some make a point of being deliberately understated, while others claim to wear the kimono every day, having forsaken Western clothes completely. Some are weekend wearers. Others might be wearing a kimono for the first time, usually betrayed by their nervous demeanour and slightly awkward appearance. The kimono is not the most forgiving garment: to the trained eye, minor mistakes and a less than smooth appearance immediately reveal the wearer's level of familiarity with the garment.

KdJ members speak of being *kinarete iru* – this means 'being used to wearing a kimono'. *Kinarete iru* refers not only to being used to wearing the kimono but also of giving the impression of being used to the kimono. That sense of effortlessness, of having 'tamed' the kimono, as if it were an alien being, is conveyed through the skill with which the kimono is worn, the aesthetic choices (often discussed and commented on at length) that are made. A person's level of comfort with the kimono is detectable through the ease with which they walk, sit or stand. Being able to give off an aura of ease and confidence is something which all members aspire to, consciously or not.

On this day, I am one of the nervous ones. I haven't worn the kimono very much, not at this stage in my fieldwork, and my discomfort shows. So too does my tall, white, blond foreignness. But Kyoko, Takashi and their friends act as kind and protective guardians to me, as they do with all beginners, ready with advice, ready with accessories to lend or give to me, and ready to defend to others my awkward choice of dress. As we move through the Nagoya Agricultural Centre, peering into pens holding various breeds of chickens and their small fluffy yellow chicks, people aren't really taking in the agriculture. They are watching each other.

What are you wearing? How are you wearing it? Are you wearing it well? What colours and what accessories do you choose? Were they expensive? Is it a brand I know? Where did you get them, and more importantly, where can *I* get them? Kyoko was later to tell me, when she had fondly made matching pairs of *tabi* socks for herself and for me, that even if you were 'bursting with the need to show people, you still had to wait for them to notice'. We had worn our matching *tabi* on another occasion when we were out in kimono together. Dutifully, I waited, as I was instructed. In due course, someone noticed the purple cat Kyoko had stamped on my *tabi*. I watched her grin, and the grin spread on my face too. She was right – it was satisfying to have waited. Better, to have been noticed.

Kimono de Jack holds six gatherings a year, one every two months. Participation is free, and events are specially chosen to allow participants to move freely within venues that, in the vast majority of cases, do not charge. The idea developed as a way to give people an opportunity to wear kimono, and to stir a wish within onlookers to wear it too. The formula is always the same: you can come when you like, you can leave whenever you like. The organisers take two group photos at different times so as to make sure that people arriving late or leaving early do not miss a photo opportunity. They also do a headcount to see how many people came to the event. One of the photos will always feature the Jack members lifting a fist as they say 'Jakku da!' ('We are Jack!'). The other will feature participants lined up with their left foot slightly forward (to show off their *zori* shoes and *tabi* socks).

The success of the Aichi division of KdJ has much to do with its leader, Yoshihide Shibakawa. Shibakawa-san owns Azumaya, the kimono shop where Kyoko works, located about 40 minutes southwest of Toyota in the small town of Nishio (see Chapters 5 and 6). Although Shibakawa-san himself prefers not to mix his life as a retailer with his activities in KdJ, some of the members are Azumaya customers, and those that aren't will know of Azumaya. Azumaya doesn't stock many bolts like the special silk one Gotō-san showed me and my mother. Instead, the ones they stock are more likely to be colourful, cheaper and made of cotton.

Like the home of the Gotō family, Azumaya is both family home and kimono shop. After a KdJ event, it is common for kimono-clad members to descend on Azumaya for an after-party. On one occasion after a KdJ gathering, a core group of about 15 members flocked to the shop, even though it was about 40 minutes away from the KdJ venue. On arrival, the group proceeded to peruse Shibakawa-san's items, sit around and chat and joke with Shibakawa-san.

This, I must add here, is unusual in a kimono shop. Kimono shops are normally quite formal affairs that are typically not conducive to relaxed, informal conversation or casual browsing. In atmosphere, they are not dissimilar to boutiques selling high-end branded goods. The days of KdJ events and visits to Azumaya end happily, often in a local *izakaya* (Japanese pub).

The kimono paradox

Throughout the 12 months of fieldwork that I undertook in Japan between 2015 and 2016, my first goal was to understand how the kimono industry worked. This was not an easy task – the industry itself, apart from the shops which are more visible, is largely a hidden world in Japan, one which relatively few people know about. With patience and some lucky encounters characteristic of fieldwork serendipity, I began to get to know people working in the industry, and the whole flavour of my fieldwork changed.

Different as each business owner was, the story everywhere was the same: the industry was in crisis. People were not buying kimono, or at least, not as they used to back in the 1970s and 1980s. The refrain I heard repeatedly was, 'at this rate, we won't last ten years'.

To a reader unacquainted with the kimono, this might seem puzzling. The kimono enjoys a high level of recognition both inside and outside Japan as the ultimate symbol of Japanese femininity, an unparalleled ambassador for Japanese taste and aesthetics. The kimono continues to captivate, and the iconic image of the kimono-clad woman often circulates in the media both inside and outside Japan. The kimono's visibility and reputation do not predispose an outsider to think of an industry in crisis. Why, then, are its members so concerned?

In the post-war period, the kimono underwent a process of formalisation, with the kimono increasingly reserved for ceremonies and ritual events such as graduation or coming of age ceremonies, weddings and funerals, among others. The post-war kimono industry had made its fortune selling expensive silk kimono and obi used primarily for such formal occasions. Gotō-san's customers are not wrong when they say they have *too many* kimono. Nakamura Kenichi, the managing director of a chain of second-hand kimono shops named Tansu-ya, told me in an interview that, according to an estimate he had made, there are roughly 800 million kimono and obi 'sleeping' (*nemutte iru*, as they are said to be in Japanese) in their *tansu* (see Chapter 7). Of these, he guesses, about 10 per cent might be used occasionally. An excess of kimono exists in Japan, fuelled by high sales between the 1960s and 1980s, but the kimono as formal wear is now selling far less well than it used to. This narrative of crisis and difficulty was omnipresent, and yet there was a confusing countervailing force at work.

In events such as KdJ gatherings, there seemed to be a budding kimono culture that was very much alive, a culture based on lifestyle in which the goal was not to present yourself and your family well at a ceremony or ritual, but rather to express yourself and showcase your own style. The attendees of KdJ were varied in their backgrounds, ages and occupations, and their purchases too were varied. Among the people who had adopted a 'kimono lifestyle' were some who bought bespoke kimono in standard kimono shops, but there were also second-hand kimono enthusiasts and those who experimented with combining kimono and Western clothes – something that goes against standard kimono aesthetics. For yet more, the kimono is something they collect, obsessively in some cases; they blog about their own particular 'style', inspiring others to imitate them. I saw a culture that was very much alive, and, strikingly for a so-called 'traditional' garment, this culture was one which belonged to the world of fashion, consumption and lifestyle, a world in which traditional dress is typically considered irrelevant. I would not suggest that the kimono does not count as 'fashion'. The argument that the kimono is, and has always been, closely linked to fashion, has been made ably by other scholars (Francks 2015, Cliffe 2017) but there remains a strong perception that the aesthetics and codes that govern traditional clothing more generally speaking are frozen in time, or at least change at a slow pace, and are not subject to the ever-changing whims of fashion in the same way that the globalised, mass-produced clothing industry is.

From seeking to simply understand how this little-known industry functioned, my attention was tugged towards an apparent paradox: a kimono culture that appeared to be both in crisis and very much alive. To solve this paradox, it became crucial to grasp not only the cultural changes that affected how the kimono is worn and by whom, but also to understand the people who make, market and sell the kimono. The ways in which they choose to retail the kimono change the nature of the kimono itself. This book is born out of this paradox, and explores the lived experience of what it means for a traditional industry such as kimono-making to be 'in crisis'. This crisis takes the shape of falling sales, the result of a broader economic recession in Japan, and customer tendencies to shift away from the expensive, made-to-order kimono purchases that retailers relied upon fairly consistently in the post-war period. But I was also driven by the wish to portray the many-layered nature of contemporary kimono culture, pun intended, and show that there is more to the kimono than the staid image of a 'traditional' Japanese woman, or a geisha, with which the kimono remains stubbornly associated in Western imaginations. The kimono is undoubtedly an ambassador for a certain image of Japan: refined, intricate, elegant, and unmistakably feminine,[4] but the agents of its creation, craftspeople, retailers and wholesalers, remain largely unknown, as do the challenges that they currently face. Instead, the kimono tends to be associated either with geisha, or with controversies surrounding the appropriate use of the kimono which appear in the news on a regular basis. Accusations of cultural appropriation levelled at the Boston Museum of Fine Arts for their much-debated use of a kimono replica, based on Monet's painting of *La Japonaise*, in 2015 were plastered over Western media, but left many Japanese people quite indifferent (Valk 2015).

A key purpose of this book, then, is to situate the kimono firmly in its home context through detailed ethnographic work, and provide an inside look into an industry which is both in crisis and undergoing tremendous change. Traditional culture, particularly traditional clothing, is often examined primarily from a cultural or historical perspective separate from the economic processes of production and distribution that govern its creation. However, by investigating the lives, struggles and hopes of insiders in the industry we can see how the generation of kimono culture is intimately linked to those who create, market and sell kimono, making them agents of both economic and cultural production. Further, this book investigates an industry facing either inevitable decline or radical change from the perspective of those whose livelihoods hang in the balance. The example of the kimono industry suggests that economic crisis is not necessarily a purely negative phenomenon – the disruptive nature of crisis breeds adaptability, resilience and creativity in the 'survivors' of the crisis, and for others it also provides an opportunity to hope for a different future for the kimono.

Crisis and hope

Now, if you wanted to play devil's advocate, you might be tempted to ask: why does this matter? Why might the fate of the kimono industry be important? The cold, unfeeling answer is that, as a retailer in my research bluntly put it, 'Japan will be just fine if the kimono disappears'. Certainly, the country will not cease to function if the kimono vanishes. However, from the perspective of cultural heritage, it is self-evident that Japan has much to lose in terms of the sheer range of techniques of weaving, dyeing, sewing and embroidery connected to the production of the kimono. In addition to the wealth of cultural and symbolic significance encoded in the kimono's patterns, colours and shape (Dalby 2001: 7), the kimono also maps the history and transformation of the Japanese state itself, changing from everyday wear before the Meiji Restoration in 1868 to formal wear in the post-war period. The kimono documents shifting conventions and national sartorial choices, reflecting the gradual Westernisation of Japanese mores, aesthetics and fashions. The kimono's ability to represent and encapsulate Japanese culture is linked to the role it plays in Japanese ceremonial and ritual life, but is also due to the kimono's symbiotic link to Japanese traditional arts, such as tea ceremony, flower arranging, Noh and Kabuki theatre, as well as religious dress in both Buddhism and Shintoism. For each of these 'types' of kimono, ceremonial or religious, there is a specific branch of the industry with its own craftspeople, retailers and wholesalers. From a cultural perspective, much is at stake, but so are the livelihoods of those involved in its production and distribution within an industry that is largely invisible both to the public eye and within academic scholarship.

My research participants were often deeply aware of the fragility of their livelihoods. Many could quote the figures representing how the market size shrank from its heyday in the 1970s to 2016 off the top of their heads. The banking crisis of the early 1990s caused a large number of retailers and wholesalers to close, and the ongoing downturn since the 1990s has significantly reduced demand for the kimono, particularly the bespoke, expensive kimono worn by women for ceremonial occasions that was the mainstay of kimono sales in the post-war period. For the last two decades of the 20th century it became increasingly acceptable to wear formal Western clothes for ceremonial events such as graduation ceremonies, tea ceremonies, weddings and funerals among others. Prior to this, wearing a kimono was considered to be the best form of dress for ceremonial wear for women (Goldstein-Gidoni 1999, Dalby 2001). In addition, customs that reliably delivered large sales of kimono have also declined dramatically in popularity from the 1970s onwards. One such custom, the mass purchase of kimono to give to a daughter about to get married as part of her bridal trousseau, consistently brought about purchases of kimono throughout the year, but today this custom has all but faded into non-existence (see Chapter 3). Socio-cultural change relating to ceremonial and ritual life in Japan, as well as economic factors, have created significant difficulties for the industry.

The 1970s represented the peak of sales and demand, according to my research participants. This is corroborated by figures from market research conducted by the Yano Research Institute, which reveal that the domestic kimono market has shrunk to 271 billion yen in 2017.[5] A press release from the Yano Research Institute in June 2020 estimated that the market in 2019 would further shrink to 260.5 billion yen. As a result of the Covid-19 pandemic, the market for 2020 was forecast to fall to around 238 billion yen.[6] In 1981, however, the market size was 1800 billion yen (Donzé and Fujioka 2018: 258). The Nishijin weaving district in Kyoto, famed for its silk brocade obi, once one of the most productive and lucrative production sites in Japan, has seen its sales plummet: sales in 2008 were around 20 per cent of what they were in 1990 (Moon 2013: 73), a dramatic decrease in the space of a decade, reflecting the ongoing impact of the economic crisis of the 1990s. These figures, reports of closures and declining sales were confirmed by my research on the ground; a representative from a *tonya* ('wholesaler') in Kyoto told me of the firm's survival while prestigious *tonya* folded all around them in the 1990s (as I explain in more detail in Chapter 4). At the same time, craftspeople informed me that it is now difficult for their children to follow in their footsteps because it would be so hard for them to make a living. Everyone I met in the industry was preoccupied with the fate of their business and the sustainability of the industry more generally speaking. A kimono designer told me that 'we have to get young people interested in buying the kimono. At this rate, the industry won't last two or three years, let alone ten'.

This sense of crisis is of course not unique to the kimono retail industry. Crises of all kinds, financial, social, demographic, culture and environmental, have been part of the national discourse in Japan for decades, with the result that a pervasive sense of hopelessness, in particular economic hopelessness, has become the norm (Kavedžja 2016). The confident optimism of the 1970s and the heady consumerism of the 1980s has been replaced by the pessimism of the post-1990s economic crisis and the 'lost decades' of financial instability and growing unemployment (Fletcher and von Staden 2013, Funabashi and Kushner 2015). Masahiro Yamada has famously described Japan as a *kibō kakusa shakai*, a 'hope/expectation differential society' in which neoliberal policies caused spiralling social inequality, separating people into those who either 'win' or 'lose' at the game of life – in terms of securing employment and marriage, both seen as key to a Japanese version of the 'good life', as indeed they are in many places (Yamada 2004). 'People who lose', broadly speaking, include those in irregular employment, NEETS (Not in Education, Employment or Training) and the *hikikomori*,[7] those who shun social interaction (Miyazaki in Miyazaki and Swedberg 2017: 6). The total number of this group varies according to estimates, but is thought by some to be in the millions and has been a regular source of moral and social panic in Japan for years. Allison also notes that rates of poverty, particularly among the isolated and the elderly, have been on the rise (Allison 2013: 5). Social anxieties, such as increasing rates of loneliness and solitude, unemployment rates among the young, but also the erosion of social and kinship ties through declining marriage rates and birth rates, all contribute to a sense of crisis in Japan. And the twin disasters of the 2011 Tōhoku earthquake and tsunami which damaged the Fukushima Daiichi nuclear power plant left both a nationwide trauma in terms of loss of life and damage, and a seemingly unending headache for a national government unable to resolve the issues of displaced residents, a nuclear power plant to decommission, and contaminated land and materials. In 2020, the Covid-19 pandemic impacted economies worldwide, including Japan's. The pandemic also attacked narratives of hope and renewal in Japan, in particular since the 2020 Tokyo Olympics, which had for years been a symbol of hope due to their promise of an economic revival, were postponed. Early reports on the outcomes of the pandemic indicate a substantial shrinking of the Japanese economy,[8] although at the time of writing this book it is still too early to tell what the long-term effects will be. Within this bleak picture, traditional industries such as kimono-making struggle quietly in the background, and their fate goes largely unnoticed.

Since the 1980s, as noted by Sherry Ortner, anthropology has become increasingly preoccupied with the 'dark' aspects of social life: adverse economic conditions, increased poverty and oppression, often entwined with the rise of neoliberalism (Ortner 2016). Neoliberalism, with its core ideology of free markets and free trade, has encouraged the pursuit of profit, leading to downsizing, slashing public aid, removing safety nets and promoting privatisation (Harvey 2005, Ortner 2016). Economic anthropology in particular has sought to explore the fallout from neoliberal practices and policies and has increasingly turned to studies of 'crisis', precarity and instability. In terms of definitions, I take my lead from Susana Narotzky and Niko Besnier: '"crisis" refers to structural processes generally understood to be beyond the control of people but simultaneously expressing people's breach of confidence in the elements that provided relative systemic stability and reasonable expectations of the future' (Narotzky and Besnier 2014: S4). The field of economic anthropology is by no means a unified discipline – indeed, Chris Hann has remarked that 'subcommunities within economic anthropology tend to talk past each other' (Hann in Callan 2018: 3). Nonetheless, recent studies in the field show a pattern of interest in economic crisis broadly speaking, particularly in the wake of the 2008 financial crisis (see Blim in Carrier 2012, for example). Precisely because of economic anthropology's commitment to examining economic processes embedded in their socio-cultural contexts, the field is uniquely positioned to examine the effects of economic crisis and volatility 'on the ground', as they affect people in their day-to-day lives. These effects have been examined among groups as varied as Wall Street investment bankers, whose lives are characterised, as Karen Ho puts it, by a culture of 'instability and crisis' (Ho 2009: 6); and the Mongolian women who strive to achieve balance in economic conditions characterised by flux and uncertainty (Empson 2020).

The difficulties and hopes of the kimono retail industry speak directly to this body of work on crisis and economic decline, but also question the nature of 'crisis' itself: this book is a story about resilience, hope and transformation in an industry against which all the odds appear to be stacked. Horacio Ortiz notes that, in addition to exploring situations of crisis on the ground, it is also the place of anthropologists to question the nature of the crisis, its definition, and 'even the assertion of its existence' (Ortiz in Carrier 2012: 587). In showing how crisis has also proved to be fertile ground for both hope and creativity among retailers in the industry, I will demonstrate that as anthropologists we can fruitfully question the meaning of 'crisis' and reveal that economic crisis is not necessarily purely negative. Anthropologists have already pointed out that the word 'crisis' implies a negative process, in direct opposition to a previous state of affairs in which things were somehow 'better' (Ortiz in Carrier 2012: 585). This certainly fits into the narrative of crisis in Japan more generally speaking, in which the 'good old days' of the 1970s and 1980s are thought of as a time of wealth, stability and mass consumption.

In tandem with a growing body of literature concerned with crisis and instability linked to neoliberalism and the global market economy, there has also been an increasing focus on hope, in particular since Vincent Crapanzano's 2003 article, in *Cultural Anthropology*, which exhorted anthropologists to look more closely at hope as an analytical category. Hirokazu Miyazaki has taken up this appeal in his examination of the tensions generated by an attitude of hope among Japanese derivatives traders (Miyazaki 2006, 2013). Economic anthropologists can provide insights into the categories of hope and crisis, as the economic activities they observe among their chosen participants are inherently linked to the categories of risk and hope: making a living, in whatever form that may take, is often a mix of anxiety and optimism. While they may be oriented towards past hopes and problems, crisis and hope

12 The paradox of contemporary kimono culture

are also future-oriented: future revenue and future loss, future success and future failure, and future possibilities and problems (Narotsky and Besnier 2014: S4–5). This book adds a voice to the conversation between crisis and hope by highlighting how crisis encourages, indeed at times forces, kimono retailers to become creative and ingenious, and how this in turn translates into broader changes within kimono culture itself.

In many ways, the recent history of the kimono, both cultural and economic, is a story in which crisis and hope are in constant conversation. From the time that Western clothes were introduced to Japan in the second half of the 19th century, the kimono has had to compete against a form of clothing to which the entire world had begun to conform. By the end of the 20th century, the clothing industry had become a global behemoth operating within the framework of a globalised market economy. By contrast, the kimono industry is a stubbornly domestic market which still contains elements of a distribution system and a division of labour rooted in the feudal era (see Chapter 2). The influence of Western aesthetics and fashion since the 19th century has been almost unstoppable and many parts of the world have now adopted Western styles of dress in some form or other (Maynard 2004: 5). The kimono's entrenched position in Japanese society, both as ceremonial wear and as a cultural symbol, speaks to both the importance attached to the kimono in cultural terms, and to the ingenuity of the kimono retail industry in adapting to changing social, cultural and economic landscapes.

As this book will cover in Chapters 5, 6 and 7, a segment of the kimono industry has used crisis to its advantage: the economic crisis of the 1990s had the effect of disrupting established wholesalers in the industry, shaking their long-established hold over the distribution of kimono. Until this point, there was little communication between craftspeople and retailers, as wholesalers stood in between. Subsequently, with fewer wholesalers and those remaining in weaker positions, new creative avenues have appeared, with new possibilities for young independent designers and for collaborative relationships to be established between retailers, craftspeople and consumers (this is further explored in Chapters 6 and 7). Retailers are pressured by the crisis into questioning both themselves and their sales methods, pushed to carve out new markets and to explore ways of selling the kimono that better suit an interested Japanese customer. What the resilience of these retailers shows is that creativity in the face of crisis is an avenue for hope: hope for change, for a better industry, and quite simply, for the future of the kimono itself.

Clothing and anthropology: a new focus

A further contribution this book seeks to make is to bridge a gap between two fields of anthropology: economic anthropology and the anthropology of clothing. Although anthropologists have always collected objects and material culture in their field sites, among which clothing featured prominently, it took until the second half of the 20th century for anthropological works focused solely on clothing to appear (Taylor 2002: 194). Susanne Küchler and Daniel Miller argue that Western anthropologists 'struggle with [...] a very specific Western idea of being, in which the real person, myself, is somehow deep inside me, while my surface is literally superficial, [...] somehow less real and certainly less important' (Küchler and Miller 2005: 3). This in turn has led to clothing being overlooked in anthropological literature as a topic worthy of investigation (Küchler and Were 2005: xix). Since becoming more firmly anchored as a field, the anthropology of clothing has tended to focus on the link between clothing and identity. Even though much of contemporary material culture studies is theoretically indebted to consumption and thus intrinsically linked to economic processes, when it comes to clothing, analyses tend for the most part to focus on selfhood, identity and belonging (see Eicher, Roach-Higgins and Johnson 1995, Tarlo 1996, Woodward 2007 and Margiotti 2013 among others). Of course, this approach produces excellent anthropology, and it is an entirely logical choice since, as Terence Turner famously noted, clothing's position on the skin allows for a unique relation with both the personal, physical self and the social self, perceived by others (Turner in Cherfas and Lerwin 1980: 112). Anthropologists have naturally gravitated towards clothing's powerful multi-faceted way of expressing both social and personal identity, and certainly any work dealing with clothing should bear these facets in mind. Indeed, looks, aesthetics and fashion – in other words, our personal choices as well as our ability to self-perceive how others see us – are something apparel industries of any kind have to bear in mind.

Some works in the anthropology of clothing deal with the economic workings of the fashion industry, such as Warner Wood's work on Zapotec weavers and their place in the global crafts market (Wood 2008) or Lucy Norris's analysis of second-hand clothing in India (Norris 2010). However, analyses which place the material culture of dress and clothing in their economic context as items which are produced, sold and circulated remain relatively few, and this is especially the case when it comes to 'traditional' clothing such as the kimono.

This book acknowledges the importance of this body of work on clothing and identity, in particular in Chapters 5, 6 and 7 which explore how shifting the focus away from the kimono as ceremonial wear to the kimono as fashion wear is key to new marketing strategies that boost sales. However, a key aim is to locate this shifting discourse of what the kimono should be within the context of its economic production and distribution. Against the grain of much work on clothing that has examined either the production or the consumption of clothing and the role subsequently played in the construction of a person's social and individual identity, this book will examine both production and consumption as interdependent and interrelated processes.

Methods and field sites

The book draws on twelve months of fieldwork in Japan, during which I was based in the city of Toyota in Aichi prefecture. My fieldwork also took me to nearby Nagoya and Nishio, as well as Kyoto, Tokyo, Kanazawa and Yonezawa, all towns and cities with kimono retailers, craftspeople and wholesalers (see Figure 1.2).

Located in the centre of Japan on the historic Tokaido road that links Tokyo with Kyoto, Aichi prefecture is a hub for industry and technology and is particularly famous for its aerospace and automobile industries. Toyota is, unsurprisingly enough, home to the headquarters of Toyota Motors. The city used to be named Koromo, and was renamed Toyota in 1959 to reflect the importance of the company to the city. Toyota Motors remains, to this day, one of the main employers in the city. For many in the city, life is in some way connected to the company.

Toyota city is often thought of as wealthy by other Japanese people due to its connection with the headquarters and factories of Toyota Motors.

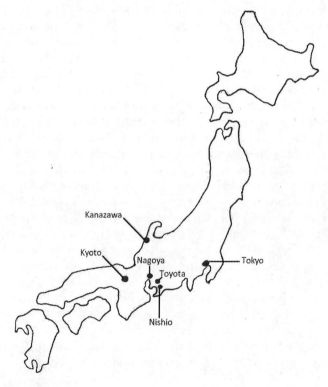

Figure 1.2 Main field sites.

Toyota, with a population of just over 420,000, is dwarfed by its much larger neighbour Nagoya, which has a population of approximately 2.29 million people. This makes Nagoya one of Japan's largest cities. As well as their difference in size, there are also cultural differences between the two cities. While Nagoya belongs to the Owari region of Aichi prefecture, Toyota belongs to the Mikawa half. The two 'halves' have slightly different dialects and customs.

During the twelve months that I stayed in Toyota, I lived with a Japanese host family comprised of my host mother Sachiko,[9] two of her three daughters and a student from America that Sachiko was also hosting during the time that I was there. I had set out to study the kimono during my doctoral research, and full of anticipation and expectation, I started with the people I had closest to hand, and to do that I needed my closest ally.

Sachiko, I can say without exaggeration, is a woman with a magnetic personality. She credits her sociability and sense of humour to her upbringing in Osaka, a city with a reputation for producing fun-loving comedians – indeed, many comedians on Japanese television are immediately recognisable through their Osaka dialects. In addition to being a well-known figure in her neighbourhood, Sachiko runs her own henna hair-dyeing business from her home. This meant that there was a constant flow of women coming to the house that I could talk to and get to know. Many an hour was spent sitting with them and asking them stories about their kimono. During that time, I was struck by one recurring theme: every single one of these women had at home large numbers of kimono that, for the most part, they did not wear – exactly as the Gotō family told me. I asked Sachiko and her friends and immediate social circle to show me their often impressive collections of kimono, which ranged anywhere between 15 and several hundred kimono and obi sash belts. These often took up considerable space in their homes, and were at times a source of anxiety to the women in my research as they did not always know what to do with them (Valk 2020). Intriguingly, women right across the social spectrum owned such collections: everyone from elderly women from farming backgrounds to middle-class housewives in their 50s whose husbands worked for Toyota Motors. Even in more modest homes, these collections were considerable. They were also, for the most part, quite old, having been bought mostly at the time when my participants were getting married and their parents were preparing a bridal trousseau for them.

The evidence of this consumption of kimono in the past, to the point of excess, was particularly striking, and all the more so as many of these women were no longer buying kimono. In addition, women in their 40s, 30s or 20s did not tend to own the collections that their mothers and grandmothers owned. This uneasy combination of past excess with current lack of consumption piqued my interest in the industry itself. The patterns of consumption I observed hinted at spikes and troughs, and I was curious to find out more.

At first, my efforts to meet retailers were rarely successful. In spite of the crisis, there is no shortage of kimono shops in Japan. However, approaching owners by simply walking into their shops without prior introduction turned out to be futile in all but one case, that of the Gotō family. They were unusually open and welcoming, and the only kimono shop happy to speak with me without a prior introduction. Culturally, introductions are of crucial importance. The contributors to the volume *Doing Fieldwork in Japan* consistently 'emphasize the need for introductions from a third party in order to obtain research access' (Bestor, Steinhoff and Bestor 2003: 14). They also note that 'such introductions involve the standard Japanese cultural practice of borrowing trust from other people in order to gain access to a new situation, which carries complex obligations to act responsibly and not misuse or damage the trust' (Bestor, Steinhoff and Bestor 2003: 14). So, in expanding my network of retailers, again, Sachiko and my network of contacts in Toyota came up trumps, as many had some kind of connection with retailers in the industry and were willing to vouch for me as trustworthy. Thanks to them, I grew to know the local shops well.

One particular connection was especially fruitful. A friend of Sachiko's introduced me to Kyoko, my Kimono de Jack companion, who became a close friend and key gatekeeper in my fieldwork. She will feature prominently throughout this book, but especially at the beginning of the next chapter. Kyoko's part-time job at Yoshihide Shibakawa's kimono shop, Azumaya, meant that through meeting her I had stumbled on one of my main field sites (see Chapters 5 and 6, in particular). As is often the case with anthropological research, serendipity can lead to some of the most interesting participants and field sites.

The Gotō family and the Shibakawa family both proved invaluable. Each family kindly introduced me to their contacts in the industry, putting me in touch with wholesalers, craftspeople and retailers. Through the Shibakawa family in particular, I met a loosely connected group of craftspeople, retailers, wholesalers, writers and independent designers who, for the most part, agreed that the kimono had largely untapped potential as 'fashion wear'. Unlike the more 'traditional' side of the industry making mostly ceremonial wear, this was a group who had taught themselves marketing fit for the 21st century. Social media-savvy, they had mastered sales strategies that were more like those of entrepreneurs and social media influencers than the descendants of traditional, family-owned businesses. This group, that I name the 'kimono fashion network' (Chapter 6), were actively re-branding the kimono as fashion wear and as a lifestyle, and in so doing were carving out new markets for their business. For them, fashion held the key. Re-aligning the industry with a globalised discourse on fashion and self-expression capable of appealing to more customers is a source of hope, not just for their future but for that of the kimono. Gaining traction with their sales and with the loyalty of a consumer niche interested in the kimono as fashion, this group had even won the attention of the Ministry of Economy, Trade and Industry (METI). Under its aegis, they had formed a 'Committee for the Revival of Japanese Dress' tasked with outlining strategies for increasing public interest and sales.

Tracing working and social relationships in this way enabled me to map effectively who was connected to whom, how these relationships had been built over time, and what sort of shared narratives were being created around kimono retail and the purpose of the kimono more broadly. In addition to conducting participant observation in Azumaya and three shops in Toyota, I also conducted interviews with craftspeople, retailers and wholesalers and members of government in the Agency for Cultural Affairs and the Ministry of Economy, Trade and Industry (METI).

Structure of the volume

Chapter 2 sets the scene for the rest of the book by providing background on the particularities of the kimono as an item of clothing, and by giving an overview of the development of the kimono industry itself. The sartorial logic of the kimono differs significantly from that of Western clothes, and the norms of how to wear a kimono, the body techniques required to wear it, have evolved over time. In 21st century Japan, few people now possess the skills to wear a kimono, and those who want to wear one usually have to learn how. This learning is both physical, in terms of getting to grips with how to put the kimono on your body, but also abstract: learning the aesthetic codes, matching of colours and the meaning of patterns on the kimono. Chapter 2 also outlines the way in which the kimono retail industry is structured, delving briefly into its history and exploring how the structural elements remaining from the feudal period continue to shape the industry today. While large parts of kimono production have been automated and mechanised, this is not systematic across the industry and mass production has not reached levels similar to those in the standard apparel industry. Further, there are aspects of kimono-making that prohibit mechanisation, and in some sectors of the industry the prestige attached to hand-made, textile masterpieces has precluded the use of machines in production.

Chapter 3 explores the gradual formalisation of the kimono in the 20th century, and the retail industry's hand in shaping a kimono culture primarily geared to ceremonial and ritual life. I trace the ways in which the kimono industry chose to focus its production on increasingly luxurious wear predicated on the idea of the kimono as ceremonial wear. In doing so, the industry positioned itself not only as kimono makers and retailers, but also knowledge experts capable of advising customers whose knowledge of the kimono rules had become shaky as a result of the kimono being less frequently worn in Japanese society. By commercialising knowledge in this way, the industry accelerated the kimono's formalisation throughout the 20th century. I also explore the post-war markets for formal kimono, paying particular attention to the custom of the bridal trousseau, according to which young women about to get married were given large supplies of kimono.

Chapter 4 focuses on resilience within the kimono industry, as a strategy deployed by business owners to keep going in the face of difficulty and falling sales. The concept of resilience offers alternative images of not just the kimono industry but Japanese society as a whole, as a site of creativity in the face of crisis. I also examine some of the public perceptions of the kimono industry.

Chapter 5 focuses on the kimono shop Azumaya, in the small town of Nishio, owned by Yoshihide Shibakawa. Azumaya is part of a growing network of kimono makers and retailers who are promoting the kimono as a fashion item for both women and men rather than a prestige item for women only. Azumaya's stock is mostly casual wear and is often made of cotton rather than silk. Shibakawa-san is a trend-setter who takes an active role in designing kimono in collaboration with craftspeople and wholesalers, unlike previous models of retail in which shop owners took little or no part in the design process. I also examine how the site of Azumaya itself is envisioned as the 'home' of a community of people who wear the kimono as fashion.

In Chapter 6, Shibakawa-san's journey to rejuvenate his industry and reinvent himself is further contextualised within what I have described above as the 'kimono fashion network': a group of retailers, independent artists, craftspeople, bloggers, writers and consumers. Making the most of the decentralisation and fragmentation of the industry, this group has generated a network beyond the hubs of production and distribution in Kyoto. Keen to break down the barriers between customer and providers, the network promotes the idea that they are a community revitalising the kimono as lifestyle fashion. Borrowing from a globalised discourse on fashion, members of this community develop their own tastes and ways of wearing the kimono and tread a delicate line between flouting and respecting convention. Theoretically, this chapter draws on the concepts of 'taste' and 'lifestyle'.

In Chapter 7 I explore further the effects of the fragmentation of the industry with the rise of second-hand retail, but also independent retailers and designers. The growing share of sales made by online retailers and second-hand retailers is testimony to an industry moving away from traditional shops run by families or chain shops in department stores, and towards an ever more fragmented style of distribution. Chapter 8 brings together the themes of the book in terms of the inter-connectedness of crisis and hope, an economic and cultural process that is bringing about a paradigm shift in the making, selling and wearing of the kimono.

The 1990s crisis and its ongoing effects have had a dramatic effect on the kimono industry and sales are lower than they have been in the past, but the crisis has also brought about change and creativity. The removal of barriers such as being forced to sell items through wholesalers has enabled young, independent craftspeople to market their wares in new ways. New working relationships are also being established between retailers and craftspeople.

Disrupting the balance of power in the industry has brought about a change not just in how the kimono is made and sold, but in what the kimono itself will mean in Japan. A new image of the kimono as fun and fashionable, while itself a marketing strategy, has generated greater interest in the kimono among a niche but growing market. In doing so, the same forces of hope and creativity that helped kimono businesses weather the crisis of the 1990s are in turn shaping the meaning of the kimono and its future in Japan and beyond.

Notes

1. A *tansu* is a piece of furniture specifically designed to store kimono flat in shallow drawers. Kimono are not meant to be kept in wardrobes or hung on hangers, but instead are folded according to a specific method, wrapped in *washi* (Japanese paper) and stored in a *tansu*.
2. The 'Jack' in Kimono de Jack comes from 'highjack'. The idea is to 'highjack' a particular place or venue with people wearing the kimono, thereby changing the atmosphere of the place and creating a wish among onlookers to wear the kimono.
3. Kyoko and Takashi are known to me and my family by their first names. To reflect their involvement in our lives as English speakers, I refer to them by their first names without the -san suffix.
4. The fact that kimono are now mostly worn by women is the product of historical developments in the later 19th and early 20th history. As Japan strived to modernise its economy, industry and broader culture, men were encouraged to wear Western clothes, whereas women continued wearing the kimono for much longer. This is discussed in more detail in Chapter 2.
5. From research conducted by the Yano Research Institute, available here: www.yanoresearch.com/press/pdf/1812.pdf (accessed 18/09/2019).
6. From research conducted by the Yano Research Institute, available here www.yanoresearch.com/en/press-release/show/press_id/2441 (accessed 01/09/2020).
7. The word *hikikomori* (literally, 'withdrawing inwards', 'being confined') designates people who avoid social interaction and limit their participation in society for a significant amount of time.
8. See www.japantimes.co.jp/news/2020/08/17/business/economy-business/japan-gdp-shrinks-record-coronavirus/ (accessed 01/09/2020).
9. Similarly to Kyoko and Takashi, Sachiko is also referred to by her first name without the suffix -san to reflect her involvement in my own cultural and family life.

References

Allison, A. 2013. *Precarious Japan*. Durham, NC: Duke University Press

Bestor, T. C., Bestor, V. L. and Steinhoff, P. G. 2003. *Doing Fieldwork in Japan*. Honolulu, HI: University of Hawai'i Press

Blim, M. 2012. 'Economic crisis, 2008: what happened, what can be learned about how and why, what could happen next'. In Carrier, J. G., ed. *A Handbook of Economic Anthropology*, Second Edition. Halle and Bloomington, IN: Max Planck Institute for Social Anthropology

Cliffe, S. 2017. *The Social Life of Kimono: Japanese Fashion Past and Present*. London: Bloomsbury Academic

Crapanzano, V. 2003. 'Reflections on hope as a category of social and psychological analysis'. In *Cultural Anthropology* 18(1): 3–32

Dalby, L. 2001. *Kimono: Fashioning Culture*. London: Vintage

Eicher, J. B., Roach-Higgins, M. E. and Johnson, K. K. P. 1995. *Dress and Identity*. New York: Fairchild Publications

Empson, R. M. 2020. *Subjective Lives and Economic Transformations in Mongolia: Life in the Gap*. London: UCL Press

Fletcher, W. M. III and von Staden, P. W. 2013. *Japan's 'Lost Decade': Causes, Legacies and Issues of Transformative Change*. London and New York: Routledge

Francks, P. 2015. 'Was fashion a European invention?: The kimono and economic development in Japan'. In *Fashion Theory* 19(3): 331–361

Funabashi, Y. and Kushner, B. 2015. *Examining Japan's Lost Decades*. London: Routledge

Hann, C. 2018. 'Economic anthropology'. In Callan, H., ed. *The International Encyclopedia of Anthropology*. Hoboken, NJ: Wiley-Blackwell

Hashino, T. 2018. 'The survival strategy of the Japanese kimono industry'. In Donzé, P.-Y. and Fujioka, R., eds. 2018. *Global Luxury: Organizational Change and Emerging Markets Since the 1970s*. Basingstoke: Palgrave Macmillan

Harvey, D. 2005. *A Brief History of Neoliberalism*. Oxford: Oxford University Press

Ho, K. Z. 2009. *Liquidated: an Ethnography of Wall Street*. Durham, NC and London: Duke University Press

Goldstein-Gidoni, O. 1999. 'Kimono and the construction of gendered and cultural identities'. In *Ethnology* 38(4): 351–370

Kavedžija, I. 2016. 'Introduction: reorienting hopes'. In *Contemporary Japan* 28(1): 1–11

Küchler, S. and Miller, D. 2005. *Clothing as Material Culture*. Oxford and New York: Berg

Küchler, S. and Were, G. 2005. *The Art of Clothing: a Pacific Experience*. London: UCL Press

Margiotti, M, 2013. 'Clothing sociality: materiality and the everyday among the Kuna of Panama'. In the *Journal of Material Culture* 18(4): 389–407

Maynard, M. 2004. *Dress and Globalisation*. Manchester and New York: Manchester University Press

Miyazaki, H. 2006. 'Economy of dreams: hope in global capitalism and its critiques'. In *Cultural Anthropology* 21(2): 147–172

Miyazaki, H. and Swedberg, R. 2017. *The Economy of Hope*. Philadelphia: University of Pennsylvania Press

Miyazaki, H. 2013. *Arbitraging Japan: Dreams of Capitalism at the End of Finance*. Berkeley, CA: University of California Press.

Moon, O. 2013. 'Challenges surrounding the survival of the Nishijin silk weaving industry in Kyoto, Japan'. In *International Journal of Intangible Heritage* 8: 71–86

Narotzky, S. and Besnier, N. 2014. 'Crisis, value, and hope: rethinking the economy: an introduction to supplement 9'. In *Current Anthropology* 55(S9): S4–S16

Norris, L. 2010. *Recycling Indian Clothing: Global Contexts of Reuse and Value*. Bloomington, IN: Indiana University Press

Ortiz, H. 2012. 'Anthropology – of the financial crisis'. In Carrier, J. G., ed. *A Handbook of Economic Anthropology*, Second Edition. Halle (Germany) and Bloomington, IN: Max Planck Institute for Social Anthropology

Ortner, S. 2016. 'Dark anthropology and its others: theory since the eighties'. In *Hau: Journal of Ethnographic Theory* 6(1): 47–73

Tarlo, E. 1996. *Clothing Matters: Dress and Identity in India*. London: Hurst & Co.

Taylor, L. 2002. *The Study of Dress History*. Manchester and New York: Manchester University Press

Turner, T. 1980. 'The Social Skin'. In Cherfas, J. and Lerwin, R., eds. *Not Work Alone: A Cross-Cultural View of Activities Superfluous to Survival*. London: Temple Smith

Yamada, M. 2004. *Kibō kakusa shakai: makegumi no zetsubōkan ga nihon o hikisaku*. ('The hope differential society: the despair of losers tearing apart Japan'– my translation of the title). Tokyo: Chikumashobo

Valk, J. 2015. The "Kimono Wednesday" protests: identity politics and how the Kimono became more than Japanese'. In *Asian Ethnology* (74): 2: 379–399

Valk, J. 2020. 'The Alienating Inalienable: rethinking Annette Weiner's concept of inalienable wealth through Japan's "sleeping kimono"'. In *HAU: Journal of Ethnographic Theory* 10(1): 147–165

Wood, W. W. 2008. *Made in Mexico: Zapotec Weavers and the Global Ethnic Art Market (Tracking Globalization)*. Bloomington, IN: Indiana University Press

Woodward, S. 2007. *Why Women Wear What They Wear*. Oxford and New York: Berg

Chapter 2

The kimono and the kimono industry

A conversation between cloth, body and skill: getting dressed in kimono

Kyoko slides open the door that conceals two *tansu* ('kimono chest') filled with kimono. Her *tansu* were bought for practical purposes, tucked away in the closet of the *tatami*-floored living room of her modern house.[1] In the homes of other women I have visited, especially those older than Kyoko, the *tansu* would be a more lavish affair, most likely received when the owner got married, as part of her bridal trousseau. I visited 21 households in Aichi prefecture and Kyoko's was different from all the others: her *tansu* and kimono were not part of a bridal trousseau, and she was also younger (in her early 40s) than the other women. Most of the women I met in their 50s or older had been gifted a bridal trousseau, including large *tansu* containing sets of kimono. Ordinarily, these kimono would have been made for a range of occasions, such as weddings, graduation ceremonies and funerals. But Kyoko has bought almost all the kimono that she owns, and she wears the kimono because she enjoys it: it is part of her lifestyle, one that she shares, rather unusually, with her husband Takashi.

I had known Kyoko for nine months at this point. Our friendship has grown since we first met and she introduced me to the kimono shop Azumaya, where she works part-time. She has become a special kind of research participant: the provider of many key introductions, but also a close friend. Often there while I conduct my research, we also spend a lot of time together, shopping, cooking or sightseeing. Quite a lot of this is done while wearing a kimono, quite simply because Kyoko enjoys it.

It is unusual for women Kyoko's age to throw on a kimono to go to a museum, just because they feel like it. For starters, most women do not know how to put on and wear a kimono, or at least not confidently. By this point in my fieldwork, I can put on and wear a kimono by myself, and I have picked up a range of tips and advice from different sources – many from my host, Sachiko. Other tips I have learnt from *kitsuke* ('kimono dressing') classes I have taken. But much guidance also comes from Kyoko. Kyoko herself had taken classes in how to wear a kimono. Indeed, most women who want to wear a kimono have to find someone who can teach them.

So, I have asked Kyoko to select a kimono and allow me to record her process of getting dressed. Why, you might ask? Getting dressed in a kimono is a complex process, very different from putting together an outfit of Western-style clothes. Rather than a habit, getting dressed is a skill, one which has to be learned. The act of getting dressed in a kimono itself deserves attention, as it illustrates a central aspect of modern kimono culture and a key consideration for its retailers. Conveying the complexity of 'getting dressed' in writing is difficult; the medium is poorly adapted to convey the challenges of wearing a kimono. Nonetheless, with the help of Kyoko, I attempt here to set the scene for the rest of this book by explaining the complex relationship between body, skill and kimono.

For this task, we choose a kimono that is very Kyoko: it is stylish, with black stripes and subdued shades of grey. Kyoko has a preference for muted styles, with perhaps a sharp colour accent present in the *haneri* (the underkimono collar which remains visible in the final outfit) or the *obiage* (the obi 'scarf' which is visible just over the top of the obi). Kyoko's is a fashion-forward style. She sources her outfits mainly from Azumaya, which belongs to a section of the industry which sells the kimono as fashion rather than only as formal, ceremonial wear (see Chapter 5).

After the kimono, we then choose all the accessories: the obi sash that will go around Kyoko's waist, wrapped twice and tied behind her back in the *otaiko-musubi* style.[2] We also select the underkimono, referred to in Japanese as *nagajuban*, and all the other elements, such as small belts and clips, that are used to keep the underkimono and kimono in place. It is a common misconception outside of Japan that the kimono is a robe-like piece of clothing tied at the waist, but the reality is much more complex. The kimono in its current iteration is comprised of at least 14 different elements, each with a role to play in the dressing process.

Kyoko's kimono and accessories

1. Kimono
2. Obi sash
3. *Nagajuban* (underkimono)
4. *Haneri* (a decorative collar cover sewn onto the *nagajuban* – sometimes left plain white)
5. Collar core (plastic or cardboard core slotted into the collar of the underkimono in order to facilitate leaving a gap between the collar and the nape of the neck)
6. *Datejime* (a thin band used to flatten the area around the waist; two are often used: one over the underkimono and one over the kimono itself, before tying the obi)[3]

7. Anywhere between three and five *himo* (thin belts used to keep kimono and underkimono in place, and to help tie the obi)
8. *Maeita* (a piece of stiff plastic or card wrapped around the waist that helps the obi sit comfortably)
9. *Obimakura* (a padded cushion used to create one of the most common forms of obi tie, known as *otaiko-musubi*)
10. *Obiage* (usually a silk cloth, plain or patterned, used to cover the *obimakura*. Since it is slightly visible, choice of colour is often a subject of great debate)
11. *Obijime* (one of the most important elements: in many styles of obi tying, this tie is used to keep the obi in position once it has been tied)
12. Clips (used temporarily to help keep the obi in place when tying it – these are removed later)
13. *Tabi* socks (these divide the big toe from the rest, to facilitate wearing *zori* shoes)
14. *Zori* shoes (shoes that resemble flip-flops in structure, but are ornate and decorated)

Kyoko starts with a white shift, crossed over the chest, that is often used as the first layer of a kimono outfit. After that, she puts on her *nagajuban* (underkimono). At this point, the position of the collar on the nape of the neck has to be established, and the collar has to be crossed, left over right, and held in place with a *himo* (belt). This part is very important: placing the collar right over left is the way that the dead are dressed at funerals, and is possibly the single biggest mistake that can be made when wearing a kimono. The potential pitfalls and faux pas of wearing kimono are many, but no mistake is bigger than a kimono collar worn right over left.

After she has tied her *nagajuban* in place using a thin *himo* belt and the *datejime* belt, Kyoko puts on her kimono. She has to concentrate, applying the right amount of tension to the fabric, the right amount of strength as she wraps the kimono around her body. Every movement has to be calculated in advance, with the next step in mind, in order to produce the polished, elegant look that is in vogue.

With that done, Kyoko has to be mindful of two key features of the kimono. Women's kimono (this feature does not exist with men's kimono) are tailored longer than the woman's actual height. In order for the kimono not to drag on the ground, a fold named *ohashori* is made at the waist. Current aesthetic conventions call for this fold of fabric to be made as smoothly and crease-free as possible. It also needs to be just the right length: the length of an index finger beneath the navel, I am told, by Kyoko and other women who have shared their know-how with me.

Various tools, such as a *maeita*, are then used to flatten the kimono around the waist and prepare a smooth surface for tying the obi. Obi tying is especially complex: while kimono are at least somewhat person-shaped, allowing for a more intuitive approach, obi are long, wide pieces of fabric. This requires careful learning, and an ease with abstract thinking and shapes is most useful here, something which Kyoko has in spades. *Otaiko-musubi*, one of the most common ties, is also among the more complex, with many different methods for achieving the final result.

The entire process of getting dressed in a kimono is a careful tug of war with the fabric which is never quite the same each time. Kyoko is experienced, and wearing the kimono for her requires little effort, but it is a body of knowledge acquired consciously, gradually, with a considerable investment of time and energy.

Putting the kimono on is complex enough, but there is possibly an even greater level of difficulty in choosing a combination of kimono and obi. The politics of choice and aesthetics governing the initial purchase of a kimono are equally intricate, and the wearer has to ask herself (usually, it is a woman) a number of questions: is the kimono for a particular occasion and, if so, is it formal enough? Does she have the right kind of obi and accessories, as there are rules associated with kimono types and obi types depending on the level of formality? Is the kimono type correct for the season? What colour is appropriate for the wearer's age, but also suits her tastes?[4]

Now, Kyoko poses for the finished result (see Figures 2.1 and 2.2). She is a perfectionist, and today, as on other occasions, she finds something she would have liked to arrange better. But Kyoko is skilled, she can get dressed quickly and without help. This time, donning the kimono is just for the purpose of my recording, but often we have dressed in kimono, and spent days out together.

Situating the kimono in the anthropology of clothing: the kimono as dressed practice and communication

It might seem strange to think that you would need to learn to wear clothes: in many parts of the world, young children learn to wear T-shirts, trousers and underwear and rarely have to think about it too much during adulthood, except perhaps in the case of more complex items of clothing that are not often worn. But putting on a kimono requires a different kind of embodied knowledge, one which has to be consciously learned, usually later in life by observation, experimentation, taking classes or watching videos online. To wear a kimono is to engage in an ongoing dialogue between the body and the fabric. Parts of the kimono need adjusting throughout the day as the body moves the fabric and threatens to undo the careful work done in putting it on.

For most of us, getting dressed is part of our *habitus*, in the sense famously employed by Pierre Bourdieu: a set of physical dispositions, skills, customs and behaviours that we acquire, for the most part, without having to think about them too much (Bourdieu 2013 [1977]: 73). Learning to clothe ourselves starts as acquiring a skill, but eventually turns into an unconscious and embodied skill and habit.

Figure 2.1 . Kyoko's kimono and obi (front).

Wearing a kimono involves stepping *out* of a familiar habitus, and making the process of getting dressed conscious. This is because the kimono requires an entirely different skill set, which most people need to actively learn in order to become proficient. This was not, of course, the case prior to Western clothing becoming the norm in Japan – a gradual process throughout the first half of the 20th century – but in present day Japan the sheer difference of the kimono and the difficulties involved in wearing it prove to be a significant barrier to people wanting to wear it.

In many ways, getting dressed in a kimono is close to practising an art or playing music: the outcome might be slightly different each time. There are parallels with other forms of clothing across the world. Mukulika Banerjee and Daniel Miller explored in their book *The Sari* how a young woman first learning to wear the sari struggled to get to grips with the unfamiliar garment, 'engaged in a constant battle to make a five-metre piece of rectangular cloth obedient to her will' (Banerjee and Miller 2003: 70). They note how acquiring the skills to wear the sari takes time and willpower, and this

Figure 2.2 Kyoko's kimono and obi (back).

process is often helped by other women and their experience. Although the sari and the kimono are very different garments, their similarity lies in that they both belong to a category of clothing that is wrapped around the body, and therefore requires adjusting throughout the day. Banerjee and Miller write that 'in striking contrast to most stitched clothing, which once put on in the morning can be largely taken for granted for the rest of the day, the sari forces a continued engagement and conversation with its wearer' (Banerjee and Miller 2003: 71). Much the same can be said about the kimono.

Many academics working on clothing and dress have emphasised the relationship between clothing and the body, in particular Joanne Entwistle, who stressed that clothing should be considered a 'situated bodily practice', in other words calling attention to the embodied and socially situated practice of dress (Entwistle 2000: 325). Getting dressed and presenting ourselves clothed to society is a daily routine across the globe, replete with significance related to our social worlds of hierarchy, gender, ethnicity, age and occasion, and inner worlds of emotion, personal aesthetics, comfort and self-expression. In the 1970s and 1980s, analyses of clothing in the social sciences focused on the idea of clothing as communication – a language through which the wearer and viewer communicate about the identity of the wearer, in particular in terms of age, status, gender, and so on (see Lurie 1992 [1981], Barthes 1983). Since then, anthropology has increasingly turned towards the 'other' side of clothing, namely the embodied, inner side, rather than the outer social side. This change in perspective has occurred in tandem with growing focus on agency and process in anthropology (Hansen 2004). Terence Turner highlighted this two-sided nature of clothing, and its role as the interface between the individual 'as a biological and psychological entity' and the wider social world on the outside of the body (Turner 2012: 486). The kimono is indeed a form of communication as much as it is a form of dress practice, particularly since it conveys a large number of cultural signs and symbols, as well as codes for seasons, age, gender, and occasion, among others. Looking closely at the process of getting dressed in a kimono usefully highlights that the kimono is both a system of communication and an embodied dress practice.

As the kimono is such a cultural icon, the actual process of putting the garment on, and its relation to the body tends to be overlooked. However, these are important, especially because the complexity of the kimono makes it difficult to wear, which in turn impacts the kimono industry as a whole. The complexity of the kimono as an item of clothing reveals clues as to its development throughout the 20th century, and the hand of the industry in this development.

Historical development of the kimono

The kimono as we know it today derives from the *kosode*, an undergarment worn by court nobility in the Heian period (794–1185) (Jackson 2015: 8). In the centuries that followed the Heian period, the *kosode* was increasingly lengthened and worn as the outer layer of clothing, and the *kosode* became the standard form of clothing for women of the samurai class in the Edo Period (1603–1868).

The next landmark on the road from *kosode* to kimono was the Meiji Restoration in 1868, which marked the return of political power to the imperial family, and started the Meiji period (1868–1912). Until this point, the word kimono itself was not in common usage. 'Kimono', meaning 'thing to wear', is thought to have emerged during the mid-19th century amidst the increasing exposure to and influence of Western clothing and in response to a need to have a word to describe what Japanese people wear, in contrast to Western-style clothing (Milhaupt 2014: 21, Dalby 2001: 9). In the Edo period (1603–1868), Japanese society was stratified using the social classes of samurai, peasant, artisan and merchant. While the samurai were considered to be at the top of the hierarchy, they were not always wealthier than the artisans or merchants, and wealthy merchants were often the trend-setters of the day (Milhaupt 2014: 32). When Edo period classes were abolished in the wake of the Meiji Restoration, women from all walks of life aspired to the elegant *kosode* that were associated with beauty, style and wealth.

The idea that the kimono is an item of clothing for women only is one of the many entrenched notions about the kimono outside of Japan. Kimono for men do exist, and always have existed, but it is true that the kimono nowadays is mostly worn by women. The gendered dimension of the kimono is a product of the late 19th and 20th century. Margaret Maynard notes that in many cultures across the world, it generally seems to be men who adopt Western clothing the fastest (Maynard 2004: 5). After the Meiji Restoration in 1868, in the race to 'catch up' with the West and become a modern nation with a Western-style military, a national education system, and a modernised industry and government (Pyle 1996: 92), men were encouraged to wear Western clothes. This was to be read as a sign that Japan had understood the codes necessary to be taken seriously in a global sphere of politics dominated by Western sartorial aesthetics (Koike, Noguchi and Komura 2000: 102). By contrast, women continued to wear Japanese dress well into the 20th century, with the lasting effect that the kimono is now primarily associated with them. A male version exists and is quite similar, although some features are different, as well as the way in which it is worn (see Figure 2.3).

Figure 2.3 Differences between women's and men's kimono.

Women leave a gap between the collar and the nape of the neck, requiring a collar core in order to maintain the shape. Men do not leave a gap, and the collar sits against the neck. Men's obi are longer and narrower than women's, and worn around the hips rather than around the waist. As previously mentioned, men also do not have the *ohashori* feature, where a fold of fabric is gathered and folded beneath the obi.

Modern kimono, for both men and women, are T-shaped constructions that are tailored in a very different way from Western clothes. Western clothes are tailored to fit the body, whereas kimono, along with the sari and Southeast Asian clothing, are wrapped around it. The kimono uses no buttons or zippers but is held in place with various belts and the obi sash. Although kimono can be made from a number of fabrics, and a number of retailers now specialise in 'atypical' fabrics such as denim, typically fabrics made especially for kimono are purchased in a kimono shop. Many of these are family-owned and have been in a single family for generations. Azumaya, the kimono shop where Kyoko works, for instance, is a family-owned business with a single shop that has been in the Shibakawa family for three generations (Kyoko herself is not related to them). There are also kimono shop chains that can be found in department stores. In addition, some prestigious department stores have their own kimono shops, such as Takashimaya or Mitsukoshi. While kimono can sometimes be purchased as prêt-à-porter, they are usually sold to the customer in the form of a *tanmono* (bolt of kimono cloth), which is mostly between 11 and 12 metres long and between 34 and 40cm wide[5] (Milhaupt 2014: 21). Although this is subject to variation, an average price for a new silk kimono is usually somewhere between 150,000 (£1068) and 500,000 yen (£3685), although *tanmono* costing over a million yen can also be found in upmarket kimono shops. These prices are an estimate, as kimono prices vary widely depending on the fabric, how it was made, where it was made and how it was priced.

The contemporary kimono is one that has retained many features of the *kosode*, in particular its shape (see Figure 2.4). The kimono's expanse of fabric is similar to the canvas of a painting, allowing the whole body to display a particular pattern. This might seem similar to a long dress, but the sleeves of a kimono allow for an extra surface on which pattern can take centre stage. The kimono is also typically understood to have a longer lifespan than regular clothes, and this is reflected in the materiality of the kimono: as it is cut along straight lines, it can be taken apart and re-sewn into bolt form. This allows the kimono to be re-dyed and even re-stitched to fit a new person – typically a female relative to whom the kimono has been passed on. In practice this is not done as frequently as it used to be (see Valk 2020), but during my fieldwork I did speak to some women who took advantage of the mutability of the kimono in this way.

Both the process of tailoring and the process of putting on a kimono belong to a different sartorial logic than Western clothes. As Toby Slade writes, 'the kimono creates a certain understanding of the body, as something

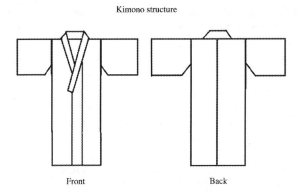

Figure 2.4 Kimono structure.

to be wrapped' (Slade 2009: 54). As with South Asian and Southeast Asian clothing, the kimono belongs to a category of clothing which wraps the body rather than fitting it, as Western tailoring traditionally has. Although the kimono has gone through several stylistic and aesthetic permutations over the centuries, the basic form of the kimono was in place by the 14th century (Slade 2009: 53). The enduring nature of the basic form of the kimono is remarkable, but this presents difficulties for modern-day consumers who are accustomed to different types of dress in their day-to-day lives. In the latter half of the 20th century especially, the kimono came to occupy a very different role in Japanese society as it became increasingly separated from daily life.

'Separation from the kimono' in the late 20th century

Over the course of the 20th century, Japan underwent a process known as *kimono-banare* in Japanese, meaning 'separation from the kimono'. Kazuko Koizumi pinpoints the real shift from Japanese clothes to Western clothes to the Shōwa period (1926–1989), and the final stage of this 'clothing revolution' took place from the mid-1970s to the mid-1980s, in which Koizumi observed that even older women in the countryside had stopped wearing mourning kimono to funerals (Koizumi 2006: 14). World War Two was instrumental in accelerating this shift. The production of kimono, considered to be luxury items, was restricted during the war (Nakamura 2006: 150), and in the immediate poverty-stricken post-war period fabrics were rationed and most clothes were made at home from whatever was available (Gordon 2012: 190–191). Silk kimono remained the privilege of the wealthy, as indeed silk had been in previous centuries (Slade 2009: 53). This changed after World War Two and the Japanese economy recovered. Now, women in the growing middle class aspired to own silk kimono, and the industry developed an entire business model on the basis of providing what had once been a luxury item available to only a limited section of society. This is fully explored and developed in Chapter 3. For now, suffice to note that World War Two proved to be a turning point for the kimono, both in terms of the fabrics from which it was made and in terms of when and on what occasion it was worn.

One major, and important, barrier emerged for women wanting to wear a kimono. Until World War Two, the knowledge of how to wear the kimono was taught in the home, a set of body techniques that were part of day-to-day life. Marcel Mauss suggested that we have culturally constituted 'body techniques'. These are the ways in which we walk, run, sit, swim and use tools such as digging with a spade (Mauss 1973: 71–73). While we learn many of these techniques (e.g. through swimming lessons,) some of these are so mundane, so reinforced through day-to-day repetition, that we often fail to see them as culturally produced and, potentially, culture-bound. Our relationships with our clothes involve a set of body techniques that we rarely question, but by the second half of the 20th century, the body techniques related to the kimono were no longer second-nature. This means that a conscious process of learning about, and relating to, the fabric of the kimono is necessary when a woman (or, less commonly, a man) decides to learn to wear a kimono.

Although some women still learn from their mothers or grandmothers, transmission of knowledge in the home is not assured. Another layer of complexity was also introduced: with the kimono increasingly being re-invented as formal wear and ceremonial wear throughout the second half of the 20th century, wearing a kimono became increasingly demanding. The body techniques needed for dressing became increasingly rigid and complex to fit the image of the formal kimono. The dominant aesthetic was one of neatness, smoothness and attempting to achieve 'perfect' presentation for ceremonial wear, an aesthetic that remains deeply entrenched today.

The kimono industry and other sources, such as women's magazines and kimono dressing academies, reinforced the idea that the kimono was bound by three key factors: Time, Place and Occasion. These English words are used in a Japan-made acronym, TPO, to describe clothing which is appropriate for a given situation. There is in Japan a great deal of literature on how, when and where to wear a kimono. A typical example of this literature is the *Kimono no Jiten: Utsukushii Kikonashi no Rūru* (Ōkubo, 2012) ('The Kimono Dictionary: Rules for Beautiful Mastery of the Kimono'; my translation of the title) which is a dictionary of all things kimono, laying out major dye and weaving techniques, types of kimono and advice on when to wear which type, explanations of patterns and family crests, as well as guidance on how to care for kimono. Japan has a prolific 'advice literature' industry catering to a population eager to do things 'correctly', and there is a large amount of advice literature available on the kimono. While there are a number of formal guides like this book, there is also a plethora of more informal guidance on how to wear the kimono available online as well.

Prior to 20th century standardisation, styles and ways of wearing the kimono were subject to considerable variation across region and class, but in the 20th century this became fixed into a set of rules, which consisted of aesthetic norms and guidelines for proper wear. Failing to conform to these rules was viewed as a social faux pas and continues to be considered this way even today. This fear of 'getting it wrong' exerts a considerable amount of influence over customer choices and the way women feel able to present themselves when they wear the kimono. Understanding TPO fully means acquiring and becoming proficient in a considerable body of knowledge. As the expression might suggest, the rules concern kimono type, but also season and age-appropriateness. Almost all kimono fall into one of two types: formal (*reisō* or *yosoiki*) and non-formal (often known as *fudangi*). Non-formal kimono are an ambiguous category, since they can also contain kimono that are expensive and use refined regional craft techniques, but are not necessarily appropriate for formal occasions. The appropriate obi also needs to be matched to the kimono, and there are generally speaking three main types: the *fukuro-obi* (formal) the *Nagoya-obi* (semi-formal) and the *hanhaba* or half-width obi, considered to be casual wear and usually associated with the summer *yukata* (light cotton kimono).

TPO also covers seasonal rules. Typically, there are three seasonal kimono types: lined kimono (*awase*), which are worn from October to May, unlined kimono (*hitoe*), which are worn in September and June, and summer kimono which are worn in July and August. Kimono and obi patterns, particularly with formal kimono, are coded for seasonality. As Inge Daniels has noted, rituals of domestic consumption in Japan draw on a sense of aesthetics grounded in seasonality: 'seasonal kimono codes change almost monthly with the appearance of new plants and flowers' (Daniels 2009: 174). This means that a kimono featuring irises is to be worn in May when irises flower or just before: anticipating the season is considered to be good taste, but overshooting and wearing an iris pattern too late would not be. A woman wearing a floral pattern featuring a flower that is quite limited in time means that her kimono is also limited in time – this is turn reflects her good taste, but also the ability of her household to finance this type of purchase. An obi with *sakura* (cherry blossom) can technically only be used in February, March and April, but many of my participants found creative loopholes in these rules, especially for common patterns such as cherry blossom: cherry blossom, they argued, was a symbol of Japan, and therefore could be worn all year round. Other participants ruled that, if the cherry blossom was on a branch, then the seasonal rule applied – if it was just the flower, then it was simply a decorative pattern and could be used all year round. Advocates for looser rules around kimono wear do exist when it comes to TPO, as I shall explore in later chapters, but it takes courage to flout the rules. In several interactions, my participants complained of the *kimono keisatsu* ('kimono police'): usually older women who would see someone wearing a kimono and take it upon themselves to say that they had something wrong: either the pattern, or colour, or a fold wasn't quite right. The stress of being observed, and possibly critiqued, can be enough to put people off trying to wear the kimono. I was approached by the 'kimono police' several times in Japan, although the mistakes I made were often imputed to the Japanese people near me who, it was thought, had failed to educate me appropriately. One participant remarked, frustrated, 'the worst thing about these people is that they want to correct what you're wearing but they are always wearing Western clothes!'

A concern with form, presentation and the 'right' way of doing things has been identified by academics as an important force in Japanese society. Takie Sugiyama Lebra described the importance of 'face', in other words a person's sense of self, but also their esteem in the eyes of others in Japanese culture. Further, this sense of face is under scrutiny by the wider world and social group, or *seken*, upon which the successful upholding of face is reliant (Lebra in Rosenberger 1992: 107). Thus, Japanese people often feel under pressure of judgement or evaluation in public places, and this is even more the case when wearing the kimono. Not only does the kimono stand out in a world of Western clothes, it is also a powerful signifier of Japanese culture and femininity. Many academics working on Japan have pointed to the discursive ways in which the 'Western' and the 'Japanese' are constructed in Japanese culture, often in opposition to one another (Goldstein-Gidoni 1999: 353). Marilyn Ivy argues that 'chopsticks, kimono, and sushi materially demarcate the Japanese "thing"' (Ivy 1995: 11). Wearing a kimono, then, means to engage with the legacy, however altered and transformed, of a past way of life, one which has evolved to carry powerful cultural signifiers of Japaneseness. As Liza Dalby notes, 'to wear a kimono is, inevitably, to make a statement' (Dalby 2001: 126): a statement about who you are as a woman, about your age and social status, about your relation to kimono aesthetics and how you relate to Japanese culture. Thus the way the kimono is worn (neat, tidy or rumpled) and the aesthetics that are chosen (traditional or modern, perhaps even flouting convention) invite intense scrutiny.

The complexity of wearing a kimono in contemporary Japan is three-faceted: it means (a) being able or willing to purchase a kimono and all its accoutrements, (b) mastering putting it on and (c) engaging with the rules of the kimono aesthetics and TPO.

The kimono retail industry

Historical development: a long-standing connection with wealth and luxury

Having given you a sense of how the kimono evolved to be as it is today and why it is currently so complex, the purpose of the following section is not to sketch an entire history of the development of the kimono industry, but rather to present an overview of how kimono-makers came to be associated with luxury and to give you a sense of how the present-day industry is structured, in order for the following chapters to delve deeper into the reasons for the crisis facing the kimono industry. This chapter will not, then, trace the myriad of weaving, sewing, embroidery and dyeing techniques that have evolved over the course of centuries in Japan; such an enterprise would be enough to fill books and books.

Many works dealing with the kimono focus on the cultural or symbolic meanings attached to the kimono (Dalby 2001), or make a reading based on gender and cultural nationalism (Goldstein-Gidoni 1999). Ofra Goldstein-Gidoni has examined the way in which the kimono is associated with a particular discourse of Japanese femininity. Her analysis of a beauty parlour examines the way women are dressed in *furisode* (literally, 'swinging sleeve' kimono) and men are dressed in Western suits for their coming of age ceremony at age 20 in terms of a binary between women as models of Japaneseness and men as models for action. Accordingly, the act of dressing a woman in kimono symbolically associates her with the canon of gentle, traditional femininity based on the Meiji era (1868–1912) slogan of the *ryōsai kenbo* ('good wife, wise mother'). In contrast, suits symbolically prepare men for a life of action and productivity in the workplace (Goldstein-Gidoni 1999: 352). This interpretation is connected to the creation of a particular version of Japanese femininity. This is an approach I will return to in later chapters, but the main focus of this book will remain on the socio-economic processes that came to govern the production of the kimono in the late 20th and early 21st centuries. In doing so, I will demonstrate how the cultural dimensions of 'traditional' material culture cannot be viewed as separate from the conditions that govern their economic production.

It is worth also pausing briefly here to consider the use of the term 'traditional'. I use this term in part to reflect the original Japanese terminology, *dentō* (tradition), which is often used to characterise kimono and the kimono-making industry. The word in English is a somewhat loaded term. As Richard Bauman notes, the most standard interpretation of the word refers to the passing down of past practices and customs through the generations. In his words, tradition is the 'element of historical continuity or social inheritance in culture' (Bauman 2015 [2001]: 503). However, multiple scholars, in particular Eric Hobsbawm and Terence Ranger, have discussed the ways in which tradition is essentially 'invented', often in support of modern, nation-building exercises (Hobsbawm and Ranger 1984). This has also specifically been applied to Japan in Stephen Vlastos' volume dissecting the 'invention' of various traditions in Japan (Vlastos 1998). Addressing Lee Thompson's chapter on the *yokozuna* title and the championship system in sumo as invented tradition in Vlastos' edited volume, Marshall Sahlins commented on the idea that the modern embellishments or alterations of rituals invalidated the meanings held by the ritual because they were not as old as people assumed them to be; for Sahlins, the ability of tradition to change represented not an 'invented' nature, but rather an 'inventiveness' – in other words adaptation in changing contexts (Sahlins 1999: 408–409). So in this book I use the word 'tradition' and 'traditional', partly to reflect the Japanese wording, and partly because it is helpful in drawing a distinction between Japanese clothing and craft industries which undeniably have continuity with the past. I also understand the modern iterations of the kimono in the way Sahlins does, in other words as examples of the 'inventiveness' of tradition.

Returning now to the industry itself, the kimono industry is known as *gofuku gyōkai* in Japanese. The word *gyōkai* simply refers to an industry, but rather than the word kimono, the word *gofuku* is used.[6] The *gofuku* industry has a very long history, with roots in the retail systems of the Edo period (1603–1868). Naoko Takesue argues that the current industry owes much of its structure to how it was organised during the Edo period (1603–1868) (Takesue 2014: i). There is also a long-standing connection between the kimono-producing industry and the idea of 'luxury'. Being able to enlist the services of someone else to make you a kimono was, for much of Japan's history, only available to the wealthier echelons of Japanese society. Many people instead made their own clothes (Milhaupt 2014: 23). Individual households gathered the materials for their everyday clothes and made them themselves. According to Toby Slade, until the end of 15th century, one of the materials preferred by commoners for kimono was flax linen, but from the 15th century onwards, flax faced competition from the emerging cotton industry (Slade 2009: 53). Although wool was introduced through trade with Dutch, Spanish and Portuguese merchants in the late 16th century, its imports were limited and as domestic production of wool did not take off, woollen fabric remained uncommon (Slade 2009: 53). The first domestic woollen mill opened in 1878 (Nakagawa and Rosovsky 1963: 68).

Most households had the know-how to take the kimono apart in order to wash it but also to resize the kimono for someone else in the family. It was commonplace for everyday kimono, in other words those which were not kept for special occasions, to be worn until they could be worn no more and then the fabric would be reused for other items around the house (Milhaupt 2014: 23). My research participants recalled that dishcloths or sleepwear were among the more common usages for old kimono cloth. This practical knowledge of how to handle, sew and repair kimono was passed down between different generations of women in the home well into the 20th century. Kazuko Koizumi, who was born in 1933, recalls her mother's knowledge: 'as was the case in many households in the past, my mother took care of all things related to the kimono: from sewing to cleaning and care, right up to re-using the fabric for other things. She did it all herself' (Koizumi 2006: 26; my translation). Given that Koizumi's mother was asked by relatives and friends for help with their kimono, she was perhaps especially skilled, but Koizumi notes that knowledge of how to care for one's own kimono was commonplace in her mother's generation (Koizumi 2006: 26).

Who, then, made kimono for other people? In the Edo period (1603–1868), these were 'loosely affiliated' groups of craftspeople working under the direction of a producer who interfaced with customers (Milhaupt 2014: 23). These customers belonged to the wealthy ruling classes prior to the Edo period, those who could afford to have clothes made rather than having to make their own. Many of the techniques that go into making the kimono have roots in methods of dyeing and weaving on the Asian continent. According to Okpyo Moon, the techniques that made the fame of the Nishijin weavers in Kyoto, such as gold brocade and silk damask, have their origins in China, while other fabrics such as figured satin and velvet were introduced from Portugal and Spain (Moon 2013: 75). But it was during the Edo period (1603–1868) that these methods diversified and flourished. The Edo period allowed many arts and crafts in Japan to develop further than they had before: following a long period of civil war and political conflict, the Edo period brought stability and relative economic prosperity, which in turn brought an appetite for clothing. The increase in size of cities in the Edo period encouraged the development of consumerism and an early market economy (Francks 2009: 12). The development of the city and the proto-market economy also strengthened the production of textiles. Several major Japanese department stores have their roots in kimono retail businesses that became successful during this period (Koizumi 2006: 68). For example, Takashimaya started out in 1831 as a shop specialised in kimono materials (Matsunaga 2000: 12; see also various chapters in Macpherson 1998).

The main customers of luxury kimono at this time belonged to the merchant class. The Tokugawa Shogunate imposed a rigid, Confucian social order in which people belonged to one of four classes: samurai, farmers, artisans and merchants (Hall 1974). The merchant class, though considered 'lowly' in terms of this Confucian hierarchy of value, became wealthy in the Edo period, and it was in part their appetite for clothing which allowed the kimono retail industry to grow to unprecedented levels. During this time, the loose division of labour mentioned earlier retained its structure: craftspeople worked on the different elements of a kimono based on the requests placed by a producer. The division of labour among craftspeople became more complex at this time, with increasing consumerism driving a diversification of styles and fashions. Different craftspeople handled different sections of the kimono: making silk, weaving silk (much of this often took place in people's homes as a side-business), weaving, dyeing (including stencil dyeing, tie-dyeing and wax-resist dyeing), embroidery and sewing, to name a few. This division of labour, with craftspeople overseen by producers, remains largely the same today, although it has been considerably disrupted by the recession of the 1990s and the advent of online retail. Later chapters will focus on these disruptions.

During the Edo period (1603–1868) fashion trends emerged, supported by the distribution of pattern books. These pattern books were in many ways similar to catalogues, and according to Terry Satsuki Milhaupt, they 'served three interrelated functions as kimono makers' manuals, consumer catalogues and fashion plates or advertisements' (Milhaupt 2014: 32). Seiko Sugimoto further argues that fashion and publication were interlinked from the late seventeenth century, and that *ukiyoe* (woodblock prints) featuring fashion leaders such as high-ranking courtesans, Kabuki theatre actors and young, urban women were used to promote particular patterns, styles and fashions (Sugimoto 2020: 158), in much the same way that fashion icons do in the 21st century in online and print media. The Edo period was a conflicting time when it came to fashion, however, as the Shogunate also regularly imposed sumptuary regulations on clothing aiming to draw a clear distinction between the four classes and to limit what the government considered to be profligate spending on the part of the wealthy merchant class in particular (Shively 1964). This was mostly because, although the merchants were considered lowest in the hierarchy, the richness of their garb outstripped their rank, and made instant recognition of social status through clothing difficult. Some of these sumptuary regulations were ineffective: merchants found other ways to express themselves through clothes, such as using extravagant linings inside their kimono and overcoats. Appetite for silk grew, paving the way for Japan's early industrial revolution and for Japan to become a major exporter of silk in the late 19th century.

The end of the Edo period brought about a period of tumultuous social, political and economic change. Power was transferred back from the Tokugawa Shogunate to the Meiji Emperor in the momentous event of the Meiji Restoration in 1868, which brought about sweeping political, social, cultural and economic change. With the abolition of the class system after the Meiji Restoration, dress codes were no longer fixed by class, and the erstwhile lower classes of Japan aspired to the styles of the old samurai class and the imperial court (Slade 2009: 129). This led to the establishment of new dress codes for formal occasions, creating a new kind of formal wear that was available across classes (Koizumi 2006: 39). Rika Fujiwara notes that women in the early 20th century began to attend public events, and as a result, they needed a new kind of formal wear (Fujiwara 2006: 39). Although at this time wearing silk was no longer the privilege of the upper classes or the wealthy who could afford to circumvent the rules, silk remained prohibitively expensive and out of the reach of most Japanese people. Although Western clothes were introduced in this period, and men began to adopt Western attire, the kimono industry did not suffer. In fact, it benefited from industrialisation and the increased usage of power looms and chemical dyes among other new technologies, which increased output and the production of textiles (Hall 2018). This mechanisation of textile production effectively divided it into two: the production of textiles aimed at export, and a smaller-scale production of textiles aimed primarily at the domestic, kimono-making market (Francks 2009: 103). Nonetheless, technological innovation and the introduction of imported textiles as well as chemical dyes allowed for a greater variety of styles and fashions.

One famous example of this innovation is *meisen* textile. Featuring bold patterns and colours, *meisen* was very popular among city dwellers in the

1920s and 1930s. Such was its cultural influence that, after a period of being set aside and forgotten, *meisen* kimono have become valued once more today by those who wear the kimono as fashion (see Chapter 7). Another invention on the part of the industry was the *hōmongi* kimono, a dyed, expensive kimono type, in the Taishō era (1912–1926), which is now women's formal wear par excellence (Koizumi 2006: 39). To this day, this kimono is used to attend formal events, such as graduation ceremonies and weddings.

A significant blow was dealt to the kimono retail industry during World War Two. With industry largely mobilised for the war effort, the kimono industry was restricted. Kimono themselves were deemed to be too 'luxurious' and unsupportive of the war, so women were encouraged to wear *monpe* (a type of trouser and upper body wrap combination) which were considered more practical, more economic and less wasteful (Milhaupt 2014: 234). At a time when food became scarce and making ends meet was difficult, the silk kimono that women had in their *tansu* ('kimono chest') could be bartered for food (Dalby 2001: 146). Some of my research participants recalled members of their own families trading silk kimono for food in the war years and just after. Even after the war, it took some time before the kimono retail industry got back on its feet. In the years immediately after the war, Japan was a poor country with a weak economy. At the time, many households made their own clothes, and sewing machines on which Western clothes could be run up cheaply became popular (see Gordon 2012 for an in-depth discussion of the role of sewing machines in post-war Japan). Many of the kimono from this period are quite modest items made from wool, with simple patterns. They were often produced as *ansanburu* (from the French *ensemble*) which comprised a kimono and overcoat with the same pattern. Many of the homes that I visited in the Toyota area still have a number of this type of kimono *ansanburu* which often belonged to older family members.

Kimono retained their dual classification system of *fudangi* (everyday wear) and *yosoiki* (formal wear), but by the 1970s formal wear had far outstripped *fudangi* and formalisation of the kimono continued unabated. There are many social, cultural and economic factors underpinning this process. One aspect of this transformation was that the lifestyle of the Japanese had changed in the immediate post-war period. American culture flowed into the homes of the Japanese during the Occupation (1945–1952) and thereafter home life was transformed. Homes became Westernised, and the kimono was ill-suited to the practicalities of day-to-day life, such as driving. It was, however, this retreat of the kimono from day-to-day life that enabled its role as ceremonial, formal wear to become so strong. As Liza Dalby writes, 'the everyday activities of modern life are not easily carried out in kimono. Yet in spite of its commonly acknowledged disfunctionality, the kimono has not simply disappeared. As kimono's social sphere has contracted, its symbolic importance has intensified' (Dalby 2001: 125). Another aspect is, as we have already seen, the role filled by the kimono as formal wear and the cultural capital that it came to embody for women in the emerging middle class of the 1960s.

Toby Slade writes that by the Taishō period, department stores, many of which started out as kimono shops, were involved in marketing trends in kimono style (Slade 2009: 132; see also Milhaupt 2014: 104–105). In this way, the industry was instrumental in establishing not just trends but the modern rules of the 'kimono canon' itself. Many of these rules had not existed before the 20th century. This is the reason why there was a proliferation of types of kimono for women and very few for men: by the mid-20th century, men wore Western suits for formal events, but there was a lucrative market in selling formal kimono to women. Diversifying formal kimono types was a good idea to ensure that women would not be content with one or two formal kimono.

'Traditional' clothes do not exist in a vacuum, separate and distinct from economic forces, which may be one of the most powerful driving forces behind their creation. Broadly speaking, the kimono can rightly be viewed as a stage upon which the major social, political, economic and cultural changes of modern Japanese history have occurred. Trends are certainly complex, and what starts as a trend may be comprised of a number of social, cultural and economic forces, but the kimono industry has had a long history associated with the production of luxury, and this connection has only increased further with the formalisation of the kimono in the 20th century. This connection will be explored in Chapter 3, and, as we will see, it is not just a recipe for success.

Structure of the kimono retail industry

Researching the kimono industry means looking for a new frame of reference within anthropology. This is because the subject matter does not fall neatly into existing research categories. One might look to the anthropology of work or 'organisational' anthropology, which typically focuses on businesses, banks and other organisations. The kimono industry produces a very specific type of product that has its roots in a pre-capitalist, pre-industrial industry, and so one might think that it could be better explored through the lens of 'craft'. But equally the kimono retail industry cannot easily be classified as a 'craft' industry. Craft itself is difficult to define exactly: what does, and what does not, count as craft? At what point does craft stop being craft? When production is mechanised and extends beyond the boundaries of the original producing community? The definition of craft is so tricky that the editors of a volume on craft practices published in 2016, Alicia DeNicola and Clare Wilkinson-Weber, quite simply chose not to define it at all (see DeNicola and Wilkinson-Weber 2016: 4). On the one hand, the word 'craft' can refer to any item that is made by hand, by a single person. A knitting project with no commercial value and with no ultimate transaction, for instance, can be a craft. But it can also refer to a product destined for sale and consumption, made by a wider group of people. The similarity remains in the sense that production methods are largely understood to be artisanal and hand-made, potentially also labour-intensive. There is an understanding in anthropology that 'craft' takes place in the context of a particular community, with specific modes of production and manufacturing, and often, if not always, relating to the cultural or social identity of a specific locality. So far, the kimono seems to fit the bill. However much of the anthropology of craft is focused on either the way in which craft techniques are acquired or the place of craft in global markets. The first aspect is theoretically linked to anthropological literature on knowledge and skill. The connection between craft and skill-acquisition was made by Jean Lave and Etienne Wenger's work on legitimate peripheral participation – the process by which a skill is acquired within a community (Lave and Wenger 1991). This concern with knowledge transmission is reflected in subsequent work on craft, such as Soumhya Venkatesan's research on the process by which Labbai mat-weavers learn to weave in Pattamadai in South India (Venkatesan 2010). The second, and more economic, approach has been to examine how craft producers tackle or relate to globalisation and international markets. This approach is characterised by a concern with how 'authenticity' is constructed, and the perception of 'craft' by Western markets. An example of this approach is William Warner Wood's work on Zapotec weavers (Wood 2008).

The kimono retail industry does not fit comfortably into either of these approaches. The former would be useful for approaching craftspeople and their skill acquisition, but would not address the severe difficulties facing the craftspeople in terms of falling demand and a lack of apprentices to take over from ageing craftspeople. Further, the kimono industry is a stubbornly domestic market which has made minimal inroads into the international market. This is partly because the looms are designed to make bolts that are roughly 39cm in width, and they are not easily adapted to other forms of clothing. In addition, kimono themselves are uncompromising in their sartorial logic. Kimono for women drag on the floor if not properly folded at the waist, and the sleeves get in the way of day-to-day activities. They are challenging clothes for the uninitiated. On the other hand, while the market is domestic, often production takes place abroad. This is especially the case for the production of rental kimono, which are most often used by young women for coming of age *furisode* ('swinging sleeve' kimono) at age 20. Raw materials, such as silk, are also often produced abroad. As a result, the industry does not fit the usual craft 'model' of a commodity produced locally and then entering the international market – rather production is often outsourced, as it is for Western clothing, but the market itself remains domestic.

Secondly, the industry is not a typical craft industry in the terms that anthropology usually understands it. Although it has reduced dramatically in size since the 1970s, the industry's market size was still 271 billion yen in 2017.[7] The industry is also well-integrated within the domestic market structure and within the world of Japanese retail. Even though it is not exactly a mainstream industry, neither is it on the fringes of the market. As a result, the kimono industry cannot easily be compared to other studies on craft in anthropology – rather, it is best to understand the kimono industry as something of a hybrid: an industry that is fully integrated into a domestic capitalist market economy, while retaining a structure which has its roots in a pre-market feudal society.

One of these pre-market features is that many parts of the industry are still comprised of family businesses. Many kimono shops are family-owned, and many craft workshops are also family-owned businesses. In some cases, particularly in craft centres such as Kyoto, these businesses have been owned by the same family for generations, in some cases hundreds of years. In terms of means of production, some areas of the kimono industry are entirely mechanised and some textiles are produced in large quantities, while others are made by hand, making the industry very difficult to classify as either craft or not. It must be said here that many of the Japanese craftspeople I interviewed did not like the English word craft, claiming that the word has a lightness and frivolity to it that is not conveyed by its Japanese counterpart, which is *kōgei*. Not easily translated, *kōgei* might be closer to the French *artisanat*, which conveys a sense of artistry and finely honed skill.

So far, I have referred to the structure of the kimono retail industry without a detailed explanation of exactly who the major players in the industry are. It is crucial to go into depth here, as this structure is extremely important in understanding who the power brokers in the industry are – in other words, who gets to decide what type of kimono is made and to whom it is sold. In the early stages of my fieldwork, when I got to know the Gotō family featured in Chapter 1, I was struggling to wrap my head around how the industry functions. From the outside, it appeared very opaque. How did the goods end up in the shops that I saw? Who made them, and how were they distributed? Who chose what to make, and why? Luckily, Takaharu Gotō, the son of Gotō-san (see Chapter 1), understood my confusion. On one of the occasions that I came to visit his shop, he explained the inner workings of the industry with a clever analogy:

'Think of it this way. The kimono industry is a lot like the film industry: you've got the actors, right? Those are the craftspeople. And then you've got the manufacturers, they oversee the craftspeople, so they're like the film directors. After that, you've got the producers. That's the wholesalers. They oversee both the director and the actors. So what about the shop? The shop is the cinema. And then, of course, the customers are the cinema-goers. Does that make sense?'

The structure that Gotō-san described is in fact the structure that most industries adopted in the Edo period (1603–1868). A sophisticated system of distribution was required because the Tokugawa Shogunate established its capital and stronghold of Edo 600 kilometres away from Kyoto and Osaka, which were centres of commercial production for goods ranging from food to clothing (Tatsuki 1995: 71). Pursuing Gotō-san's analogy to its fullest extent,

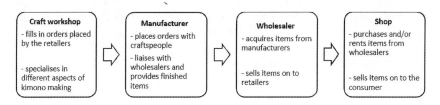

Figure 2.5 Distribution in the kimono industry.

it is of course the case that cinema owners have little to do with the actors in the films they show. In much the same way, kimono shop owners hardly ever have anything to do with the craftspeople who make their goods. As we will see in Chapters 5, 6 and 7, this is changing, but up until the economic crisis of the 1990s, there was usually little contact between between craftspeople and retailers. Mariko Tatsuki further writes that while American marketing strategies were brought into Japan in the post-war Occupation (1945–1952), industrial growth was faster than change in the distributive system, meaning that traditional structures remained in place (Tatsuki 1995: 71). This is likely even more so the case with traditional industries. For a simplified diagram of how the kimono chain of distribution works, see Figure 2.5.

In reality, and especially since the economic crisis of the 1990s and the ensuing recession, this chain of distribution has become more flexible, with shops purchasing directly from manufacturers or craftspeople, and customers purchasing directly from craft workshops, for instance. There are also new, hybrid enterprises which combine both the roles of the manufacturer and the wholesaler.

For decades, of the four major elements of the industry, that is to say, the craftspeople, manufacturers, wholesalers and retailers, the wholesalers had a considerable amount of sway. This is because they were the only agents in the chain to be able to influence 'both' sides: their orders give work to the manufacturers, and this is in turn influences the trends in terms of what kinds of kimono get made and to which retailers they are sold. For the most part, craftspeople in the industry do none of the marketing and trend research work – their job is much the same as that of their forebears in the Edo period (1603–1868): to take care of one stage in the process of making a kimono, such as dyeing or weaving, among many others. Typically, craft workshops specialised in one stage of the kimono-making process only, resulting in a highly specialised division of labour. Rarely, an unusual type of kimono may require a craftsperson to handle all stages of the process, but generally they are involved with their specialist stage only. It is this highly specialised process of creation, driven by an appetite for luxury and high-prestige kimono in the Edo period, and subsequently in the post-war period, that brought about both a wide variety of kimono types and a complex division of labour.

As a result, however, craftspeople have for the most part been out of the loop when it comes to choosing what to sell, usually receiving their instructions from manufacturers. Manufacturers, too, lead quite similar lives, receiving orders from the wholesalers, passing them on to the craftspeople and collecting the completed orders. Although some of the wholesalers also have their roots in the Edo period, they are the ones who most benefited from the integration of the kimono into the market economy. The kimono needed an 'official' system of distribution that could connect manufacturers with nationwide stores, and wholesalers filled that niche, deciding on the one hand what would sell and what to make and, on the other, who to sell it to. Importantly, kimono prices are not fixed, meaning that pricing varies widely. This leads to the common and slightly wry statement that *kimono ha nedan ga nai* ('kimono have no price') as prices for the same bolt of fabric may vary wildly. A research participant who enjoys buying kimono had the following insight into the industry:

> There are lots of stages between the craftsman and the customers which make things expensive. Say a kimono costs 150,000 yen (£1068) to make, with the tools, the dye and the cloth and everything. Then the *tonya* [wholesaler] take their premium, so that could double the price, or even triple it. Then the retailers take *their* premium, and so you can end up with something that took 150,000 yen (£1068) to make but the consumer buys for 400,000 (£2849) or 500,000 yen (£3685)! It's because they are so expensive that kimono are dying out. That and the fact that people can't wear them. Wealthy people can afford kimono, but not regular people. You'll find that kimono always have something to do with money.

They are referring here to the expensive formal kimono that became the mainstay of the post-war Japanese kimono industry. This is why it is important to think of the kimono as an economic object embedded in a system of circulation, distribution and profit-making. It is of course also a vehicle of cultural symbolism and 'tradition', and a stage upon which market preferences are played out (see Chapters 5, 6 and 7) but the kimono and its relation to money, for both producers and consumers, is a key factor that has defined what type of kimono are made and to whom they are sold. For decades, the wholesalers had significant sway over this process. Retailers were often locked in particular deals with certain wholesalers (or, alternatively, locked out of them) and even if they approached other business partners, they might be turned down.

The system, however, is breaking down. The steady decline in sales of kimono since the 1970s did not in and of itself shake the hold of the wholesalers. Instead, it was the economic crisis of the 1990s, and the ensuing recession, that did. This economic downturn shook the kimono industry to its core, creating a situation of crisis that continues to this day. It also changed the power structure in the chain of distribution. As I will explore in following chapters, this crisis deeply affected all sectors of the industry, forcing many businesses to close. Those who endured had to build resilience, while others sought out creative ways to ensure that their businesses survived.

Notes

1 *Tatami* is traditional Japanese flooring made of rushes and straw.
2 This way of tying an obi, in particular Nagoya obi and *fukuro* obi types, is one of the most common (although the technique varies for these two types of obi) but it can be quite difficult to grasp.
3 Additionally, there are also *zori* or *geta* shoes, *obidome* (decorative pieces worn on the *obijime* belt), kimono bags, shawls, overcoats (*haori*) and *netsuke* (decorations that can be slipped into the obi). According to the dressing style the woman has used, the number of accessories such as thin *himo* belts, may vary, and differences in accessories and dressing style are very common.
4 Colour in Japan is highly coded for age. Generally, women over the age of 35 choose to avoid bright colours, instead preferring a more muted palette of grey, blue, black or beige – this is the case both for kimono and Western clothes. I should note that there are also individuals past the age of 35 who prefer more colourful clothes, but as a rule, age seems to bring about a preference for subdued colours.
5 The width varies according to the manufacturer, when the bolt was made and whether it was intended for a woman or a man. Bolt length also varies.
6 呉服屋 is comprised of the characters 呉 (*go*) which refers to Wu, a kingdom in ancient China, 服 (*fuku*) which means 'clothing', and 屋 (*ya*) which means 'shop'. The kimono industry in Japanese does not use the word 'kimono'. 呉服 (*gofuku*), which means 'clothes from the land of Wu'. Even now, kimono shops are referred to as 呉服屋 (*gofukuya*) or 呉服店 (*gofukuten*) (Tanaka 2012: 82).
7 From research conducted by the Yano Research Institute, available here: www.yanoresearch.com/press/pdf/1812.pdf (accessed 18/09/2019).

References

Banerjee, M. and Miller, D. 2003. *The Sari*. Oxford: Berg: 2003
Barthes, R. 1983 [1967]. *The Fashion System*. New York: Hill
Bauman, R. 2015 [2001] 'Tradition, anthropology of'. In Wright, J. D., ed. *International Encyclopedia of the Social & Behavioral Sciences*. (Second edition). Amsterdam, Netherlands: Elsevier
Bourdieu, P. 2013 [1977]. *Outline of a Theory of Practice*. Cambridge: Cambridge University Press
Dalby, L. 2001. *Kimono: Fashioning Culture*. London: Vintage
DeNicola, A. O. and Wilkinson-Weber, C. M. 2016. *Critical Craft: Technology, Globalization, and Capitalism*. London: Bloomsbury Academic: 2016
Daniels, I. 2009. 'Seasonal and commercial rhythms of domestic consumption: a Japanese Case study'. In Shove, Elizabeth, Trentmann, Frank and Wilk, Richard, eds. *Time, Consumption and Everyday Life: Practice, Materiality and Culture*. New York and London: Bloomsbury Academic

Entwistle, J. 2000. 'Fashion and the fleshy body: dress as embodied practice'. In *Fashion Theory* 4(3): 323–347
Francks, P. 2009. *The Japanese Consumer. An Alternative Economic History of Modern Japan*. Cambridge: Cambridge University Press
Fujiwara, R. 2006. 'Yosoiki to fudangi' ('Formal wear and casual wear'; my translation of the title). In Koizumi, K., ed. *Shōwa no Kimono* ('A kimono of the showa era'). Tokyo: Kawade Shobō Shinsha
Hall, J. 2018. 'Digital kimono: fast fashion, slow fashion?'. In *Fashion Theory* 22(3): 283–307
Hall, J. W. 1974. 'Rule by status in Tokugawa Japan'. In *Journal of Japanese Studies* 1(1): 39–49
Hansen, K. T. 2004. 'The world in dress: anthropological perspectives on clothing, fashion, and culture'. In *Annual Review of Anthropology* 33: 369–392
Hobsbawm, E. and Ranger, T. 1984. *The Invention of Tradition*. Cambridge: Cambridge University Press
Goldstein-Gidoni, O. 1999. 'Kimono and the construction of gendered and cultural identities'. In *Ethnology* 38(4): 351–370
Gordon, A. 2012. *Fabricating Consumers: the Sewing Machine in Modern Japan*. Berkeley, CA: University of California Press
Ivy, M. 1995. *Discourses of the Vanishing: Modernity, Phantasm, Japan*. Chicago, IL: University of Chicago Press
Jackson, A. 2015. *Kimono: the Art and Evolution of Japanese Fashion: the Khalili Collections*. London: Thames and Hudson
Koike, S., Noguchi, H. and Komura K. 2000. *Gaisetsu: Nihon Fukushokushi* ('A History of Japanese Clothing and Adornment' – my translation of the title). Tokyo: Koseikan
Koizumi, K. 2006. *Shōwa no Kimono* ('A kimono of the showa era'). Tokyo: Kawade Shobō Shinsha
Lave, J. and Wenger, E. 1991. *Situated Learning: Legitimate Peripheral Participation*. Cambridge: Cambridge University Press
Lebra, T. S. 1992. 'Self in Japanese Culture'. In Rosenberger, N. R., ed. *Japanese Sense of Self*. Cambridge and Melbourne: Cambridge University Press
Lurie, A. 1992 [1981]. *The Language of Clothes*. London: Bloomsbury
Macpherson, K. L. 1998. *Asian Department Stores*. Richmond: Curzon
Matsunaga, L. 2000. *The Changing Face of Japanese Retail: Working in a Chain Store*. London: Routledge
Mauss, M. 1973. 'Techniques of the body'. In *Economy and Society* 2(1): 70–88
Maynard, M. 2004. *Dress and Globalisation*. Manchester and New York: Manchester University Press
Milhaupt, T. S. 2014. *Kimono: A Modern History*. London: Reaktion Books
Moon, O. 2013. 'Challenges surrounding the survival of the Nishijin Silk Weaving Industry in Kyoto, Japan'. In *International Journal of Intangible Heritage* 8: 71–86
Nakagawa, K. and Rosovsky, H. 1963. 'The case of the dying kimono: the influence of changing fashions on the development of the Japanese woolen industry'. In *The Business History Review* 37(1): 59–80
Nakamura, K. 2006. *Tansu-ya de Gozaru* ('Tansu-ya at your Service'; my translation of the title). Tokyo: Shōgyōkai Publishing

Ōkubo, N. 2012. *Kimono no Jiten: Utsukushii Kikonashi no Rūru* ('The Kimono Dictionary: Rules for Beautiful Mastery of the Kimono'; my translation of the title). Tokyo: Ikeda Shōten

Pyle, K. B. 1996. *The Making of Modern Japan*. Lexington: D.C. Heath and Company

Sahlins, M. 1999. 'Two or three things that I know about culture'. In *The Journal of the Royal Anthropological Institute* 5(3): 399–421

Shively, D. H. 1964. 'Sumptuary regulation and status in early Tokugawa Japan'. In *Harvard Journal of Asiatic Studies* 25: 123–164

Slade, T. 2009. *Japanese Fashion: A Cultural History*, Oxford and New York: Berg

Sugimoto, S. 2020. 'Branding Tsumugi kimono in Japan: kimono magazines as mediators between consumers and the "Mingei" movement'. In Nakatani, A., ed. *Fashionable Traditions: Asian Handmade Textiles in Motion*. Lanham, MD: Lexington Books

Takesue, N. 2014. *Daikibo Gofukushō no Ryūtsū Kakushin to Shinka – Mitsui-Echigoya ni Okeru Shōhin Shiire Taisei no Hensen* ('The Development and Reform of the Distribution System in a Large-Scale Kimono Shop – the Change in Item Stocking in Mitsui-Echigoya' – my translation of the title). Tokyo: Chikura Publishing

Tanaka, A. 2012. *Kimono Jibun-ryū Nyūmon* ('An Introduction to Kimono, My Way' – my translation of the title). Tokyo: Shogakukan

Tatsuki, M. 1995. 'The rise of the mass market and modern retailers in Japan'. In *Business History* 37(2): 70–88

Thompson, L. A. 1998. 'The invention of the *Yokozuna* and the championship system, or, Futahaguro's revenge'. In Vlastos, S., ed. *Mirror of Modernity: Invented Traditions of Modern Japan*. Berkeley, CA: University of California Press

Turner, T. 2012. 'The social skin'. In *HAU: Journal of Ethnographic Theory* 2(2): 486–504

Valk, J. 2020. 'The Alienating Inalienable: rethinking Annette Weiner's concept of inalienable wealth through Japan's 'sleeping kimono''. In *HAU: Journal of Ethnographic Theory* 10(1): 147–165

Vlastos, S. 1998. *Mirror of Modernity: Invented Traditions of Modern Japan*. Berkeley, CA: University of California Press

Venkatesan, S. 2010. 'Learning to weave; weaving to learn... what?' in *The Journal of the Royal Anthropological Institute* 16 Making knowledge: S158–S175

Wood, W. W. 2008. *Made in Mexico: Zapotec Weavers and the Global Ethnic Art Market (Tracking Globalization)*. Bloomington, IN: Indiana University Press

Chapter 3

The rise of the formal kimono in the post-war years

Selling status and commercialising knowledge

A familiar hail shower hits me as I leave Kanazawa station on a gloomy November morning. Kanazawa, with a population shy of half a million people, is on the Japan Sea coast – famous for its rain, hail, and heavy snowfall. As the locals are fond of saying: in Kanazawa, you can forget your lunchbox, but don't forget your umbrella.

Coming to Kanazawa is something of a homecoming for me. This is a town I know well – I lived there and worked in the Kanazawa city hall for two years on the JET programme[1] before my fieldwork.

The weather is said to have left its mark on the inhabitants of the city, who are often labelled as more aloof than most Japanese people. They are also described as proud, especially of their gastronomy and culture. Kanazawa's other name is 'little Kyoto' because of its scenic beauty, but also its rich history in the arts and crafts.

Kanazawa developed under the wealthy and stable patronage of the powerful Maeda clan from the end of the 16th century to the Meiji Restoration in 1868. Throughout this period, the clan poured money into the development of the arts, and borrowed extensively from court culture in Kyoto to do so. One of these Kyoto 'imports' was a famed Edo period (1603–1868) craftsman, Miyazaki Yūzen, who gave his name to a resist-dyeing technique which involves painting patterns directly onto the fabric. His artistic contribution to local dyeing techniques created a type of kimono now known as Kaga Yūzen. Kaga Yūzen is distinguished from Kyoto Yūzen by its gentle palette (usually drawing from just five colours: purple, indigo, ochre, black and red) and for its intricate designs, often comprised of leaves, flowers and birds. While there are some variations with embroidery or gold leaf, Kaga Yūzen is further distinguished from Kyoto Yūzen by its lack of embellishments and its depictions of natural imperfections such as *mushikui* ('damage done by insects') on leaves. The result is a unique and widely prized aesthetic.

The method of making Kaga Yūzen textiles is complex, requiring skill for each stage in the process. In a nutshell, the main steps of the process are as follows: patterns are usually first drawn on paper, and then white, undyed kimono cloth is placed over the paper. The craftsperson then traces the pattern using the sketch beneath the fabric with *aobana* ('dayflower') sap. While these lines initially appear as blue, when the fabric is washed later on in the process, the properties of the sap enable the lines to be washed away without trace. Dye-resistant rice paste is then traced on the outlines of the patterns to prevent the dyes from running. Colours are applied to the patterns (but not the rest of the fabric, which is dyed later). The bolt is steamed, and then the patterns are covered with paste, so as to protect them when the background fabric is dyed using a broad brush. After steaming once more, the fabric is then washed thoroughly to remove the paste. This stage was traditionally done in the two rivers that flow through Kanazawa, and gave rise to the Kanazawa tradition of *Yūzen-nagashi* (Yūzen washing), but most washing is now done in purpose-made waterways. After that the fabric is rinsed, dried and inspected for stains or imperfections.

As is often the case in the kimono industry, there are also 'Kaga Yūzen-like' kimono that are marketed based on their similarity with the original, and these may include additional features such as embroidery. Traceability is not always easy, and it can be hard for customers to trace a bolt of fabric reliably back to the source. With high-profile craft techniques such as Kaga Yūzen, customers often have a sense of what the iconic fabric should look like because the aesthetics are so striking. However, even if customers have an idea of what the product should look like, some kimono are made to look so similar to the original regional craft technique that it can be difficult to tell the difference.[2]

While I was employed at Kanazawa city hall, I translated a number of tourist leaflets and museum websites and so I was familiar with the history of Kaga Yūzen, but I did not know any craftspeople myself. I leveraged my contacts in Kanazawa: a friend who, until he retired, ran a renowned French restaurant, offered to help. He met me outside the station and drove me to Kanamaru Senko (literally 'Dye Workshop Kanamaru'), a Kaga Yūzen craft workshop by the river Sai. There are two rivers in Kanazawa: the Sai and the Asano, in which craftspeople in the past used to wash away the paste used in the process of dyeing Kaga Yūzen textiles – hence the concentration of workshops by the rivers.

We are greeted by my friend's acquaintance, Shūichi Kanamaru, a Kaga Yūzen dye craftsman. He shows us through an antechamber, welcoming us with tea and sweets. He has some sample kimono brought out, and in the small space he spreads the luxurious fabrics on the floor. Kaga Yūzen has a reputation for combining sobriety with breath-taking beauty, and Kanamaru-sensei's work does not disappoint.

'In 2020, our business will be a hundred years old. I'm the third generation of craftspeople, my grandfather was the first. Kaga Yūzen, it has brand power, you know. People can recognise it.'

50 Post-war rise of the formal kimono

Figure 3.1 Kaga Yūzen hōmongi (formal kimono) (Reproduced with kind permission from Kanamaru Senko).

This is no exaggeration. Kaga Yūzen are considered to be one of the most refined and beautiful textile crafts in Japan. Many of my research participants among the local women in my neighbourhood in Aichi prefecture would know what a Kaga Yūzen kimono looked like, and to own one would elicit admiration, even perhaps envy (see, for example, Figures 3.1 and 3.2).

'There are about 160 Kaga Yūzen craftspeople now. Among those, only about 30 or 40 are truly active. It's those 30 or 40 who have work and who have a reputation. The rest aren't producing. They do other jobs on the side. And so there are people who say "if I am going to wear Kaga Yūzen I want to wear *this* craftsman's Kaga Yūzen." For everyone else, it's a tough line of work.'

He leads us out of the antechamber and into the workshop itself, a modern building with narrow stairs and corridors. We pass by a window overlooking the Sai and Kanamaru-sensei pauses, looking out onto the river.

'You know, there used to be around 200 people working on Kaga Yūzen by the river. I remember as a child seeing craftspeople washing the fabrics in the waters. Now there's maybe five or six people still making Kaga Yūzen.'

Figure 3.2 Detail from a *kurotomesode* (formal kimono usually reserved for the mother of the bride or groom at a wedding) (Reproduced with kind permission from Kanamaru Senko).

We carry on up the stairs, into a plain room where the radio is playing. Among those working in his workshop are two craftspeople, an older man and a younger woman. The woman is Kanamaru-sensei's daughter, Emi Kanamaru, and she has learned the techniques and skills required for Kaga Yūzen dye from her father. Both she and the older man are working on the *shitae* part of the process, which involves tracing patterns onto the fabric using the *aobana* ('dayflower sap') dye. She lets me try my hand at tracing a delicate floral pattern with the dye. As she gently guides me, her passion for her work is clear.

We return to the antechamber and sit down with more tea, and Kanamaru-sensei resumes his description of the industry.

'The kimono industry, you know, it isn't really an industry anymore. It's a *reisai kigyō* [micro-sized business]. The pie has got smaller and smaller – 30, 40 years ago, parents would have kimono made for their daughters when they got married. *Everyone* wore kimono at weddings – 50, 60 years ago, kimono were *fudangi* [ordinary everyday wear], in my own mother's day. Now it's all Western clothes. And the style of weddings is now very Westernised too. Before, people would wear kimono for entrance and graduation ceremonies. Now, it's hardly a problem for you to live your whole life without wearing a kimono. And these days, of course, you can rent kimono too. Like that you don't have to look after them either.[3] It's a fact that caring for kimono isn't easy, either. Since opportunities to wear the kimono have decreased, our business has suffered.'

The Westernisation of clothing in Japan undeniably hit the industry hard, but in the 1970s and 80s, formal kimono such as Kaga Yūzen still sold well. Kanamaru-sensei has lived through that time of consumption and demand for formal kimono, but he is keenly aware that, since the 1990s, spending has decreased.

'Society has become split into extremes now – the wealthy and the poor. How do you go about selling something that costs hundreds of thousands of yen to people who barely have a chance to wear a kimono? And it's not just the kimono, either. Bear in mind that you're talking about buying *zori* shoes, an obi sash –'

'A *nagajuban* [underkimono],' I interject.

'A *nagajuban*, that's right. Then there's the cost of sewing it up to order. You easily end up with something that can cost hundreds of thousands of yen. It's hard to ask people for that kind of money now.'

I asked him about demand for Kaga Yūzen.

'Think of it as a pyramid with the wealthy at the top. Usually it's people who are well-off who buy Kaga Yūzen. But you won't get a large number of orders. We hesitate about having our children take over after us, because it's not easy to support yourself and your family in this line of work. It's fine as a hobby, it's fun, but it's hard as a job. Everyone ends up thinking about that.'

It wasn't long before the conversation turned to the role of the wholesalers.

'The process of distribution is really complex, with lots of different stages. That's why it's so expensive. It's hard, because kimono aren't something that you can sell so easily, just like that. So we need the wholesalers. And believe me, they have their troubles too! The thing is, craftspeople have to work very hard to make what they make, and the pay isn't very high. And when the kimono goes through the wholesaler, that makes the price go up. As far as the consumer is concerned, it's just too expensive. All of us in the traditional industries are going through hardship. We get recognition from the government for our craft, for sure, but you've also got to be able to make a living. The government recognises that we make beautiful things, but at the end of the day, if you can't make a living, then only a tiny percentage of people will be able to do this.'

Emi Kanamaru, the craftsman's daughter, is faced with the conundrum of how to market the skills she has painstakingly learned from her father. Between 2014 and 2016, she won three prizes for her work in exhibitions and competitions. Her patterns are often innovative, moving beyond traditional flowers and birds. She has also started a line of accessories and items such as *noren* (a type of Japanese curtain which often hangs across shop entrances), blinds and some interior decoration (see Figure 3.3). As of 2020, she manages this side of the business, which accounts for about 20 per cent of the goods they produce.

Figure 3.3 Kaga Yūzen panel depicting plum, bamboo and pine, a traditional trio of auspicious plants on a sliding door in a guest house run by the accommodation manager Comingle Co. (Reproduced with kind permission from Kanamaru Senko and Comingle Co.)

When I last spoke to Emi Kanamaru, she was on the search to expand new avenues of business. For the Kanamaru family, Kaga Yūzen and the culture of Kanazawa has been a part of the fabric of their family, but the future remains uncertain. Who will become the fourth workshop head after Shūichi Kanamaru is still undecided, but his daughter's determination, I hope, will find a way for the family's skill to live on.

Silk, luxury and formal wear: exploring the industry's formal kimono strategy in the post-war years

The Kaga Yūzen kimono made by Kanamaru-sensei and other craftspeople in Kanazawa sold well in the post-war years, but as the above vignette makes clear, this is no longer as easy as it used to be. Kaga Yūzen, among other regional craft techniques, now represents the high end of a market for expensive kimono that is shrinking. Many such crafts are the object of conservation policies by the government and receive both national and international attention for their complexity, beauty and skills. There is the designation awarded by METI – *dentō kōgeishi* ('Masters of Traditional Craft') – but recognition of kimono craft techniques has also reached the international level, with UNESCO designating the regional techniques of Shiozawa *tsumugi* and Yūki *tsumugi* as Intangible Cultural Heritage (Nakatani 2020: 157).

In the previous chapter, I explored how the kimono retail industry has historically been connected to luxury. It is this connection that enabled the development of ever more intricate techniques of embellishment and design, often connected to a particular regional technique. Kaga Yūzen is an example of this development. Why is it, however, that Kaga Yūzen and other high value, formal, silk kimono, became so popular in post-war Japan, but are now difficult to sell? This chapter unravels the complex socio-cultural shifts in the Japanese family, and the marketing and production choices which channelled the industry into a single-item strategy based on the formal kimono – and the factors that eventually made this strategy unsustainable.

Historically, going back to the Edo period (1603–1868), the market had been split into two sectors: a luxury sector and an 'off-the-shelf' sector (Donzé and Fujioka 2018: 257–258). On the luxury side, silk kimono were made to order, mostly using pattern books. These pattern books have existed at least since the Edo period, and came to be an important means through which kimono makers communicated with consumers (Milhaupt 2014: 46–47). It is only relatively recently that shops have stopped using modern versions of these pattern books. In the off-the-shelf sector, more modest offerings in striped cotton, sometimes silk, were sold, frequently by travelling salesmen (Donzé and Fujioka 2018: 257–258). These salesmen sometimes went on to establish their own kimono shops.

Luxury is associated with silk, and for a long time silk was primarily for the wealthy, and other fabrics, such as cotton or linen, were the norm for most people. In the second half of the 20th century, however, silk became the norm. The connection between silk and luxury remained, but a major difference was that, in the 1960s after Japan's economic recovery, silk kimono were now within reach for more people than in the pre-war period. By the late 20th century, the word luxury does effectively convey one type of kimono consumption. The word also summons up particular images: high priced, branded watches, hotel complexes, cars and clothes, which may seem at odds with traditional culture such as the kimono, but some of the mechanisms of luxury most definitely apply to the kimono. Luxury consumer items are designed to demonstrate wealth and status. In many ways, this is what the kimono became in the second half of the 20th century. The off-the-shelf sector, with its cotton bolts and wool kimono, continued to have a market in the immediate post-war years when women still wore the kimono regularly, but heavy blows were dealt to this side of the industry when women started making large quantities of Western style clothes at home using sewing machines, becoming what Andrew Gordon describes as 'a nation of dressmakers' (Gordon 2012: 186). These cheap, comfortable alternatives slowly replaced the everyday kimono made of cotton or wool. In this new world of Westernised homes, offices, bicycles and cars, kimono were impractical and ill-adapted: long sleeves catch on door handles, wrapped kimono panels are awkward on bicycles, and kimono are best folded flat on the ground – a difficult task if you no longer have a *tatami* floor clear of clutter. The materiality of a newly Westernised world made the kimono alien in its own home context.

This process has happened in many societies across the globe. The irresistible practicality of Western clothes appeals, as does the affordability of mass-produced clothes, but so too does the fact they *belong* in the wider material context, which is dominated by Western clothes and sartorial aesthetics. Of course, a nuanced stance takes into account the ways in which Western culture and goods are inserted into and re-made in local contexts, rather than simply replacing local customs and practices with little or no transformation. Joseph Tobin has argued, for instance, that Western culture and goods were 'domesticated' by Japan – in other words, adapted to the Japanese context and a Japanese market (Tobin 1994). Japan, as any other country, is caught in the ebbs and flows of globalisation in which people, goods, ideas and capital change context constantly – as Ulf Hannerz puts it, 'an increasingly dense web of all kinds of communication and relationships across borders and between continents' (Eriksen 2003: 25).

Japan was not, of course, simply 'made Western'. In the immediate post-war period, there was a thirst for all things Western: in the 1950s, having a black and white TV, a refrigerator and a washing machine was referred to as having the 'three sacred treasures'. This mirrors the 'real' three sacred treasures in Shintoism: the sword, the mirror and the jewel. It was common at this time to equate technological and economic advancement with religion and mythology (Yoshimi 1999: 155).

It would be naïve, however, to suggest that this influx of Western 'stuff', steady since the 19th century and reaching a crescendo in the post-war years, did not change Japan: the retreat of the kimono from day-to-day life is testimony of the changes brought about by the influx of Western things. This retreat was not, however, characterised by a total erasure. Silk kimono became increasingly luxurious and expensive, but the word luxury alone might not be quite enough to encapsulate the role that the kimono was to occupy in the latter half of the 20th century. While the kimono admittedly lost its place in day-to-day life as everyday clothing, it gained significance and importance as the item of choice for formal and ceremonial occasions, even as fewer and fewer people wore the kimono, as I explored in Chapter 2.

The kimono experienced a resurgence of interest in the 1960s (Dalby 2001: 3), and this interest coincided with Japan's economic boom and the growth of a middle class with disposable income. With middle class affluence came middle class interests, most notably the wish, as noted by Pierre Bourdieu, to acquire cultural capital through tastes, hobbies, clothing and interests that indicate good taste (Bourdieu 1986). In Japan, it was generally expected in the 1960s, 70s and 80s that caring for the household and nurturing the family would be the core part of a woman's existence, a role which was highly valued by women and society generally speaking (Brinton 1992: 12). Women were associated with caring duties, such as seasonal gift-giving, caring for ancestors and overseeing the ritual events in the family such as milestones in the development of a child (Daniels 2012: 157). These include, but are not limited to, *shichi-go-san*, a ritual collectively celebrating children aged seven, five and three, and *jūsan-mairi*, a ritual celebrating young girls entering puberty, as well as coming of age ceremonies. All these ceremonies and ritual moments in Japanese family life typically involve dressing the children/young adults in Japanese clothing, and usually the mother as well. This is still common practice in Japan, although a number of companies now offer rental services for the different kimono required. An associated practice is taking photos to record the event, which are then often placed in albums. For much of the latter half of the 20th century, the kimono was considered to be the correct attire in which to oversee all aspects of the family's ritual life, including children's school entrance and graduation ceremonies. With women in the family tasked with upholding its ritual and ceremonial life, dressing in kimono was crucial to represent the family's wealth and social standing.

The kimono became a powerful way to express a number of things in post-war Japanese society. In an interview I conducted with the managing director of the second-hand kimono shop chain Tansu-ya, Kenichi Nakamura (see Chapter 7), he told me that the wedding of Emperor Akihito and Empress Michiko in 1959 acted as a catalyst which increased women's wish to buy kimono. The figure of the new Empress inspired admiration for the elegance and beauty of her kimono-clad figure. Following a period of intense national soul-searching in the immediate post-war years, this image of unequivocally Japanese femininity struck a chord for many women in Japanese society as an aspirational image of Japanese womanhood and beauty. The kimono has become so deeply entangled with a particular image of feminine Japaneseness (I discuss in Chapters 5, 6 and 7 that men do wear the kimono as well) that the image of a woman dressed in kimono has come to symbolise Japan itself (Goldstein-Gidoni 1999: 366).

The formal, silk kimono was, therefore, a powerful conveyor of a multitude of symbols: through its design, in opposition to Western clothes, and through its regional dye and weaving techniques, but also through its patronage by the Imperial family, the kimono powerfully encapsulated the Japanese nation, in a way that contrasted with prior images of a Japan represented by a martial, masculine image. The kimono, instead, allowed for an image that focused on beauty, refinement and femininity. The combination of Japaneseness and femininity was especially alluring to female shoppers at the time. It should not be forgotten that the materials out of which formal kimono were made were especially important: silk kimono and the image they convey of genteel femininity had long been associated with the samurai class (Dalby 2001: 135) and the wealthy who could afford to possess the luxury of silk. Long after the feudal era classes of samurai, peasant, artisan and merchant were abolished in the late 19th century, silk had remained, for the most part, out of the hands of many. As a result, silk had always been the subject of longing for those who, in the pre-war period, could not afford it. Tatsuichi Horikiri, in his collection entitled *The Stories that Clothes Tell: Voices of Working-Class Japan*, recounts the story of a young woman born in 1909 into a farming family. This young woman desperately yearned for a silk kimono, even though this would be extremely expensive. She taught herself to weave mats, and while she gave the money from the sale of the mats to her mother, she would sometimes be given a bit of change. Over years, she saved money and finally, borrowing a small amount from her mother, she bought a bolt of *meisen* kimono cloth. She sewed the kimono herself, in secret, in fear of what neighbours would say if they saw her. Not only was it improper for a woman of her standing to wear a silk kimono but her family was also in debt, and if the money lender were to see her wearing silk, he might have taken the kimono from her or pressured her family to pay what they owed. It was only later in her life, after her marriage, that the farmer's daughter felt she could at last wear her silk kimono (Horikiri 2016: 47–48).

This story hints at the depth of fascination with, and longing for, silk among Japanese women. But then rising incomes after the war put silk within reach of an unprecedented number of Japanese people. Given such powerful associations with wealth, beauty, nation and womanhood, it is not surprising that demand for the formal kimono increased dramatically. In addition, for the rising middle class at the dawn of Japan's phenomenal post-war economic recovery, the formal kimono became intimately associated with wealth, status and good taste, a material manifestation both of the nation's new stability and of the family's economic and cultural capital.

Being able to wear silk kimono meant that you had 'arrived', in the sense that your family was wealthy enough for you to be able to afford one, ideally made using a technique that your peers would recognise, such as Kaga Yūzen, to formal events, such as children's school entrance or graduation ceremonies, tea ceremonies, weddings, funerals, and so on. The kimono was a tool to demonstrate economic and social status, but also cultural status in the sense that it communicated a woman's cultural capital by showing that she knew both how to wear a kimono and the aesthetic rules and codes of TPO (the Japan-made English acronym for Time, Place, Occasion – see Chapter 2).

It would be tempting, then, to see the gradual reduction of cotton and wool kimono in the immediate post-war period in favour of luxury formal silk kimono associated with ritual and ceremony as an inevitable consequence of a changing world, a Westernised world in which the kimono's role was increasingly formalised and came to epitomise a particular image of Japanese femininity. After the initially rather unpromising market of the immediate post-war years, the economic recovery of the 1960s brought about an increase in disposable income across a growing middle class. As a result, it made sense for the kimono industry to focus on the formal kimono and stimulate the market for expensive silk kimono. The Committee for the Study on Japanese Dress, organised by the Ministry for Economy, Trade and Industry (METI), found that demand for the dyed silk kimono boomed in the 1950s, and steadily increased in the second half of the 20th century. In 1981, the industry peaked, with sales reaching roughly 1800 billion yen.[4]

In the post-war decades, however, the rise in demand was very promising, and the industry had a strong incentive to focus on these types of formal kimono. Kimono with the 'brand power' of a refined, regional technique such as Kaga Yūzen were especially in demand. This particular brand power is located in the regional traditions that went into making them. Their authenticity is legitimised through their existence down the centuries and their association with particular regional craft traditions. With demand for formal, silk kimono increasing in the post-war period, the industry focused primarily on these types. Kimono made from other textiles, such as cotton, wool, linen and polyester,[5] were also produced, but not to nearly the same extent as silk kimono. Building on pre-existing cultural norms of formality and propriety governing what to wear at what occasions, the industry began diversifying formal types of kimono in order to be able to sell a range of formal wear. This is why there are so many types of formal kimono for women in Japan, and still only one type of formal kimono for men. A man's most formal kimono attire is the combination of a black kimono with a *hakama* (pleated trousers) and *haori* (overcoat). This is usually for the groom at a wedding. Women, on the other hand, not only have their own bridal kimono, but a dizzying array of different formal kimono types to choose from. I have already discussed in Chapter 2 how the industry invented the *hōmongi* kimono for formal events in the Taishō era (1912–1926), capitalising on women's increased presence in formal, public events. The industry produced a kimono related to the *hōmongi*, yet subtly different, called a *tsukesage*. The two kimono are very similar and many customers struggle to tell them apart. The only major difference is that a *tsukesage* has fewer embellishments, such as gold and silver thread, and generally speaking fewer patterns and a more staid appearance. It was marketed as a refined, plainer, potentially more versatile version of the very formal *hōmongi*. The kimono industry has been very efficient at 're-using' existing kimono types, and marketing them in different ways to suit the formal kimono market. The pull of tradition with regards to the kimono is very strong, and marketing something as traditional and suitable for specific formal events is often a powerful mechanism for securing a purchase.

If you are the mother of the bride or the groom, however, then a different kimono is required. This kimono is called a *kurotomesode* (see Figure 3.2) and is immediately recognisable because it is completely black, with the exception of patterns below the obi line, but not above. The *kurotomesode* is expensive, and only used by the mother of the bride or groom at a wedding. The industry marketed this kimono type as essential formal wear. They also generated a version of this kimono in colour, called an *irotomesode*, which can be worn to the weddings of relatives other than sons and daughters. In terms of formality this is roughly what the categories are divided into:

Kurotomesode (for married women, mother of the bride/groom)
Irotomesode (for both married and unmarried, but more likely older women)
Furisode (for unmarried and/or young women)
Hōmongi (for unmarried and married women)
Tsukesage (for unmarried and married women)
Komon (unmarried and married women; relatively informal)

Some of these categories existed before the post-war period, but the industry actively encouraged the diversification of formal wear to avoid the problem of kimono saturation. Kimono, compared to Western clothes, have long lives. They are not the product of fast fashion, clothes that are worn for a season or two and then replaced. They are designed to last for decades, even generations. Therefore, having one formal kimono, in the minds of some customers, was enough for years' worth of formal events. Consequently, the industry encouraged the idea that having a range of formal kimono was important, in order to be fully prepared for different formal events, ceremonies and rituals.

The commercialisation of knowledge

The retreat of the kimono from day-to-day life and its increased formalisation brought about a specific role for the kimono industry. The understanding of levels of formality related to the kimono types listed above used to be passed down within the family, as indeed most kimono-related knowledge was, such as the proper way to get dressed and the aesthetic codes relating to age, season and occasion ('Time, Place, and Occasion'). As Western clothing became the norm, Japan entered a stage of *kimono-banare* or 'separation from the kimono'. This separation was enhanced by the increasing formalisation of the kimono in the second half of the 20th century, because the kimono became reserved for special occasions only. As the kimono receded from day-to-day life so, too, did knowledge and understanding of the kimono. The role of cultural transmitter was instead filled by kimono retailers and, to a certain extent, *kitsuke* schools (kimono dressing academies). In other words, the kimono industry does not just sell kimono, obi and other kimono-related accessories, but they also sell a body of knowledge about the kimono. Operating as consultants, the retail face of the industry is expected to be able to impart knowledge about when to wear what, how to combine outfits, to help the buyer find the right kimono and even at times help them to wear it, as some kimono shops also offer informal kimono dressing classes.

As I have already discussed in previous chapters, Japan is a society that attaches a great deal of importance to ritual and the correct performance of ritual (McVeigh 1994). There is a gap, however, between the importance of these rituals and the knowledge that Japanese people have of how to perform them, the understanding of what to do and when that is necessary for a ritual to be ordered, effective and meaningful. Thus Japanese people often find themselves at important junctures in their lives where they need a ritual to take place – a wedding or a funeral, for example, or other occasions such as tea ceremonies or visits to religious sites – but may lack the necessary know-how. Form, etiquette and behaviour matter deeply in everyday interactions and mundane moments, and this importance is magnified for more significant occasions. Not knowing what to do can cause a certain amount of anxiety, an uneasiness which the plethora of advice literature on customs, etiquette and ways to behave on particular occasions seeks to assuage (McVeigh 1994: 58).

When times in the life cycle of the family call for a kimono (which is now becoming increasingly optional), families often find themselves at a loss about what to do: is there a kimono at home that we can use? If so, which one? How should the kimono be folded? What kimono should go with which obi? Do I have the right kimono for this occasion? Who can wear it, and can anyone I know dress me? If I combine these two items, will I get it wrong and be embarrassed? Knowledge about the kimono, how to wear it, and an understanding of the 'kimono canon' of rules and aesthetics, is unevenly distributed across Japan, regionally and in terms of age and class, and many women find their knowledge about the kimono to be lacking. As a result, customers are often reliant on the advice of retailers when they purchase a kimono, and they rely on the retailer to tell them when and where they can wear a particular kimono, what obi they can pair it with, what accessories are suitable, whether the pattern is age-appropriate, and so on.

This commercialisation of knowledge in the kimono industry has parallels with the way in which knowledge pertaining to ritual and etiquette generally has been commercialised in other areas of Japanese life. Hikaru Suzuki, writing on the commercialisation of the funeral industry in Japan, demonstrates how the funeral services took over the practices and rituals associated with caring for the dead (Suzuki 2000: 39). Katherine Rupp notes that, until the 1960s, wakes and funerals in her field site were held in the home but by the early 21st century funeral companies had entirely taken over funeral practices (Rupp 2003: 95–6; see also Tsuji 2006: 399). Nowadays, most Japanese people use the services of the funeral industry. Since they require the services and the knowledge of the funeral industry to perform the rituals and ceremonies that Japanese people consider important on these occasions, they place their faith in the expertise of the company.

A similar phenomenon has taken place in the marriage industry as well. By the 1990s, 80 per cent of urban Japanese couples chose the services of commercial wedding companies (Goldstein-Gidoni 2001: 24). Ofra Goldstein-Gidoni argues that 'among commoners and in rural areas' especially, pre-war wedding ceremonies were typically quite simple affairs. Complex wedding ceremonies only came later with the establishment of the modern marriage industry: 'the profit motive was a major reason for the development of the fixed wedding offered by the new wedding parlors, since owners wanted to reap profits from every stage of the wedding day, beginning with the preparation of the bride and ending with the reception' (Goldstein-Gidoni 2001: 24). In much the same way as the kimono industry often positions itself as an adviser to consumers who do not know as much about the kimono, wedding industry advisers see themselves as providing services and knowledge to a public that may not know as much about weddings. Walter Edwards has also analysed the growth of wedding companies and services in Japan, and describes people approaching a wedding service as follows: 'unfamiliar with the details of formality, they require patient coaching before, and skilful cueing during, the performance' (Edwards 1989: 77). He also quotes a director at the White Crane Palace wedding service saying that 'we have to coddle them [the customers] a bit [...] because they don't know all that much about ceremony' (Edwards 1989: 77). Edwards further writes that the director's words 'point to the larger process of the ordinary person's alienation from ritual expertise, a process that has accompanied the growth of the commercial wedding industry' (Edwards 1989: 78)

The similarities with the kimono industry are many: the key transition period of World War Two, the way in which family knowledge became commercialised and the manner in which customers still want these traditional forms of culture, particularly at key ritual moments in life, but are mostly reliant on professional expertise. Having the knowledge which customers may lack enables industries focusing on traditional customs and material culture to build expertise, which then becomes a key part of their service. This gives them the ability not just to change culture but also to generate it.

However, the kimono industry's business model, compared to other businesses using a similar knowledge-monopoly, is riskier in that they can only sell the one product. According to Tomoko Hashino, the prices of both kimono and obi more than doubled from 1970 to 1988 and, at the same time, the quantities purchased fell by around one-half for kimono and one-third for obi (Donzé and Fujioka 2018: 263). The kimono industry did not foresee that demand would decrease for formal kimono, and were unable to predict the decline of the markets that they relied upon. But who, exactly, was purchasing formal, luxury kimono when the industry was doing well?

Post-war markets for formal kimono: women, family and the bridal trousseau

The formal kimono strategy was both a product of circumstance and a strategy that the industry used, for survival at first, and then for profit. This might seem to be a significant risk to take, but at the time in the 1960s and

1970s, it did not appear to be so because formal kimono sold well. Because the industry could point to several key markets for formal kimono, they actively stimulated and encouraged women in these markets to buy kimono. In this section, I take a closer look at these specific markets, drawing on the qualitative data I obtained from 21 homes that I surveyed in Aichi prefecture, mostly in Toyota, drawing on the connections of Sachiko, my host with whom I stayed for the duration of the twelve months of my fieldwork. I would spend several hours at a time with my participants, most of whom were in their 50s, 60s or 70s, often with their friends as well, and together we would look at their collections of kimono. I was invariably struck by the sheer quantities of kimono that my research participants possessed, often dozens of kimono and obi and, in a couple of memorable cases, hundreds. It should be said that Toyota is a relatively wealthy part of Japan, and that my middle-aged participants, even though from modest backgrounds, had benefited from the economic growth of the 1970s and 1980s. Many of my participants had some connection with the headquarters and production sites of Toyota Motors, with relatives employed in the company. Their collections of kimono comprised a number of different types and styles, and came from multiple sources. Some of these kimono they had bought for themselves, in the case of women who practised tea ceremony or other forms of Japanese art, or those who wanted to wear kimono for formal events and knew how to dress themselves. As I have already discussed, in the post-war period, the formal kimono became an important means of establishing a family's economic and cultural capital, and women's ability to wear the kimono and display their understanding of its aesthetics was a part of how they demonstrated their social standing. My participants in the city of Toyota, as women who grew up in the post-war period, occupied an interesting position: on the one hand, they were sensitive to this role of the kimono, and in their middle age often gravitated towards it, taking *kitsuke* (kimono wearing) lessons or traditional Japanese arts that required it to be worn. On the other hand, their generation had enjoyed the influx of Western goods and culture that came into Japan in the post-war period. Some of my participants had worn the kimono quite regularly throughout their lives and did so confidently, but many had more difficulty. In most cases, they did want to wear kimono, but this wish was not always realised in the face of the difficulties, especially their lack of confidence. Among the more confident kimono-wearers, many had regularly bought kimono for themselves, but for the majority, their collection came from gifts from older family members. I have explored elsewhere how the kimono is supposed to function as inalienable wealth, in the sense coined by Annette Weiner (see Weiner 1985, 1992). Female family memory is passed down from one generation to the next through the kimono, in opposition to the traditional understanding in social theory of Japanese kinship that places emphasis on family transmission through the male line, in particular the family name (see Valk 2020). Clothing is unique among material culture for its ability to powerfully evoke the presence and essence of another person (see Woodward 2007 for detailed investigations into the relationship between clothing, memory and identity). With their added importance in ritual and ceremonial life, and the economic investment that goes into their acquisition, kimono are items of especially charged importance, and their transmission between generations is still expected, although many of my participants struggled to ensure that these collections would be passed on (Valk 2020).

Almost always the largest category in the collection of the women I visited was their bridal trousseau. Women in their 50s and 60s at the time of my research all possessed bridal trousseaus with kimono, regardless of the fact that few wore them often. Bridal trousseaus were a major market for the kimono industry in the post-war period, as rising prosperity in the growing middle class made this custom wide-spread across Japanese society. The bridal trousseau, or *oyomeiri-dōgu* in Japanese ('items for brides') typically refers to items such as kimono, linen, furniture and other household goods that new brides traditionally brought with them to their new household (Koizumi 2004: 252). Inge Daniels' work on Japanese homes in the Kansai area in Japan revealed that the majority of middle-aged women in her study possessed *oyomeiri-dōgu* that they had brought with them to their new homes (Daniels 2010: 142). A major element of the trousseau is the *tansu* in which the new bride's kimono are stored. The word *tansu* can be used to refer to any piece of traditional Japanese furniture that is used to store household items and its shape is determined by the items it is intended to house (Koizumi 2004: 276). A traditional kimono *tansu* is typically made of three parts that can be taken apart to facilitate transportation. For the most part, these sections can then be stacked on top of each other. More modern versions of the *tansu* may not have these features, although they will most certainly have the same types of shallow, wide drawers capable of accommodating kimono. The *tansu*, in many of the homes that I visited in Toyota city, was part of the bridal trousseau given to women, now in their 50s, 60s and 70s, when they got married.

The practice of putting together a full kimono trousseau for daughters who were getting married is an old custom for the wealthy and the elite. Kimono were one element of the trousseau which also comprised household goods, among other items. Citing the work of the historian Kazuko Koizumi, Inge Daniels notes that the custom of female contribution to her new household had developed among the social elite by the 17th century (Koizumi 1995: 258–64 in Daniels 2010: 142). Reliable examples of the detailed kimono contents of bridal trousseau in the Edo period also exist (see Tamura 2004: 263–6 in Francks 2009: 33). Kazuko Koizumi identifies that, with some significant regional differences, commoners had begun to imitate the custom of the bridal trousseau which was more prevalent among what was then the wealthier classes (Koizumi 2004: 254). It was not until the beginning of the Taishō era (1912–1926) that the custom became widespread enough to be considered a nationwide phenomenon (Koizumi 2004: 258). While it might have been possible to assemble household items and *tansu* for lower income families, kimono, especially silk kimono, were an unaffordable luxury for the majority of the Japanese population before World War Two. It was only after the war and Japan's subsequent economic success that it became possible for the average family to afford silk. Because kimono were seen as indispensable, if seldom worn, Japanese parents felt compelled to provide them, and because of Japan's new wealth, they were able to do so on an unprecedented scale. The formal silk kimono boomed in post-war Japan, in part because rising incomes generally meant that more families could afford to spend money on customs such as the bridal trousseau. As a result, in the post-war period there was a reliable market for kimono both from women who wanted kimono for themselves and for those buying for their daughters when they married, or for other special occasions such as the coming of age ceremony at the age of 20. This market was not as stable and secure as it seemed, however, and it has proven to be especially vulnerable to the socio-cultural shifts away from the kimono as the ideal piece of formal wear, as well as to the economic crisis which hit in the 1990s.

Many of my participants hoped to make trousseaus for their daughters, but few had successfully done so. It was no longer considered necessary, at least from their daughters' point of view. The reasons behind this rejection of the kimono and the tradition of the *tansu* are both social and economic. First of all, social norms surrounding marriage have changed in the late 20th and early 21st century. Women who grew up in the 1960s and 70s had an understanding that they would marry *into* a household (*oyome ni iku*), often moving in with their husband's family and parents, particularly if he was an elder son (Hendry 1981). Households in Japan were traditionally referred to as the *ie*, a household unit characterised by a system of familial rank, headship (usually by a man) and transmission of headship to the oldest son,[6] with a strong imperative to transmit the family name, as well as ancestor worship (see Shimizu 1987). In the context of relationships between households, it was key to provide a bridal trousseau and a *tansu* that were lavish enough to match the social and financial status of the husband's family so that the new bride could join them without feeling any shame about her own family and origins. It was also the case in the 1960s and 70s that, on the wedding day, the neighbourhood and family of the bride and groom could actually open the drawers of the *tansu* and inspect all the other items in the trousseau.

So the bridal trousseau was a way for the bride's family to both anchor their status by showing the neighbourhood their wealth and their ability to 'provide' properly for their daughter, and also to express their sense of parental obligation or devotion towards their daughter. My participants frequently referred to the wish on the part of parents (particularly mothers) to provide kimono for their daughters as *oyagokoro* (literally, 'parents' heart'). The gift demonstrated their wish to care for her by making sure that she had a lifetime's supply of kimono, that she would be respected in her new home where her status as a daughter-in-law would be quite low, and that she had a safety net for her family in the form of kimono that she could sell if need be. In times of financial difficulty, as was the case during World War Two, a *tansu* full of kimono could also provide a daughter with emergency funds should she need to provide for her new family in place of her husband, or, in a worst case scenario, should she need to escape her new family's household and return to her old family. Providing a trousseau was taken for granted, and while this custom had, in the past, only been available to wealthy families, with rising prosperity post-war, the custom spread and the industry enjoyed a boom in sales as a result.

For women growing up in the 1980s and 1990s, the idea of marrying into an *ie* has considerably weakened. Although the ideal of the housewife remains strong and men are almost always designated as head of the household, women now in their 20s and 30s have typically stayed in education longer than their mothers and have typically stronger career aspirations. Japanese women overall are marrying less frequently and, when they do, they marry later than their mothers (see Tokuhiro 2010 and Vogel and Vogel 2013 for detailed discussion on the evolution of marriage in Japan). The overall trend is towards less marriage or late marriage, and fewer children. Women's increased involvement in higher education and employment, together with shifting family structure and marriage norms in late 20th and early 21st century Japan are significant contributing factors to these changes (Retherford, Ogawa and Matsukura 2001: 65).

When women do marry, they are likely to move into an apartment with their new spouse rather than into their husband's home with his parents, which means that there is less room for a cumbersome *tansu*, and the community would not generally be welcome to inspect the contents of the new bride's wardrobe. Marriages have become a more private affair. While it might be premature to say that all the characteristics of the *ie* system have vanished, it is clear that Japanese society has moved from the multi-generational *ie* towards a model of family based on the nuclear family with the couple at its centre (Tokuhiro 2010: 12). Accordingly, with this shift in social patterns, what is deemed acceptable to wear to important events, such as weddings and funerals, has changed. It is now perfectly acceptable to wear a dress to a wedding and a black suit to a funeral, and as a result the formal kimono seems less of an obligation and more of an unnecessary complication, particularly when invitations arrive at short notice (Valk 2018). Some of the women in their 50s and 60s that I spoke to felt the need to prepare at least a few kimono for their daughters when they got married, out of a lingering sense of parental obligation, but in most cases these trousseaus were not the formidable *tansu* laden with dozens of silk kimono that their own mothers prepared for them.

The bubble economy of the 1980s encouraged lavish spending and many well-to-do housewives who pursued tea ceremony, *kitsuke* classes or flower arranging had money to spare on kimono. However, the bubble burst in the early 1990s (see Chapter 4), putting a break on consumption practices (Yoshikawa 2007). Secure employment, which had previously been taken for granted, was now much harder to achieve, and the insecurity of the 1990s likely encouraged Japanese people to save money (Francks 2009: 208). The children of the wealthy post-war generation were coming of age at this time, and the economic crisis deeply affected both their social mores and their consumption practices. Whereas their mothers may have been housewives who had the freedom to buy kimono and spend on leisure and hobbies, this generation of women is concerned with practicality and thrift. The owner of a kimono shop in Toyota told me that kimono shop owners face a very different market today because 'now people use their money differently. They would rather use it on school fees or to buy a car. It's a tough situation. We have a very small profit margin. It's worrying for the future.'

The kimono was becoming less and less of a mandatory item for women, and while the 'swinging sleeve' *furisode* worn by young women during coming of age ceremonies remains much more deeply entrenched (even though in most cases today it is rented rather than bought – see Chapter 4), the bridal trousseau has very much declined. Many of my participants had asked their daughters if they wanted a kimono trousseau, to which many reportedly replied that they did not. Some of my participants nonetheless still bought kimono for their daughters, but mostly the daughters did not take the kimono with them, preferring to leave them with their mothers, particularly since they are usually even less sure than their mothers about how to wear the kimono. So their mothers keep their daughters' (often unworn) kimono at home, and at the same time their own mothers, now elderly and rarely in need of a kimono, give them their own kimono to be looked after. Other elderly relatives may well do so too. Many women in their 50s and 60s thus end up being a kind of kimono caretaker, storing the kimono of three or more women in their home, and, for the most part, these kimono lie unused (see Valk 2020). The current situation is that most homes have a kind of 'kimono saturation', comprised of formal kimono. This drives demand down even further, as customers are less likely to buy new formal kimono when they feel that (a) Western clothes will do anyway for a formal occasion, and (b) if they did want to wear a kimono, they could simply choose one of the ones already in their home. The reality for many of my participants was that plans to wear a kimono could be easily scuppered: forgetting how to tie a particular obi, heavy rain or hot weather, a tiring schedule, the tempting alternative of convenient Western-style formal wear and worry about damaging the kimono, but also kimono after-care such as folding or airing it, – these were all factors that often made women choose not to wear the kimono. Of course, there were some participants who had more confidence and who enjoyed the process but, overall, the picture is of decreased use, even for formal, ritual occasions.

To summarise, the rise in popularity of the formal silk kimono in post-war Japan coincided with rising incomes and the growing prosperity of Japanese society. In a society in which middle-class status was partly mediated through consumption, beautiful, formal silk kimono made using regional techniques became an important way of demonstrating both a conspicuously Japanese femininity and cultural and economic capital. This state of affairs was soon to change, with a society increasingly distancing itself from the kimono and a major financial crisis on the horizon in the 1990s. Both of these factors were to significantly damage the kimono industry, which had focused on the formal kimono almost to the complete exclusion of other types of kimono.

Notes

1 The JET programme has two streams: one stream employs young, mainly English-speaking, people from abroad and the other employs people with a relatively high level of Japanese language fluency to be placed in local government and assist with interpretation, translation and community events. I was employed in the latter scheme.
2 I encountered this problem myself. A friend got in touch with me after a relative of his wife had died, and he asked me to collect her kimono as nobody else was willing to take them. The collection included a kimono which I initially thought was a Kaga Yūzen. The colours and patterns were right, and it also had a red stamp which usually marks the kimono as having been made by a craft master. I took it to one of my field sites, the kimono shop Azumaya, to authenticate the kimono. Shibakawa-san, the owner, deliberated with his parents, and in the end concluded that the kimono must be a 'Kyo-Kaga Yūzen' – a kimono made in Kyoto but designed to look like a Kaga Yūzen. This was their verdict, but even for professionals this kimono was hard to trace, showing just how tricky the understanding of brands and regional production can be.
3 Kimono require a certain amount of 'aftercare' after being worn: because they are washed professionally, which can be costly, people try to avoid getting them dirty. They have to be aired in order to make sure sweat does not stain or permeate the fabric. Leaving kimono unaired for long periods of time is thought to encourage mould. They also need to be folded carefully according to a specific order which ensures that they will not become creased. Often, people do not know how to fold them.
4 From page 6 of a White Paper produced by the Ministry of Economy, Trade and Industry, available here: https://www.meti.go.jp/committee/kenkyukai/seizou/wasou_shinkou/report_001.html (retrieved 10/03/2021).
5 Broadly speaking, textiles for kimono tend to be ranked according to formality. Silk is usually the most formal, with cotton, linen and polyester occupying lower rungs on the ladder of formality. Regarding polyester in particular, some of my participants enjoyed the fact that polyester is usually cheaper and easier to look after than silk, but others disliked the feel of polyester. Participants who wore the kimono often were actually aware of the difference in 'feel' between textiles, and I noticed a frequent preference for natural fabrics such as silk, cotton or linen.

6 There is also a system which allows for successfully continuing the *ie* even if there are no sons. In some cases the oldest daughter's husband can be adopted into the family and take on the family name, thereby allowing for the continuation of the *ie*.

References

Bourdieu, P. 1986. 'The forms of capital' in Szeman, I. and Kaposy, T., eds. 2011. *Cultural Theory: an Anthology*. Oxford: Wiley-Blackwell

Brinton, M. C. 1992. *Women and the Economic Miracle: Gender and Work in Postwar Japan*. Berkeley, CA: University of California Press

Dalby, L. 2001. *Kimono: Fashioning Culture*. London: Vintage

Daniels, I. 2010. *The Japanese House: Material Culture in the Modern Home*. Oxford and New York: Berg.

Daniels, I. 2012: 'Beneficial bonds: luck and the lived experience of relatedness in contemporary Japan'. In *Social Analysis* 56(1): 148–164

Edwards, W. 1989. *Modern Japan Through Its Weddings: Gender, Person, and Society in Ritual Portrayal*. Stanford, CA: Stanford University Press

Eriksen, T. H. 2003. *Globalisation: Studies in Anthropology*. London and Sterling, VA: Pluto Press

Francks, P. 2009. *The Japanese Consumer. An Alternative Economic History of Modern Japan*. Cambridge: Cambridge University Press

Goldstein-Gidoni, O. 1999. 'Kimono and the construction of gendered and cultural identities'. In *Ethnology* 38(4): 351–370

Goldstein-Gidoni, O. 2001. 'Hybridity and distinctions in Japanese contemporary commercial weddings'. In *Social Science Japan Journal* 4(1): 21–38

Gordon, A. 2012. *Fabricating Consumers: the Sewing Machine in Modern Japan*. Berkeley, CA: University of California Press

Hashino, T. 2018. 'Chapter 13. The survival strategy of the Japanese kimono industry'. In Pierre-Yves Donzé, P.-Y. and Fujioka, R., eds. *Global Luxury: Organizational Change and Emerging Markets since the 1970s*. Singapore: Palgrave Macmillan

Hendry, J. 1981. *Marriage in Changing Japan: Community & Society*. London and New York: Taylor and Francis

Horikiri, T. (edited and translated by Wagoner, R.) 2016. *Working Class People in Early 20th-Century Japan. The Stories Clothes Tell: Voices of Working-Class Japan*. Lanham, MD: Rowman & Littlefield

Koizumi, K. 1995. *Shitsunai to kagu no rekishi* ('A History of Home Interiors and Furniture'), Tokyo: Chuo koronsha. In Daniels, I. 2010. *The Japanese house: Material Culture in the Modern Home*. Oxford and New York: Berg.

Koizumi, K. 2004. *Tansu*. Tokyo: Hosei University Press

McVeigh, B. 1994. 'Ritualized practices of everyday life: constructing self, status, and social structure in Japan'. In *Journal of Ritual Studies* 8(1): 53–71

Milhaupt, T. S. 2014. *Kimono: A Modern History*. London: Reaktion Books

Retherford, R. D., Ogawa, N. and Matsukura, R. 2001. 'Late marriage and less marriage in Japan'. In *Population and Development Review* 27(1): 65–102

Rupp, K. 2003. *Gift-giving in Japan: Cash, Connections, Cosmologies*. Stanford, CA: Stanford University Press

Shimizu, A. 1987. '*Ie* and *Dōzoku*: family and descent in Japan'. In *Current Anthropology*. 28(4): S85–S90

Sugimoto, S. 2020. 'Branding Tsumugi kimono in Japan: Kimono magazines as mediators between consumers and the "Mingei" movement' in Nakatani, A., ed. *Fashionable Traditions: Asian Handmade Textiles in Motion*. Lanham, MD, New York, London: Lexington Books

Suzuki, H. 2000. *The Price of Death: The Funeral Industry in Contemporary Japan*. Stanford, CA: Stanford University Press

Tamura, H. 2004. *Fuasshon no shakai keizai shi* ('The socio-economic history of fashion'). Tokyo: Nihon Keizai Hyoronsha. In Francks, P. 2009. *The Japanese Consumer. An Alternative Economic History of Modern Japan*. Cambridge: Cambridge University Press

Tobin, J. J. 1994. *Re-made in Japan: Everyday Life and Consumer Taste in a Changing Society*. New Haven, CT: Yale University Press

Tokuhiro, Y. 2010. *Marriage in Contemporary Japan*. London and New York: Routledge

Tsuji, Y. 2006. 'Mortuary rituals in Japan: the hegemony of tradition and the motivations of individuals'. In *Ethos* 34(3): 391–431

Valk, J. 2018. 'From duty to fashion: the changing role of the kimono in the twenty-first century'. In *Fashion Theory* 22(3): 309–340

Valk, J. 2020. 'The Alienating Inalienable: rethinking Annette Weiner's concept of inalienable wealth through Japan's 'sleeping kimono''. In *HAU: Journal of Ethnographic Theory* 10(1): 147–165

Vogel, S. H. with Vogel, S. K. 2013. *The Japanese Family in Transition: From the Professional Housewife Ideal to the Dilemmas of Choice*. Lanham, MD: Rowman and Littlefield Publishers

Weiner, A. B. 1985. 'Inalienable wealth'. In American Ethnologist 12(2): 210–227

Weiner, A. B. 1992. Inalienable Possessions: The Paradox of Keeping-While Giving. Berkeley, CA: University of California Press

Woodward, S. 2007. *Why Women Wear What They Wear*. Oxford and New York: Berg

Yoshikawa, H. 2007. 'Japan's lost decade: What have we learned and where are we heading?'. In *Asian Economic Policy Review* 2(2): 186–203

Yoshimi, S. 1999. 'Made in Japan': the cultural politics of 'home electrification' in postwar Japan'. In *Media, Culture & Society* 21(2): 149–171

Chapter 4

The path of resilience

Weathering the economic crisis and managing public perceptions

Although the economic crisis of the 1990s has severely affected the kimono retail industry, and even though Japan's economy has never fully recovered, kimono shops are still a visible presence in Japan. Many large department stores, for example, will have a substantial section dedicated to selling kimono. Most department stores have their own kimono shops, but independent chain shops also exist, such as Yamato, which owns over 100 shops across Japan as of mid-2020.[1] Walk down the streets of any city and any town, and sooner or later you will come across a family-owned kimono shop, such as Azumaya, which is described in the following chapter.

Not so visible are the wholesalers, the businesses who provide bolts of kimono cloth to the shops. Some wholesalers deal with a range of items, while others tend to specialise – some handling bolts and others accessories such as bags and *zori* (kimono shoes) that complete the outfits. It is straightforward enough to go into kimono shops and speak with the assistants, but for the most part, establishing a deeper relationship with shop owners required an introduction from a trusted customer or member of staff. As I explained in Chapter 1, part of this is integral to the fabric of Japanese society: introductions by trusted third parties are the norm, and are expected. In the context of the kimono industry, where people are not expecting to be interviewed by someone who has just walked in, least of all by a non-Japanese person, introductions are crucial. Nonetheless, shops were relatively accessible because you can simply walk in. Craftspeople are also relatively accessible because many craft workshops have open days or showcase their skills in department stores or during special events. Encountering those who work between craftspeople and retailers, the wholesalers, was not so straightforward. The relationship between shop owners and wholesalers can sometimes be fraught, and is mixed in with politics, monopolies, and the importance of maintaining good social relationships. Once established, a shop owner's relationship with a particular wholesaler may be hard to break, and an alliance with a particular wholesaler may preclude establishing relationships with others. When kimono still sold well prior to the 1990s, shops with lower profiles might have found their requests to do business with a wholesaler denied if they were not considered suitably 'established'. For many in the industry, the benchmark is 100 years, at which point they are entitled to call themselves a *shinise*, or 'established business'.

It was only after I had spent time building up relationships with shop owners that they were happy to introduce me to their wholesalers. It was one such introduction that led me to Kyoto on a cold day in February, to a district renowned for its wholesalers. My appointment is with a representative of a large wholesaler, but when I arrive at my destination, I stand outside a tall sleek building, unsure I have the correct address. As is not uncommon with wholesalers, from the outside nothing predisposes you to think that the building has a connection with the kimono industry.

I am welcomed by a woman in uniform who confirms that I do indeed have the right address, and who asks me to wait. As I do so, I take stock of my surroundings: the building has several floors, and while women are wearing uniforms, men are wearing suits. Everyone goes about their business with purpose. The representative comes to greet me, and leads me into a small neutral meeting room. I sit, and wonder how many business deals have been struck at this table.

'I am not entirely sure how best to help you,' the representative tells me politely. 'After all, the world of the kimono, it's very deep and complicated, you know. Kimono are very different from Western clothes. I am not sure what would help you best.'

At first, he speaks to me with detailed knowledge of the kimono itself, the process of making silk and extracting silk from silkworms. He speaks with a quiet, refined cadence, and it is clear that his interest in the subject extends beyond mere professionalism.

'People think that kimono colours and fashions don't really change, that they always stay the same, but that's not actually true'.

I nodded. I had heard this several times before. Many people in the kimono industry pointed out that there was a general perception among Japanese people (and I would add beyond Japan as well) that the kimono is an unchanging entity, subject entirely to its own aesthetics and rules of wear which reach far back in time and are resistant to change and evolution. This is an illusion created, perhaps, in comparison with Western fashions that appear to be moving at a faster pace.

'You have to stay on top of things,' he continued. 'New items and new techniques are constantly being introduced. We have sales events at the beginning and the middle of the month, and then each season is sold well in advance. Summer kimono, the unlined ones,[2] for example, are sold by January or February. We have clients from all over the country come here, but sometimes we also go on sales events in different parts of the country too. But it's difficult now. It used to be that if you wanted people to think well of you, you would put on a kimono when you go and see them. Now, that's not the case anymore, you don't have to do that. That being said, the rental kimono business is growing in Japan, so that's one way that people might start having an interest in the kimono again. It's not a bad thing.'

Historically, the main centres for wholesalers in Japan were Tokyo, Kyoto, Osaka and Nagoya, the latter two being now much diminished. The whole of Japan used to be split between these four distribution hubs which each handled dispatching kimono, obi, and kimono-related accessories to their section of Japan. Each of the cities had its own established wholesaler district, but of the original four, Tokyo and Kyoto are now the main centres.

Overhead, the loudspeakers installed throughout the building call out for various staff members to attend meetings or pick up files. Taking advantage of a pause, I prompt him to speak about the industry, and the effects of the recession.

'Ah, well 20 or so years ago,[3] it was like a great tempest. The area was devastated: firms folded one after the other. Places that were hundreds of years old, places that sold as much as 20, 30 billion yen a year, they folded one after the other. In Kyoto, our companies had formed an association in the 1970s, with 670 companies. To give you an idea, that number is now in the 150s.'

The representative painted a vivid image of wholesaling as an ecosystem, with each wholesaler relying on the other for goods and services as the kimono moved towards the finished product. There are big firms such as the one he belonged to, which stock many different types of kimono ranging from informal *yukata* (light summer wear similar in style to a kimono) to specialised formal wear such as *ubugi*.[4] There are also smaller 'specialist' wholesalers (*sanchidonya*) which stock a particular kind of item, usually locally produced in the area. An example of the latter type are the local wholesalers of the Nishijin district in Kyoto, who specialise in the items produced by the famous weavers of the Nishijin district. Large wholesalers buy their wares from the specialist wholesalers (*sanchidonya*), but also directly from producers.

To say that wholesalers are merely the link between producers and craftspeople at one end, and shops and customers at the other, then, is in fact an over-simplification.

'What you've got to understand is that we are all linked, we all do business with each other. Those wholesalers who sell the items on to the chain shops and the family-run shops, if they fold, then the other wholesalers fold too. There are so many different parts in the system: the wholesalers that provide plain undyed cloth, those that provide kimono lining, those that provide kimono accessories like shoes and bags... It's like dominos, if one goes down, so do the others.'

'How did your firm manage, then?' I asked.

'It was a really difficult time, but we pulled through somehow. We took a conservative line, and didn't try too many "adventures"', he says with a wry smile.

A conservative line without 'adventures' enabled this particular wholesaler to keep going into the 2010s. The same was not true of the other wholesalers mentioned by the representative – even prestigious, powerful wholesaling companies had not been able to withstand the crisis. The picture he painted was of a business choosing the path of resilience and enduring against the odds – a mode of existence that has enabled more than just kimono wholesalers to keep going in the face of economic crisis in Japan.

Economic crisis and resilience in Japan

Kimono sales were already falling from the 1970s onwards, but nothing could quite have prepared the industry for what was to come next. In the 1990s, a banking crisis struck Japan in the shape of bad loans and a speculative bubble bursting, causing a large number of financial institutions to fail, with wide-ranging consequences for the economy and industry as a whole. In the period between 1990 and 2003, economic growth slowed to 1 per cent per year (Fletcher III 2012: 150). This period of intense economic and industrial crisis followed a period of almost continuous economic growth between the 1960s and 1980s (Cwiertka and Machotka 2018: 15). The country had emerged as a leader in development, stability and industrial growth in the region, prompting scholars to look for the reasons behind the Japanese 'miracle', locating the mysteries of Japan's post-war success in Japanese management styles, cultural traits and corporate strategies (see Vogel 1979 for a classic example of this literature). Japan became the world's second largest economy and has only relatively recently slipped into third place behind China. Japan also emerged as a consumer society, with the dramatically increased standards of living in the post-war period fuelling an appetite for comfort, convenience and consumption (Francks 2009, Cwiertka and Machotka 2018), as I have described in Chapter 3 – the appetite that allowed the industry so successfully to market its expensive formal wear and craft pieces. By the end of the 1990s, however, academics went from examining the reasons behind Japan's economic success to exploring the reasons for the dramatic bursting of the bubble economy and the ensuing economic crisis of the 1990s, 2000s and 2010s. The decade following the bursting of the bubble is frequently referred to as the *ushinawareta jūnen*, or 'lost decade'. In view of the instability that continued into the 2000s, the term is often used in the plural: Japan's 'lost decades' (Funabashi and Kushner 2015: xx).

The crisis, as described by the representative of the wholesaler, had a dramatic effect on kimono wholesalers. While shops and craftspeople were also affected, the middle section of the chain of distribution was especially badly impacted. The representative described in vivid detail how wholesalers who reliably turned a major profit each year were forced to close. Crisis, it seems, closed in on the industry from all sides: the bubble bursting in the 1990s and the ensuing financial difficulties caused firms to close and led to major disruption in the industry, perturbing established distribution routes that had existed for decades. In parallel, demand for the formal kimono, that sold so well when Japan's economy was booming, was declining. Although as Katarzyna Cwiertka and Ewa Machotka indicate, the bursting of the bubble and the recession did not change the nature of Japan as a consumer society and consumerism remained a firmly entrenched principle (Cwiertka and Machotka 2018: 16), many Japanese consumers were confronted with the reality of an increasingly insecure employment landscape and lowered household incomes. This would conceivably have encouraged a more conservative approach to household purchases. As Yoshihide Shibakawa, owner of the kimono shop Azumaya (see Chapter 5) is fond of saying, kimono are *shikōhin* – which can be roughly translated as 'luxury items'. Because they were, increasingly, not considered necessary for various formal occasions, their place on the priority list of family purchases dropped significantly. In addition, the role of the kimono in establishing a women's cultural capital was waning, and purchasing the kimono in order to represent the face of the family to society was losing its importance. The fact that families now had less spending power to purchase expensive kimono compounded this socio-cultural change.

Where, then, does this leave the industry, and wholesalers such as the one described above? Much of the recent literature on the current economic, social and cultural state of Japan gives a portrayal of a society in seemingly perpetual crisis. And, indeed, 'crisis' seems to describe the situation rather well: with the poor economic climate ongoing since the 1990s, the crisis of 2008 further worsened the economy, and then in 2011 Japan was hit by the dual disasters of the Great Earthquake and the nuclear meltdown at Fukushima. In the years following, Japan suffered a number of further, smaller earthquakes, but also typhoons and landslides. While none of these came close in scale to the disasters of 2011, and indeed Japan is used to weathering such disasters, they still claimed lives and caused extensive damage. Now, at the time of writing this chapter in mid-2020, it is hard to see how the global pandemic of Covid-19 can avoid causing further damage to Japan's economy, particularly since the Olympic Games of 2020, scheduled to take place in Tokyo, have been postponed.

Anne Allison evokes a general condition of *ikizurashisa* ('difficulty to live') in a post-disaster Japan whose economic ill-health devoured the comfortable post-war certainties such as life-time employment, secure family units with a clearly defined gendered division of labour and middle-class lifestyles. The general sentiment in Japan, she argues, is as follows: 'proclaiming Japan to be hopeless has become something of a national pastime, with a reference point clearly set in the past. Japan has broken down, dissolved, been irretrievably lost' (Allison 2013: 82–83).

Yet, as Yoichi Funabashi and Barak Kushner write, 'when visiting Japan, many foreigners are puzzled: despite all the stories, the economy seems on an even keel. Visitors scratch their heads in surprise: is the narrative of the lost decades true? The relative calmness and apparent social stability in Japan, even after such a long recession, is indeed remarkable – Japanese society is resilient' (Funabashi and Kushner 2015: xxi). While many academics across the disciplines of economics, Japanese studies and anthropology view the economic crisis in Japan and its related demographic, social and political crises as presenting a picture of a struggling country, others choose a more nuanced point of view. The volume edited by Funabashi and Kushner suggests that any appraisal of the 'lost decades' should start by unpacking the many discourses and narratives of the phrase 'lost decades' itself, beyond a purely negative portrayal (Funabashi and Kushner 2015). Ulrike Schaede takes the even more optimistic view that the lost decades were not 'lost' at all, but in fact represented a creative opportunity for change and renewal (Schaede 2012).

There is merit to considering Schaede's view on crisis as an opportunity, which I will fully explore in the following chapters of the book. I would, however, not wish to downplay the effects of the economic crisis. The vignette at the start of this chapter demonstrates just how profoundly disruptive it has been for the kimono industry. Crisis has undeniably affected Japan, on a social, economic and political level, but this strand of resilience in Japanese society has been, in my opinion, largely overlooked. The wholesaler at the beginning of this chapter, but also the Kanamaru dye workshop in the previous chapter and the Gotō family in the Introduction, are prime examples of the resilience mentioned by Funabashi and Kushner, as I show below. Resilience in the kimono industry is a trait possessed by those who did not fold, those who got by, those who are still in business but having to do business differently than they used to – in other words, by those who have weathered the storm, as Japanese people are frequently required to do, both literally and figuratively.

The concept of resilience in the social sciences is generally used in research on development, but also environmental disasters and their aftermath, to describe the ability of communities to withstand, or at least cope with, the stressors placed upon them (see Barrios 2014 and Kopnina and Shoreman-Ouimet 2016 for examples). However, the concept of 'social resilience' has also been used by anthropologists and geographers, though a general definition of the term has not emerged beyond the specific circumstances in which it is used. W. Neil Adger defined resilience as 'the ability of human communities to withstand external shocks to their social infrastructure' (Adger 2000: 361). Michael Bollig breaks down resilience into three types: ecological, social and psychological, but he does not include economic resilience in the list, which is of particular interest in the context of the kimono industry (Bollig 2014).

The consensus in the literature appears to be that resilience is a trait, or a collection of traits, that emerges in response to a negative event or adverse conditions. Resilience can be defined, quite simply, as the ability to withstand, endure or cope with difficult conditions. Almost all my interlocutors in the kimono industry exhibited resilience in some form or other. This was evidenced by the fact that they had found a way to remain in business. Resilience, I argue, can be both passive and active. Passive resilience is exhibited through tolerance or endurance of the circumstances, while active resilience is exhibited through pro-active efforts to change difficult circumstances. This latter form of resilience is characterised by a greater willingness to learn from experience (Bollig 2014: 265), but also a bolder, more creative drive to change things for the future – in other words an ability to hope for a situation beyond mere endurance.

In the kimono industry, passive resilience in particular is a direct result of the economic crisis of the 1990s and beyond, but also of the declining market for the expensive formal wear that sold well in the 1970s and 80s. Interestingly, Bruno Amann and Jacques Jaussaud argue that, based on their organisation structure and general performance, Japanese family-led firms can be said to show greater resilience than those which are not family-led. While Amann and Jaussaud focus on the Asian financial crisis of 1997 rather than the long-term effects of the recession in Japan, and while their research is concerned with relatively large firms which might not easily be compared to family-owned kimono shops, their findings comparing family and non-family businesses suggest that, overall, family-run businesses exhibit a greater degree of resilience in an economic downturn (Amann and Jaussaud 2012). Citing Diane Coutu (2002), they further identify 'inventiveness' and 'bricolage' (in the sense of improvising a solution) as a key means through which economic downturn can be weathered (Coutu, in Amann and Jaussaud 2012: 207). As we've already seen, many parts of the kimono industry are family-led – shops, craft workshops and some wholesalers – which indeed may go some way to explain its resilience and staying power.

What does this resilience look like on the ground in the kimono industry? Many of the vignettes in this book, including in this chapter, illustrate resilience in some way, shape or form, at every level of the industry. Realistically, for some shops, craft workshops and wholesalers, having to close up shop is a possibility. This is, of course, not only limited to the industries that produce kimono, but also to the other craft industries in Japan as well. Dorinne Kondo noted that small-scale, family run craft industries were struggling 30 years ago in 1990 when her book on family-run businesses was first published. She poignantly cites the example of a woodworker in Tokyo who faced the reality of having no successor for his craft. As she writes, 'the craftsmen were in a trade which, in all likelihood, was destined for extinction' (Kondo 1990: 128–129). I should point out that the difficulties faced by traditional industries are not limited to Japan. David Gordon writes that the 'sectoral devastation in many traditional industries' is a symptom of the emergence of global, multinational corporations and a globalised system of production (Kotz et al 1994: 292). The sheer speed, range of choice and price of mass-produced goods by far outstrips the capabilities of traditional industries in which production is semi-mechanised or done entirely by hand. On a fundamental, structural level, traditional industries throughout the world are caught in a David and Goliath struggle with multinational companies and mass production.

For Kanamaru Senko, the Kaga Yūzen workshop in Kanazawa that I described in the previous chapter, resilience means considering the option of decoupling their craft from the product it was originally intended to make. This involves diversifying beyond making Kaga Yūzen for kimono only, and potentially moving towards producing accessories and brokering agreements with different businesses to feature their designs.

For the Gotō family at the beginning of this book, resilience means both creativity and bricolage to transition their business gradually away from made-to-order kimono and towards selling second-hand kimono. They observed the changes in their customers' behaviour, and the declining custom in their original shop made them conclude that it was worth taking a chance on a different business model. The Gotō family also opted for a model that enabled customers to browse: small shops either in shopping centres or on the street that customers can pop into. Further, they showed the bricolage characteristic of resilience by bringing to their second-hand shop the specific know-how of an established family kimono shop. This meant offering advice and *kitsuke* (kimono wearing classes) and linking customers with particular services (such as stitching, cleaning and re-dyeing). As a result, they created a hybrid retail environment providing an alternative shopping experience and cheaper wares, while also offering their knowledge and experience in the same way they would have in their established bespoke kimono shop.

Hybridisation and bricolage are also features of other retailers I interviewed. For instance, some shops diversified beyond kimono-related goods, and started to sell Western clothes or jewellery. Pursuing this route involves relinquishing the idea of being a 'pure' kimono retailer, something which can be difficult in an industry where a lot of pride is attached to the family business and its perpetuation down the family line (Kondo 1990: 131). Doing so can provide a measure of safety, however, as it diversifies the business beyond the formal kimono, for which demand has declined. It is still a risky strategy in some ways, as it means managing two completely different systems of distribution and competition with clothing giants and multinational firms.

Other strategies to expand beyond the kimono itself involve staging particular events within the kimono shop premises. One shop hosted sales events selling luxury rice or meat, which seemed rather out of place in a kimono shop, and spoke of a need to diversify the business beyond the kimono itself. Others shops had also invested heavily in the rental *furisode* ('swinging sleeve' kimono) business for young women coming of age at 20. During this ceremony, which takes place across Japan in early January, young women and their family for the most part rent these special kimono for the day from kimono shops. This event usually involves hair and make-up services, as well as taking pictures. Many kimono shops team up with beauticians and photographers to offer these services as a package to their customers. One particular kimono shop in Toyota had opened its own dedicated photography studio to entice customers to use all its services beyond just renting the kimono.

According to my research participants, another, earlier, strategy of kimono shops had been to take customers on special trips and tours, usually (but not always) of craft workshops and textile-producing regions, which aimed at reinforcing bonds between retailers and their customers, thereby fostering customer loyalty. These tours often involved a sales event at the destination. However, this strategy is now rather less common than it was in the 1980s.

Adaptability and resilience, one can also argue, is not necessarily only a matter of choice. Retailers can be creative in their choices of strategy to tackle the difficulties faced by the kimono industry, as we will see in the next chapter, but for many there is no other option but to be resilient. Particularly in the case of family businesses, the idea of the family business having to end is especially painful. Dorinne Kondo notes that family businesses are intimately linked to the *ie*, or Japanese household unit. A key characteristic of the *ie* is the importance of perpetuation and the transmission of the family name to future generations. As Kondo writes, 'the *ie* is not simply a kinship unit based on blood relationship, but a corporate group based on social and economic ties. Thus, the *ie*, the household line, and the *kagyō*, the family enterprise, are of critical moral, social, and emotional importance' (Kondo 1990: 131). Therefore, resilience may not be a matter of choice. For family-run businesses, above and beyond economic considerations, the identity and cohesion of the family itself is also at stake. For many, finding ways to be resilient is an imperative that cannot be refused because the alternative is to allow the business to end.

Crisis and resilience, then, go hand in hand, and many parts of the kimono industry demonstrate this hidden side to the crisis: the ability to keep going and to make things work. That being said, I encountered some apprehension on the part of kimono shop customers, some of whom seemed concerned that they might be pressured into buying expensive kimono and obi. This concern is widespread enough that retailers are aware of it and may try to mitigate it. It is difficult to pinpoint the origins of this fear, although it seems to pre-date the crisis of the 1990s.

Why the idea of 'scary' kimono shops exists

For that part of the kimono retail industry which still focuses on selling expensive formal wear, its target market is women in their 50s, 60s and 70s. This is for a number of reasons: firstly, they are often, as discussed in Chapter 3 and elsewhere (see Valk 2020), the keepers of family ritual life. They are the ones most likely to attend a child's graduation ceremony or *omiyamairi* (a grandchild's first presentation at a shrine) wearing a kimono. Secondly, they are most likely to engage in a traditional Japanese art that would require a kimono to be worn, such as practising tea ceremony, and are more likely to actively pursue *kitsuke* (kimono dressing classes) with a *kitsuke* school. Japanese society is characterised by a range of different forms of learning, hobbies and leisure pursuits, often known as *okeiko*. Taking some kind of *okeiko* or lesson is so common that Takeshi Moriya described Japan as the 'lesson culture' (Moriya in Ueda 1994: 43). A legacy of Confucian and Buddhist ideals have contributed to the high status of education and the perception that education betters the self (Rohlen and LeTendre 1996: 8–9). In typical Japanese understandings of self-improvement, adulthood is not considered to be the end of the learning process, but 'an extended period rich in challenges and opportunities to improve' (Rohlen and LeTendre 1996: 11). As a result, a large number of middle-aged women in Japan, particularly those recently or not so recently freed from the duties of childcare, seek out learning and leisure activities as a form of self-fulfilment, often taking up activities that are specifically viewed as developing or refining a sense of Japanese femininity, such as the tea ceremony (see Mori 1991 and Kato 2004 for detailed discussions of women and the tea ceremony in Japan). These, then, are the women who are the most likely to buy expensive ceremonial kimono in the 300,000 to 500,000 yen (£2211 to £3685) range for themselves and their loved ones. A survey conducted in 2015 by the Ministry of Economy, Trade and Industry asked the question 'have you experienced buying your own kimono?' and found that 41.6 per cent of women aged 50 and over answered yes, compared to just 18.8 per cent of women in their 20s.[5] Middle-aged women are also the most likely segment of the population to be able to recognise a kimono made using a particular regional sewing or dyeing technique, as well as the most likely demographic to have the know-how to wear a kimono.

However, many of the women I encountered throughout my fieldwork seemed quite apprehensive about going to kimono shops. This is in some ways unsurprising, as kimono shops can be quite intimidating places because they provide a very different 'shopping experience' than almost every other retail environment in Japan. They are quite often empty, with shop attendants waiting to greet potential customers. Unlike shops selling Western clothes where one is free to browse, going into a kimono shop typically means a lot of interaction with the staff. While some department stores have opted for a more 'browsable' option that customers can enter and leave the same way they would Western clothes shops, the unfamiliarity of these spaces is potentially daunting for Japanese customers. Entering a kimono shop usually means entering into a discussion, potentially a negotiation, with a kimono retailer, and requires proceeding with caution given the potentially large sums of money involved. Many customers feel out of their depth in an unfamiliar environment, and worry that their lack of preparation or knowledge might lead to them being talked into buying something expensive or something they might not necessarily have a use for.

I observed that my participants, even in the case of kimono shops that they were familiar with, tended to prefer to go in pairs or groups. This behaviour was something I witnessed on several occasions during my fieldwork. One kimono shop owner told me that people may see kimono shops as *kowaii* ('scary') and that it could take some courage to go there. I had my first insight into this phenomenon when I lived in Japan in 2013, two years before the start of my research. At that point, I was taking *kitsuke* (kimono dressing) classes from a specialist teacher, and given that my height and proportions differed significantly from a typical Japanese woman, it was decided that a custom-made kimono would be best for me to be able to learn to wear a kimono properly.[6]

The teacher had selected a handful of bolts beforehand that fitted my budget of 40,000 yen (£256). She gave me careful instructions before we entered the shop: 'Do not touch anything. And even if you don't buy a kimono today, you have to buy something, no matter how small it is.' I followed her instructions, with some trepidation, and I did buy a bolt of kimono cloth that was then sewn up to my size. It was a pale purple polyester bolt that I had picked because polyester was more affordable than silk. It is possible that my teacher was unusually tense or worried, but in my experience, her worry at entering a kimono shop and carrying out a purchase was not completely out of the ordinary. There are several reasons why kimono shops can be considered 'scary' places by Japanese customers. The first is, as I have hinted, the unfamiliarity, since kimono shops offer a different shopping experience compared to the familiar experience of shopping for Western clothes. Even Japanese women who are well-versed in traditional culture such as tea ceremony and flower arranging, are not entirely sure how kimono are made and why they are sold the way they are. Typical shops do not sell kimono as such, but rather *tanmono*, the bolts of cloth, mostly silk, which are then made up into kimono (see Figure 4.1). The *tanmono*, usually between 11 and 12 metres long and between 34 and 40 centimetres wide[7] (Milhaupt 2014: 21), are marketed to customers in terms of the cloth's quality, the regional particularities of the techniques used to make them and the occasion for which the kimono can be used. One *tanmono* can cost anywhere between 20,000 yen (£147) and 3 million yen (£22,113), depending on the type of fabric, where it was made and who made it, and, importantly, who priced it; the kimono industry typically does not fix prices, so the same bolt of cloth may be priced differently in different shops. After the bolt is purchased, the customers' measurements are taken, and the bolt is sewn up using a particular sewing technique that is known as *wassai*.[8] Measurements are not usually made using the metric system (which Japan uses in most other circumstances) but the *shakkanhō*, a traditional system of measurement with which only the most hardened of kimono aficionados are fully familiar. In some shops other fees are levied, such as for the washing of the cloth before it is sewn. Some shops will also suggest that the bolt undergo a waterproofing procedure that goes some way to protect the kimono from damage that might be caused by rain or spilled drinks and food. Silk in particular is a fragile textile, prone to shrivelling if exposed to water. Since most expensive kimono and formal kimono are made of silk, many customers buying these costly and vulnerable kimono opt for

Figure 4.1 Ōshima tsumugi specialist Tetsuya Ueda showing *tanmono* ('bolts') of the fabric which is particularly prized for its lengthy and labour-intensive production process (Reproduced with kind permission from Tetsuya Ueda).

this relatively expensive procedure. As a result, customers are never sure what the end price will be, and they worry that it will be higher than the number on the price tag.

The second reason is a concern for customers that they might be persuaded into purchasing an expensive kimono, or something turns out not to be a 'good buy'. This might be because the kimono does not go with what they already have, or because the kimono isn't right for the occasion they purchased it for. Because kimono shop owners are experts, or at least have considerable knowledge about kimono bolt types, it is possible for customers to feel at a disadvantage and some customers may worry about the extent to which they can trust a retailer's sales pitch. This is, of course, not unexpected: when the goal is to make a sale, many retailers in different sectors and not just the kimono industry will encourage potential consumers to buy. As a result, a somewhat adversarial relationship in retail is inherent to the idea of salesmanship. With kimono, because the price can be high, the stakes are also higher if customers allow themselves to be persuaded into making a purchase. The level of trust between a retailer and their customer is therefore very important, because all but the most knowledgeable of customers have to rely on the retailers for advice and expertise.

As discussed in Chapter 3, building the post-war kimono retail industry involved the commercialisation of knowledge and the recreation of retailers as 'experts'. It is this gap in knowledge that some customers are uneasy about. Place of origin, for instance, is extremely important in determining the price and quality of a kimono, and retailers sometimes whet the appetites of their customers by telling them about the prestigious origins of their bolts. Such examples include Ōshima or Yuki *tsumugi* which come from several locations in Japan. An important feature of both Ōshima and Yuki *tsumugi* is that they are perceived by many people with a little knowledge about the kimono as representative of good taste and quiet refinement, and many of my participants saw them as such. They are usually very expensive: kimono pricing varies wildly, but a typical asking price, my interlocutors in the industry informed me, is around 300,000 yen (£2211). They are also tricky to wear, since they are technically not considered to be 'formal' wear, and thus cannot be worn to weddings or other ceremonial occasions, but equally they are not exactly casual wear either. Many of my participants considered that they are not appropriate for tea ceremonies, since the nature of the woven fabric makes a rustling noise when the wearer moves, unlike the soft fabrics of formal dyed kimono which are almost completely silent. This noise is considered disruptive in the quiet atmosphere of the tea ceremony. Nonetheless, they have been marketed as a prestige item, the mark of the true kimono connoisseur. The key here is that many customers will have heard of Ōshima, and know it to be a particular refined kind of woven fabric and thus a prestigious kimono to own, but in most cases they would not know the details about this fabric and how its authenticity is certified, because there is a level of complexity and skill involved in understanding what exactly guarantees authenticity. There are stamps confirming authenticity on the end of bolts, but these can be difficult to decipher without the customer knowing exactly what to look for. Stamps nevertheless inspire confidence in the buyer because they make the bolt look more authentic, even though there is a possibility that it might not be. I once purchased a kimono bolt from a second-hand shop for 3000 yen (£22) out of curiosity since it was stamped as 'Authentic Ise Katagami [stencil dye from Ise]'. I brought the bolt to the kimono shop Azumaya (see Chapters 5 and 6) to authenticate the bolt, and the verdict was that the bolt, while reasonably good quality, could not possibly be a handmade fabric since handmade stencil dye leaves a small patternless border on the outer side of the fabric. The patterns on this bolt reached the outer side of the fabric, indicating that the bolt was machine-dyed. There can, therefore, be a level of vagueness in the marketing of bolts, with words such as 'authentic' implying something hand-made or adhering to traditional techniques when this is not necessarily the case.

Without research, a casually interested customer can become bewildered. I have met many well-informed, even passionate shop owners with a great deal of knowledge, but it can potentially happen that the retailers themselves have incorrect knowledge about what they are trying to sell. It can also be the case that some retailers omit certain facts or foreground others in order to close a sale. Ima Kikuchi, a writer and kimono fashion guru (see Chapter 6), describes a personal experience in her book *Kikuchi Ima ga Tsutaetai! Katte ha Ikenai Kimono to Kimono Mawari* (2013) ('Kikuchi Ima Wants To Tell You! Kimono and Kimono Accessories That You Shouldn't Buy'; my translation):

> I had slipped into a special sales event at a wholesaler that you can normally only get into on invitation. The normal entrance was closed, and you had to go in round the back. The back entrance had a red and white hanging across the door, the female staff were the sales girls, all manic enthusiasm and excitement, and the atmosphere was like what you would expect in a festival. Everyone was swept up in the feverish excitement, and a buying frenzy kicked in! Purse strings were being loosened left right and centre. A saleswoman saw me with a grey criss-cross pattern on a white bolt draped over my right shoulder[9] and she exclaimed, 'you've got a good eye! That's a Shirotaka Omeshi[10] from Yamagata, that is! They're lovely *and* rare, that's a bargain you've got there!'
>
> I myself am from Yamagata, so that really spoke to me. After all, here I was, making my way in the Tokyo desert. I made my decision instantly and I asked them to sew it up for me. I think it was about 200,000 yen.[11] For me that was a tremendous splurge. The kimono became a great favourite of mine. One day when I was folding it, I noticed there was a tag on the reverse of the collar. It said, 100% polyester. I was shaking all over. A polyester Omeshi, not a silk one. And to think that this had been called a Shirotaka. I'd been tricked! And I'd worn it for years without realising! The worst case scenario here is a fake 'brand' kimono being sold as the real thing, something that would be disrespectful to the Shirotaka producers. This is why you always have to check the part of the bolt where the weaver started to weave, since the place of manufacture and other information will be listed there.
>
> Kikuchi 2013: 10–11 (my translation)

Ima-san (as she is usually known) goes on to indicate that not only should you check tags like the one she found in her kimono, but also the start of the bolt (before the kimono is sewn up) for guarantees of authenticity, as there may also be discrepancies between the two. When in doubt, she argues, the start of the bolt is the most reliable source of information (Kikuchi 2013: 11).

Customers are aware that they can be potentially vulnerable. This leads many to be careful when they choose kimono shops and some savvy customers to make creative choices in the acquisition of their kimono. One such person is Nakasaka-san, a woman with a bright and fun-loving disposition in her early 60s. I have known her for several years through Sachiko. Nakasaka-san loves traditional Japanese culture, such as kimono and tea ceremony, as much as she does Western art, aesthetics and food. The daughter of a *ryokan* (traditional Japanese inn) owner in Kyushu, she had plenty of opportunities to wear the kimono growing up and she continues to wear the kimono to this day, something which she very much enjoys. Nakasaka-san puts a lot of thought into the kinds of kimono that she buys. She has cultivated a relationship with a kimono craftsman, ordering many kimono from him throughout the years and entrusting him with the task of making her daughter's coming of age *furisode*, complete with all accessories, referred to as *tōtaru kōdinēto*, 'total coordinate', meaning that all parts of the outfit match. She thus gets exactly what she wants at a lower price, since she can avoid the commission levied by the wholesalers and the retailers. There is evidence that, increasingly, customers are seeking alternative routes to kimono and avoid going through shops, preferring instead to deal directly with craftspeople or manufacturers. This increasing diversification of distribution routes is explored in greater detail in Chapter 7.

As we saw in Chapter 3, younger women generally no longer receive a bridal trousseau, and for most of them, their first and possibly only experience of wearing the kimono might be the *furisode* at their coming of age ceremony at 20 years old. Kenichi Nakamura, managing director of the second-hand chain Tansu-ya (see Chapter 7), writes that a great many women's first experience of the kimono is the *furisode*: 'all of a sudden they are confronted with the very utmost in formal wear, and it baffles them.' He goes on to explore the results of a survey in which women answered 'no' to the question 'Do you like kimono?' Among those respondents were women whose image of the *furisode* had been overwhelmingly negative. 'They had been dressed up, and it was uncomfortable – they couldn't move, couldn't eat and they didn't feel good, among other things' (Nakamura 2006: 151; my translation). Further to these barriers of physical discomfort, the kimono's price continues to be an obstacle, especially for younger women with different spending priorities. Part of a survey conducted by the Committee for the Study on Japanese Dress affiliated with the Ministry for Economy, Trade and Industry (METI) found that the price of the kimono and the difficulty involved in wearing it were indeed described as the biggest barriers to wearing a kimono. Many women further pointed out that kimono pricing was unclear and they did not fully understand why kimono had certain prices and were not sure what to wear for what occasion. In addition, the women in the survey also worried that they did not know how to properly care for kimono, i.e. how to fold them, put them away and what to do if they became dirty or stained.[12] These findings were very much borne out by my research in that the complexity of the kimono, simply as a thing to wear, was enough to put potential wearers off, especially younger women who do not feel compelled to wear a kimono for ritual or ceremonial events, and who might feel that their lack of knowledge would cause them to be judged. In my interviews with mostly younger women in their 20s and early 30s, many expressed an interest in the kimono and an admiration for its aesthetics, but their interest stopped there: they knew that the kimono was expensive and difficult to wear. In addition to that, they would have relatively few occasions to wear it. It should be highlighted though that many people also simply may not have a wish to wear the kimono, and thus have no motivation to overcome these barriers, particularly when financial cost is incurred.

The outlook would appear to be quite bleak. The kimono industry is in the grip of a threefold crisis: the declining popularity of the formal kimono as ceremonial wear, the ongoing effects of the economic crisis of the 1990s, and an overall image that can at times be less than positive. These factors, combined together, present a picture of crisis that would appear difficult to overcome. And yet, the industry continues to show a resilience that has allowed some retailers, craftspeople, wholesalers and manufacturers to endure. For some, however, the crisis and its effects on the chain of distribution have presented opportunities to shake up their business models and greater freedom to re-shape their business as they choose. The following chapters demonstrate how, for these retailers, crisis has led to opportunity, creativity, and hope for the future of the kimono.

Notes

1 www.kimono-yamato.co.jp/en/about-us/profile/ (retrieved 03/06/2020).
2 Summer kimono are divided into two types: the first, known as *hitoe*, are kimono that do not have an inside lining. Typical rules of wear indicate that *hitoe* are only worn in June and September. Currently, there are more and more people arguing that the *hitoe* should be worn not only in June and September. The second type of summer kimono are lighter kimono, designed to make wearing a kimono in the summer heat of July and August more bearable. Both types are a specialised market within the already specialised market of kimono.
3 Mid-1990s.
4 A special kimono made to drape across a new-born baby and over the shoulder of the person (usually a mother or grandmother) carrying the infant for their first visit to a Shinto shrine. The *ubugi* is made in different colours and patterns for girls and boys.
5 From page 13 of the *Wasō Shinkō Kenkyūkai* ('Report on the Research Meeting for the Promotion of Japanese Dress'; my translation of the title). Accessible at: 'www.meti.go.jp/committee/kenkyukai/seizou/wasou_shinkou/pdf/report01_01_00.pdf (retrieved 17/09/2020)
6 It did in fact turn out to be the case that a custom-made kimono was better for me. I tried wearing a great deal of kimono, both custom-made and hand-me-downs that were custom-made for someone else, and the ones made to my measurements are definitely easiest to wear because the fabric falls exactly where you would expect it to go, so the 'finished package' is more likely to look as imagined. Many women told me that, for them as well, a bespoke kimono was easiest to wear.

7 The width varies according to the manufacturer, when the bolt was made and whether it was intended for a woman or a man. Bolt length also varies.
8 *Wassai* refers to Japanese methods of sewing, and *yōsai* refers to Western methods of sewing associated with Western clothes.
9 Kimono bolts are often draped over the shoulder to give the customer an idea of what the fabric would look like if it was sewn up as a kimono. This helps the customer decide if the colour suits them and if they like the fabric on their own body.
10 *Omeshi* belongs to a category of kimono in which the pattern is woven into the fabric during the weaving process.
11 £1473.
12 From page 18 of the *Wasō Shinkō Kenkyūkai* ('Report on the Research Meeting for the Promotion of Japanese Dress'; my translation of the title). Accessible at: www.meti.go.jp/committee/kenkyukai/seizou/wasou_shinkou/pdf/report01_01_00.pdf (retrieved 17/09/2020)

References

Adger, W. N. 2000. 'Social and ecological resilience: are they related?'. In *Progress in Human Geography* 24: 347–364

Allison, A. 2013. *Precarious Japan*. Durham, NC: Duke University Press

Amann, B. and Jaussaud, J. 2012. 'Family and non-family business resilience in an economic downturn'. In *Asia Pacific Business Review* 18(2): 203–223

Barrios, R. E. 2014. ' "Here, I'm not at ease": anthropological perspectives on community resilience'. In *Disasters* 38(2): 329–350

Bollig, M. 2014. 'Resilience — analytical tool, bridging concept or development goal? Anthropological perspectives on the use of a border object'. In *Zeitschrift für Ethnologie* Bd. 139, H. 2: 253–279

Coutu, L.D. 2002. 'How resilience works'. In *Harvard Business Review*, 80(5), 46–55.

Cwiertka, K. J. and Machotka, E. 2018. *Consuming Life in Post-Bubble Japan: a Transdisciplinary Perspective*. Amsterdam: Amsterdam University Press

Fletcher III, W. M. 2012. 'Dreams of economic transformation and the reality of economic crisis in Japan: Keidanren in the era of the 'bubble' and the onset of the 'lost decade,' from the mid-1980s to the mid-1990s'. In *Asia Pacific Business Review* 18(2): 149–165

Francks, P. 2009. *The Japanese Consumer. An Alternative Economic History of Modern Japan*. Cambridge: Cambridge University Press

Funabashi, Y. and Kushner, B. 2015. *Examining Japan's Lost Decades*. London: Routledge

Gordon, D. M. 1994. '15. The global economy: new edifice or crumbling foundations?' In Gordon, D. M. Kotz, D., Mcdonough, T. and Reich, M., eds. *Cultures of Accumulation: The Political Economy of Growth and Crisis*. Cambridge: Cambridge University Press

Kato, E. 2004. *The Tea Ceremony and Women's Empowerment in Modern Japan: Bodies Re-presenting the Past*. London: Routledge

Kikuchi, I. 2013. *Kikuchi Ima ga Tsutaetai! Katte ha Ikenai Kimono to Kimono Mawari* ('Kikuchi Ima Wants to Tell You! Kimono and Kimono Accessories That You Shouldn't Buy'; my translation of the title). Tokyo: Jitsugyo no Nihon Sha

Kondo, D. 1990. *Crafting Selves: Power, Gender and Discourses of Identity in a Japanese Workplace*. Chicago, IL: University of Chicago Press.
Milhaupt, T. S. 2014. Kimono: A Modern History. London: Reaktion Books
Mori, B. L. R. 1991. 'The tea ceremony: a transformed Japanese ritual'. In *Gender and Society* 5(1): 86–97
Moriya, T. 1994. 'The lesson culture'. In Ueda, A. and Eguchi, M., eds. *The Electric Geisha: Exploring Japan's Popular Culture*. Tokyo and London: Kodansha International
Nakamura, K. 2006. *Tansu-ya de Gozaru* ('Tansu-ya at your Service'; my translation of the title). Tokyo: Shōgyōkai Publishing
Oliver-Smith, A. 2016. 'Adaptation, vulnerability, and resilience: contested concepts in the anthropology of climate change'. In Kopnina, H. Shoreman-Ouimet, E., eds. *Routledge Handbook of Environmental Anthropology*. London and New York: Routledge
Rohlen, T. and LeTendre, G. K. 1996. *Teaching and Learning in Japan*. Cambridge, New York and Melbourne: Cambridge University Press
Schaede, U. 2012. 'From developmental state to the "New Japan": the strategic inflection point in Japanese business'. In *Asia Pacific Business Review* 18(2): 167–185
Valk, J. 2020. 'The Alienating Inalienable: rethinking Annette Weiner's concept of inalienable wealth through Japan's "sleeping kimono"'. In *HAU: Journal of Ethnographic Theory* 10(1): 147–165
Vogel, E. F. 1979. *Japan as Number One: Lessons for America*. Cambridge, MA: Harvard University Press

Chapter 5

Azumaya

The 'nail that stuck up so far that no one could hammer it down'

With summer fast approaching in the small town of Nishio, the display in Azumaya's shop window has changed to reflect their summer wares: *yukata*, light summer kimono, are now in pride of place (see Figure 5.1). Azumaya specialises in *fudangi* (non-formal) kimono, which are usually not worn for ceremonial occasions. Azumaya does sell some that are formal, but the shop window mostly showcases fashion kimono rather than formal kimono.

My introduction to Azumaya came through Kyoko, who works in the shop part-time (see Chapters 1 and 2). Kyoko is a childhood friend of the owner, Yoshihide Shibakawa. Her magnetic personality and sharp mind make her an asset to Azumaya well beyond the work she provides, usually behind the scenes.

Aware of my interest in kimono shops and eager to introduce her unusual kimono shop to me, Kyoko brought me there for a first meeting with Shibakawa-san in mid-December 2015.

'You'll see when we go there,' she told me. 'There aren't many places like our shop. The owner wears kimono every day.'

In most kimono shops, the employees do not wear kimono. The exception might be the *okami-san* (the senior female worker in a shop, sometimes the owner, or the wife or mother of the owner), but it would be unusual for other workers, and it was especially unlikely that male workers would wear kimono at work.

'For the Shibakawa family, the kimono is both lifestyle *and* work, you see. The *okami-san* has her sleeves tailored specially, so they don't get in the way. Sometimes she keeps them in place with elastic bands. Their house is attached to the shop, so they're cooking, fetching the kids from school… Everyone rides a bike, too.'

'Really? A bike? In kimono?' I couldn't help but interrupt, sceptical.

'Really!' she grinned, amused at my disbelief. 'You'll see.'

As I mentioned in Chapter 1, Kyoko first took me to visit Azumaya after I had joined a Kimono de Jack (KdJ) meeting in December 2015 (see Chapters 1 and 6). Azumaya is linked to KdJ because Yoshihide Shibakawa is technically the leader of the Aichi KdJ division. I had spent the day with

Figure 5.1 Azumaya shop front in early summer.

Kyoko, her husband Takashi, and about ten different members of Kimono de Jack, and we had inspected the site of a KdJ gathering of kimono aficionados to take place in mid-January 2016. After the meeting was over we descended upon Azumaya, which was, as I was to find out later, quite a normal thing for them to do. Azumaya is usually open late and has an open-door policy.

As I stepped inside Azumaya, I immediately noticed a difference compared to other kimono shops I had visited. The shop had a communal feel, and everyone seemed to know each other. Shibakawa-san was in the centre of the group, sitting on a chair and chatting. He might have been a little nervous to speak with me at first, but after Kyoko had introduced me the nerves melted away, revealing an approachable man with a self-deprecating sense of humour that was very infectious. I started by asking him what seemed obvious to me looking around his shop with its many kimono-clad women, and, interestingly, kimono-clad men: had people started wearing the kimono more frequently?

'There's been an increase. There's undeniably an appeal to Japanese clothes so it's very important to give people the opportunity to try them. People who didn't have the courage to express themselves can do so when they wear a kimono. They find their path. It was only about five years ago that men started wearing kimono again. Before, if you were a man and you wore a kimono, you were either a tea ceremony practitioner or involved with the *yakuza*![1] Up until ten years ago, older people still wore the kimono. Now they find it too hard and too tiring, so you don't see it so much anymore. And that's the thing – the ordinary has become *natsukashii* [nostalgic].'

Like many of my other participants, he was also under no illusion that the industry was in difficulty.

'It's tough for kimono shops now. Kimono are *shikohin* [luxury goods]. They're not necessary because 99.9 per cent of people wear Western clothes. We're at a crossroads: a lot of places went bust in the economic crisis of the 1990s, except for some chains and family-owned shops. We've all understood just how bad our situation is, but I really think that for small shops, our time has come. It's not just about business. We're the ones who can tell people how great the kimono is.'

Shibakawa-san saw his role as a lot more than just a retailer. Rather, he considered himself to be a facilitator for people to get to understand the kimono better and to enjoy it as a lifestyle. He had a particular fondness for younger customers, and he saw it as his duty to make sure that they didn't choose the wrong thing or overspend. This became a running joke between him and me as the months passed, and he witnessed the growth of my appetite for kimono and kimono-related accessories. Behind the jokes, however, was a sense of responsibility. Shibakawa-san projected into the future when it came to his customers' purchases, and encouraged them not to lose their heads if they found something they liked, and to think about it first. He was also aware that, for a lot of people, kimono shops were intimidating.

'It's hard for people to just walk into a kimono shop, a lot of people find kimono shops intimidating. I want to be the opposite of that. I want my shop to be friendly, the kind of place you can just pop in to have a look.'

Shibakawa-san also worried about the future of craftspeople, and he was among the many to tell me that he thought the industry, as they all knew it, wouldn't last another ten years.

'It's a hard business for young people to break into, but I'm in a good position: this is my home, I'm with my family and I don't have any full-time staff. My clients are loyal and I can sell things as cheaply as possible. I'm surrounded by friends. There was a time when I was worried about the future of my business, but not now,' he said. 'You know the expression "the nail that sticks up gets hammered down"? Well I'm the nail that stuck up so far that nobody could hammer me down!'

The nail that sticks up gets hammered down is a Japanese expression meaning that people who stand out too much will be put back in their place. Shibakawa-san's twist on the expression meant that he had stood out so much that it was now impossible for him to be hammered down. By this, he meant that he had chosen to run his business in a different way than most of the kimono retail industry, and Azumaya is indeed strikingly different in many ways. The Shibakawa family has painstakingly generated a reputation for openness and passion for the kimono. What set Shibakawa-san apart from other business owners was his sense of mission: he saw it as his role to get Japanese people to view the kimono as something to enjoy like any other consumer item rather than only as formal wear. He has forged a reputation for himself as a go-to purveyor of cotton *fudangi* (everyday wear as opposed to formal wear) kimono and other fashionable kimono on the casual end of the spectrum. The location of his business in rural Aichi might appear to be a hindrance as it is at a distance from major consumer hubs but also centres of kimono production in Kyoto, for instance, but this location, as I explore in the last section of this chapter, is in fact a strength. Since taking the shop over from his father, Shibakawa-san has re-created it, as well as his interactions with his customers, his image and even his own identity around his narrative of what a kimono shop *ought* to be. Shibakawa-san is not afraid to be different, or to do things in a way that might be unorthodox: in his view, he is 'the nail that could not be hammered down', not by the decline of kimono sales or the prevalence of Western clothes and not by the idea of what a 'typical' kimono shop should be.

Re-invent the business, re-invent yourself: Shibakawa-san's journey to transform Azumaya

I returned to Azumaya many times over the course of my research. I would meet with Kyoko in the mornings as she drove to Nishio to work her shift in Azumaya, and as she worked, I would spend time with Shibakawa-san, his mother and his wife. At times, they were busy with orders, customers and event planning (see Chapter 6) and so I would stay out of the way, but I was always welcome.

At quieter times, Shibakawa-san would make time to sit with me and tell me about his business, his life and the changes he had seen. Shibakawa-san was often away, visiting other like-minded retailers and planning events, so at other times, his mother would give me tips on how to wear the kimono or show me what she had in mind for the displays in the window. Sometimes, she would disappear through the door at the back of the shop which lead into their house in order to fetch appetising treats which customers had brought as gifts, and we would share them together.

Over the months, I learnt that Azumaya was not always as it is now but rather that the business had undergone a long process of transformation that paralleled Shibakawa-san's journey to find his place within the industry. Azumaya as it is now is a reflection of Shibakawa-san's soul-searching, his quest for a way to reconcile what he thought a kimono shop should be with his experience of what it actually was. Shibakawa-san also found himself among a generation that was the last to experience traditional training methods, such as taking an apprenticeship in a different kimono shop, while also belonging to a generation that was faced with inevitable change and difficulty in the business. This combination of experience made Shibakawa-san feel that his generation was especially well-equipped to tackle the industry's crisis.

'I was one of the last to be trained the old-fashioned way,' he told me. 'I went straight into a five-year apprenticeship with a different shop after

I graduated from high school, aged 18. It was very strict. In the first year all I did was cleaning, odd-jobs and rolling *tanmono* [bolts]. I got very good at that!' he laughed. 'They would test your resolve. My boss would shout things at me like, "don't bother showing up tomorrow!" Of course, I would still have to show up, someone would be sent to drag me in by the ear if I didn't! They do it to toughen you up. Otherwise you wouldn't survive in an industry this tough.'

However difficult it might have been, I could tell that he was proud of his apprenticeship and the grit he felt it had given him. As a result of following a path laid out by generations before him, Shibakawa-san could feel firmly rooted in his business. This didn't mean that he took over his business from his father unquestioningly and without inner conflict. When I asked him what it was like to be in a family-owned business and to face the responsibility of taking it over, he said, half-joking, 'Well you can't really run away from it. It reflects badly on the family, so if you're going to run, do it early!' He laughed. 'We have a saying in the industry: the founder of the business, the grandfather, he does all the hard work and sets things up properly. The second family head lives off his father's success and the third destroys the business. And I'm the third.'

He laughed again, self-deprecatingly. Shibakawa-san enjoys being the butt of his own jokes and isn't averse to being made fun of either. This easy-going nature, starkly opposed to the formality of most kimono shops, is part of the charm that keeps customers loyal to Azumaya and the Shibakawa family. It makes going to Azumaya fun, and many customers come there even if they don't intend to buy anything or have any particular questions. They come simply to hang out, or to talk about fashion and style with the Shibakawa family. However, Shibakawa-san did not start out as the passionate advocate for the kimono as fashion that he is now.

'Years ago, after I took over from my father, I didn't really care much about the kimono. I didn't wear it, I didn't actually like it much. Now, when I think of Ōshima *tsumugi*,[2] for example, to me it's like the Ferrari of kimono! And frankly, it hurts to sell it for just 300,000 yen (£2211) after all the hard work of the craftspeople. If someone came in here wanting an Ōshima with no idea of the work that went into it, I wouldn't want to sell it to them.'

Over the months, I got to know Shibakawa-san and his family. Through my conversations with him and with Kyoko, who had observed his transformation in the last ten years, I came to understand that he had experienced discomfort with the typical ways in which a kimono retail business was run: he didn't like trying to get a customer to pay several hundred thousand yen for something that he himself, at the time, did not particularly like. One day someone told him that they would never buy a kimono from a shop owner who didn't wear one, and as Shibakawa-san tells it, that was a watershed moment for him. From that point on, he started wearing the kimono. Now, he no longer wears Western clothes at all. I saw him wear a T-shirt in a photo just once, for a festival in Nishio in which everyone was wearing the same design, and to see him dressed that way felt very strange to me. The kimono, it seemed, has changed him, and everyone's perception of him.

'Wearing kimono every day, that's how I came to fall in love. Before that, I didn't really see what was so good about them. They really are amazing clothes. I can see why people in the past chose to make them this way. To me, it's the number one fashion in the world. There's lots of subtleties to master, but that's only because people have forgotten what used to be common knowledge. It's such a recent change, when you think about it. It was only 70 years ago that people stopped wearing the kimono. Things have changed really fast, and the industry hasn't kept up.'

This moment of getting to know the kimono for himself had a profound impact on Shibakawa-san's life and his work. Shibakawa-san connected an emotion with his work that was to change his outlook, and that was passion. Now, he frequently refers to himself as having *atsui omoi* (literally, 'hot feelings' meaning 'strong feelings') about the kimono. Using a meaning-based translation rather than a literal one, this translates to 'passion'.

David Wright has argued that, in the bookselling trade, love and enthusiasm for books is a key means for one bookshop to obtain a 'competitive advantage' over another (Wright 2005: 308). Shibakawa-san's enthusiasm for kimono has, indeed, given him a competitive edge, but this was not so much a strategy to become more competitive as it was a fundamental process of transformation. Much of the anthropological literature on clothing documents how wearing different clothes produces different moods and can have a profound effect on the wearer. Rejecting the idea that clothing is simply a means to express the inner self, Sophie Woodward, in her work on women and their wardrobes, has emphasised the transformational power of clothing: 'rather than just allowing women to express their inner selves, the particular item of clothing enacts an internal and behavioural change in the woman: wearing the tailored suit helps create a powerful, confident and in-control woman' (Woodward 2007: 21). Usually, these behavioural and emotional changes are temporary and end when the clothing is removed. But for Shibakawa-san the change effected upon him by the kimono appeared to be permanent, as he did not revert back to Western clothes.

As explored in Chapter 2, the kimono is an embodied dress practice (see Entwistle 2000), and the physical sensations and the interaction between the wearer and the cloth is evidence, as Webb Keane argues in the context of dress switching in Java, of the connection between materiality and transformed behaviour and social practices, habits and cues (Miller 2005: 195). Since the kimono also affects the way the wearer feels, walks and moves, it makes possible a different way of being, moving and feeling in the world. This bears similarities with Pierre Bourdieu's *habitus*, which is a set of bodily dispositions that are passed on to different generations in a largely unconscious fashion (Bourdieu 2013 [1977]: 73). However, in this interpretation of the theory, we can examine *habitus* at work on an individual level, through the body's relationship with clothing. In Shibakawa-san's case, the change in *habitus* brought about by choosing to wear the kimono daily is a conscious choice. His family, too, adopted the kimono on a day-to-day basis. As his enjoyment of the kimono increased, his personal relationship with the kimono now fed his role as a retailer. David Wright contends that 'over-identification' with products can impact bookshop workers' sense of self' (Wright 2005: 304), but my participant observation at Azumaya led me to understand this was not the case here. Shibakawa-san's enthusiasm and desire to transmit his knowledge about the kimono both fuels his sense of mission in getting others to enjoy the kimono and forms part of an effective business model. It is tempting to view marketing strategies as cold and calculating, and divorced from true enthusiasm or human feeling. But for Shibakawa-san it appears to be the case that genuine enthusiasm, as well as charisma, knowledge and humour, work as a marketing strategy because they draw and retain customers.

This chapter is an ethnographic exploration of the way in which Shibakawa-san chose 'sticking out' to the point that being 'hammered down' was no longer possible. This was a way to adapt to the crisis, but also to thrive. 'Sticking out', for Shibakawa-san, involved reinventing himself and his business. It not only involved selling something new and different, but also forging new business contacts, going beyond traditional channels of distribution, creating strong bonds with customers, and learning new skills that stand out from the crowd. Standing out is, in other words, the recipe of hopeful creativity that means the Shibakawa family have risen to the challenge of selling the kimono at a time when sales continue to decline and the industry's overall crisis deepens.

In the second part of this chapter, I take a closer look at the rootedness of Azumaya within the community of Nishio and the shop's project of place-making. Azumaya as a space is crafted in such a way that it is more than a shop: it is the 'home', both physical and metaphysical, of a lifestyle community which enjoys wearing the kimono as fashion. The way customers engage with Azumaya as a home-like environment points to a nostalgia or longing for home and rootedness in a community that is characteristic not just of Japan, but of industrialised nations more generally.

'Sticking out' to beat the crisis: being different as a means for success

The happiness factor

When Shibakawa-san started to take on more responsibilities alongside his parents, Azumaya was a relatively typical kimono shop: the family wore Western clothes, they organised group tours and events in the same way that other shops did, and they, too, sold formal kimono at the expensive end of the scale. But Shibakawa-san, like all his fellow retailers, was faced with a problem: the kimono was not selling as well as it used to, wholesalers were closing and craftspeople struggled to find apprentices. For a time, the family sold Western clothes alongside the kimono as a way to diversify income. A number of shops tried this strategy, but it was risky as it involved trying to compete with large clothing chains. Shibakawa-san told me that this approach also placed a significant burden on kimono retailers, as they had to manage two very different industries each with their own suppliers, wholesalers and accompanying rules and regulations.

Shibakawa-san wanted two things: to keep the family business going and to be happier in his work. For Shibakawa-san, happiness is a top priority. One of his favourite phrases is '*otagai ni happii*': mutually happy (using the English word 'happy'). He means this with reference to himself and his customers, but also in his business dealings with wholesalers, other retailers and craftspeople.

Generally speaking, Japanese customers have an image of the kimono industry as being a distant world which is difficult to understand, one which may require an expensive purchase from them (as discussed at the end of Chapter 4). Positive image-building is therefore extremely important in winning trust, especially as relationships with customers, once fostered, tend to last years. Shibakawa-san has gone to great lengths to establish this kind of trust. He is fond of saying that his job is as much about selling 'reassurance' (*anshin*) as it is about selling the kimono. His hope is that he sells things that people enjoy and that make them happy, in a shop that people feel comfortable to visit.

The fashion kimono

Azumaya has a speciality. While the shop stocks a number of formal kimono, their mainstay is *fudangi* (casual, everyday) kimono. This is not the typical kimono type that is sold in most kimono shops, with their focus on formal wear. Azumaya, on the other hand, has forged a relationship with a niche but fervent market of consumers who enjoy wearing the kimono more as a fashion statement and as a lifestyle choice.

Shibakawa-san is an impassioned advocate of *fudangi* kimono and of the kimono as a fashion choice more generally speaking. This is, in part, because he believes that the kimono can be used to express stylistic preferences and *kosei* ('individuality') in a way that is difficult to achieve with Western clothes. Matching a kimono and an obi produces a particular visual effect and enables a significant amount of play on the part of the consumer. Accessories, too, add accents to an outfit that allows for a particular expression of taste and preference: the underkimono collar is visible, and is often covered with a *haneri* (a decorative piece of fabric sewn onto the collar of the underkimono). This might be white and plain, but it could also be embroidered with patterns or beads, or even covered with lace. Conventional kimono tastes in the second half of the 20th century dictate that both *haneri* and *tabi* socks (the socks which are split at the big toe to allow the wearer to put on *zori* shoes) should be white, but a growing number of people who wear the kimono as a life-style choice prefer patterned or colourful *tabi* and *haneri*. *Tabi* and *haneri* choices are available to both women and men, but for women, obi accessories are especially important: choosing an *obiage* (obi scarves), an *obijime* (the special tie that goes around the obi) and an *obidome* (the decoration placed on the *obijime*) are important in creating accents and finishing off a 'look'. Collecting these items in the pursuit of a particular aesthetic is a pleasurable part of wearing the kimono as fashion, but can also be a source of anxiety if mistakes are made – such as falling in love with a kimono that is difficult to coordinate with an obi or accessories. Ima Kikuchi gives an example of how this happened to her in her book *Kikuchi Ima ga Tsutaetai! Katte ha Ikenai Kimono to Kimono Mawari* ('Kikuchi Ima Wants To Tell You! Kimono and Kimono Accessories That You Shouldn't Buy'; my translation). With her characteristic style and humorous illustrations, the writer describes purchasing a very brightly patterned kimono for which she then couldn't find an obi (Kikuchi 2013: 16–19). Without an obi, a kimono cannot be worn, so successfully combining a kimono with at least one obi is key to being able to wear the kimono at all.

Not only the kimono and obi, then, but accessories as well can be used to construct an outfit which tells a story or sends subtle messages to the viewer about the seasons, but also about the wearer's tastes and preferences. This is part of the fashion system that Shibakawa-san actively promotes, both in his own dress practice and in his shop. In order to do so, Shibakawa-san takes a different approach than other kimono shops: 'it would be very good for the kimono industry to use branding more effectively,' he told me. 'It could help save techniques from dying out. You need both marketing and design, just like Louis Vuitton.'

Up until relatively recently, the main branding strategy in the kimono industry was based on the particularities of the regional techniques of weaving and dyeing that went into making them, such as Kaga Yūzen from the Kanazawa area, described in Chapter 3. This is one of the key ways in which kimono were marketed, locating the value and authenticity of the product in the regional techniques according to which they were made. Shibakawa-san remains sensitive to the value of these techniques, as he demonstrates with Ōshima *tsumugi*, but he is also aware that these kimono are not only expensive, but belong to a very particular type of branding. A more familiar type of branding in Japan is quite simply the association with a particular brand, and the qualities and properties, as well as prices, associated with that brand. This kind of branding has started to emerge in the fashion-oriented corners of the kimono industry. Shibakawa-san determines that this is useful because it is more intuitive for customers and is easier to understand. Because Azumaya stocks a large number of these new fashion brands known by the consumers,

Shibakawa-san's shop is an excellent option for these customers. Meeting them in person allows Shibakawa-san to make lasting connections with interested customers, but he also uses social media and the Internet effectively to promote Azumaya and the brands stocked in the shop – something where more traditionally minded shops and kimono businesses tend to lag behind. Azumaya also maintains an online shop so that customers who have heard of Azumaya but live too far away can also browse and make purchases. Azumaya's pull among the circle of kimono fashionistas is significant, and visitors from distant prefectures are not infrequent.

How exactly, then, do Shibakawa-san's kimono and obi and their brands contrast with those to be found in average kimono shops across Japan? For starters, most formal kimono belong to a specific category, such as *kurotomesode* (all black except for elaborate patterns around the hem, worn by the mother of the bride or groom) or *hōmongi* (literally 'visiting' kimono, characterised by floral or traditional patterns such as stylised water patterns, Japanese musical instruments or palanquins used in the feudal era by the imperial family). Some of these formal kimono have more abstract or modern patterns but generally speaking they feature traditional patterns. In addition, these kimono are usually made of silk. Shibakawa-san does stock some kimono belonging to these types, but he also stocks a large number of kimono that are not designed to be worn for special occasions, as well as a large number that are not made of silk. Azumaya has forged a reputation for cotton kimono, which are not always readily available in other shops. Shibakawa-san has a particular fondness for cotton, which he tends to wear on an almost daily basis. Cotton has a particular significance to Shibakawa-san, as the town of Nishio in which Azumaya is located belongs to the Mikawa region, which was historically a cotton-producing area. Only a handful of cotton producers and weavers remain in the area now and Shibakawa-san stores bolts made locally. Not only is this an excellent selling point, but these bolts are, comparatively speaking, much cheaper than silk. Shibakawa-san, who often thinks of younger customers with limited budgets, or people just starting out wearing the kimono, considers the cotton kimono to be an excellent first kimono. At the lower end of the price scale, a bespoke cotton kimono bolt at Azumaya could cost around £200 (excluding tailoring costs). Azumaya also uses local seamstresses exclusively. Kimono tailoring (*wassai*) requires particular sewing skills that differ from those used with Western clothes. Tailoring usually has a separate charge from purchasing the bolt itself because the services of a specialist are required. Many shops and chains outsource the tailoring of kimono abroad as this is cheaper but even with local seamstresses Azumaya manages to keep prices low. At the cheaper end of the scale, a cotton kimono at Azumaya is likely to cost around £600, including tailoring. Overall, this is considerably less expensive than silk kimono, which, as we have seen, can cost thousands of pounds, especially if made according to a specific regional technique. This is why Shibakawa-san tries to steer first-time buyers away from silk and into the safer waters of cotton. Cotton has other advantages, too. Unlike silk kimono, which are usually cleaned professionally by specialists, many cotton kimono can be washed at home in a washing machine, meaning that wearers won't be so concerned about damage caused by sweat, dirt, food or contact with skin. Shibakawa-san has uploaded a number of videos on YouTube and the shop website offering guides to home-washing cotton kimono. Further, cotton kimono also allow for a different aesthetic appeal that harks back to the days when the kimono was everyday wear for Japanese people and cotton kimono were common.

There are many types of cotton on offer at Azumaya, and there are also a number of other textiles as well. Silk, of course, but also silk-wool mixes and cotton-linen mixes, allowing customers to choose from a varied price, pattern and colour range. Even though Shibakawa-san spoke to me often of his love of silk, cotton retains its special place in Azumaya for its adaptability, 'ordinariness' and its link to cotton production in the local area. Outside the shop front, the Shibakawa family keep a little cotton plant as a mascot for the shop.

Late in my fieldwork, I had a cotton kimono made at Azumaya from purple Enshu cotton (from the neighbouring prefecture of Shizuoka) with a discreet, tasteful pattern of eight multi-coloured threads woven into the cotton. Given that I am tall by Japanese standards, Shibakawa-san had arranged for me to meet the *wassai-shi* ('seamstress') who would make my kimono. This is not normally common practice and measurements are usually taken and sent to the seamstress. The *okami-san* (Shibakawa-san's mother), said she liked to think of me wearing the kimono as I read books and wrote up my research. 'Wear it until it falls apart,' she told me solemnly as she handed over the finished kimono to me. This refers to the custom, common in pre-war Japan, of wearing everyday kimono made from materials other than silk until they became no longer suitable as clothes and were then used as sleeping wear or as dishcloths. In contemporary Japan this practice is now rare, but for the Shibakawa family, wearing cotton kimono everyday meant that this old clothing practice could be a reality once more. This was a way for them to re-create a link with past fashions and modes of relating to the kimono. The formal kimono as we know it today is an aesthetic that was largely fixed in the post-war period. Pre-war fashions and styles, especially in the 1920s and 1930s, could be considerably more adventurous and abstract than those of the post-war period. Although without the fully formed nostalgia of vintage fashion, Azumaya does make connections with these past modes of relating to the kimono and can, therefore, lay claim to a relationship with the kimono which is more 'authentic' than other kimono shop owners.

Collaboration, cooperation and creativity

Selling the kimono as fashion and as a lifestyle choice meant changing how and who Azumaya did business with. Shibakawa-san once told me that he had decided to do 'what none of the others were doing'. Unusually for a retailer, Shibakawa-san is directly involved in the design and creation of a number of projects. One such example is his collaboration with a producer of the locally grown Mikawa cotton. Shibakawa-san's eye, like that of other retailers, is trained when it comes to selecting stock, but he is also long used to coordinating his own outfits and testing colour and textile combinations, and he has a strong interest in design. Together with a local cotton craftsman, Shibakawa-san had tested the idea of weaving together black warp (lengthwise) threads and coloured weft (transverse) threads, leading to a series of cotton bolts that became popular due to the richness and depth of colour, but also the uncanny way the colour seemed to change in the light. Now he was curious to see what effect using white instead of black for the warp would produce.

I happened to be visiting on the day he was planning to visit the cotton farm and weaving workshop, and he beamed as I arrived.

'Great timing! Hop in the car, I think you'll enjoy this!'

I got in the car with him and we drove to the craft workshop, about 45 minutes away from Nishio. The craftspeople were an elderly couple who, entirely on their own, grew local Mikawa cotton, processed the cotton and wove it, with input from Shibakawa-san. At the time, Shibakawa-san had taken on an apprentice, who was filming the meeting so as to report online to Azumaya customers who watch Shibakawa-san's weekly online broadcasts (described later in the chapter). First, we were shown the cotton drying in the sun after the harvest. We then visited the cotton fields, with fluffy white cotton balls still on the bushes.

Then Shibakawa-san and the craftspeople proceeded to carry out the test with the white warp thread but it was not conclusive. They determined that a bright colour was necessary to have a sufficient impact, but overall Shibakawa-san and the craftsman agreed that the effect was not at striking as the black warp project, which was doing well.

Shibakawa-san is involved in many such collaborative and experimental projects. Some are with local craftspeople who have limited visibility, such as the Mikawa cotton producers described above. Branding their products can contribute to bringing greater awareness of local crafts and help to revitalise ailing industries. Partly due to Shibakawa-san's work, customers have become more interested in cotton as an alternative to silk. This is just one example, but Azumaya is involved in many more collaborative ventures with other likeminded entrepreneurs, who belong to an extended 'kimono fashion network' (see Chapter 6).

By involving himself directly in the process of design and production, Shibakawa-san is subverting the formerly rigid chain of distribution (see preceding chapters) that had previously made it very difficult for retailers to take on such roles as business relationships were strictly mediated by wholesalers and manufacturers. Shibakawa-san is one of a number of business owners for whom the crisis of the 1990s and the disruption of the chain of distribution has represented an opportunity to expand their role and establish creative business relationships. I explore this trend in the blurring and diversification of roles in more depth in Chapter 7, but Shibakawa-san is an example of the motivation and creativity which can make use of difficult circumstances to effect change.

The hands-on approach

Standing out and demonstrating effort, reliability and trust to customers is key. Part of Shibakawa-san's approach is to provide a more relaxed and friendly experience, but also to go the extra mile in offering as many services as he can to his customers.

Kimono aftercare has traditionally been handled by kimono shops, although in the vast majority of cases, kimono shops have business deals with specialist companies that can wash kimono, or repair *zori* shoes for instance. The Shibakawa family has tried to acquire as many of these specialist skills as possible in order to cut out the middle-man and reduce costs. Normally, once measurements for a customer have been taken, the bolt of cloth is cut according to measure by a specialist, or by the seamstress. At Azumaya, Shibakawa-san's father has taken on the task of cutting the bolts himself. It's a nerve-wracking task – a mistake could ruin the bolt (see Figure 5.2).

Shibakawa-san himself has learnt a specialised skill. As described above, *zori* shoes have a part that goes between the toes called *hanao*, which is usually removable. These parts, as well as being functional, are also

Figure 5.2 Shibakawa-san's father, Kazuyoshi Shibakawa, in the process of cutting and preparing a cotton bolt for the seamstress.

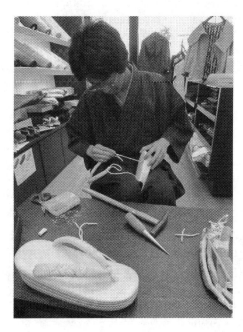

Figure 5.3 Shibakawa-san replaces the *hanao* (straps) on a pair of *zori* shoes.

decorative: changing the *hanao* means changing the look of the shoes, and can also move the *zori* up and down the scale of formality depending on the type of *hanao* and its decoration. This makes them versatile but usually a specialist with specialised tools is required to make the change. Shibakawa-san acquired the tools and taught himself to replace the *hanao* (see Figure 5.3). This means that, instead of sending the shoes away to a specialist and having the customer wait for a week or so for the shoes to come back, customers know that they can come to Azumaya a day before or even the day of an event, and have the *hanao* on their *zori* replaced before a wedding or another formal occasion. Shibakawa-san can usually make the switch in an hour.

There is, of course, genuine interest in the craft on the part of the Shibakawa family. Repairing shoes or cutting bolts all takes place in the open on the shop floor, often before the eyes of customers. The acquisition of skills is impressive in and of itself, but it also shows customers a firm wish to 'go the extra mile', which inspires trust in the customer. As Anthony Giddens notes, trust is a source of 'psychological security' (Giddens 1991: 19). In order to foster long-term customers, establishing a relationship of trust is vital for a kimono retailer. They are often required to know what the customer already has in their collection and how experienced they are with the kimono, and on that basis make good recommendations that take into account the customer's budget. The Shibakawa family is also very careful to avoid pushing customers into making a purchase, something which some customers can be apprehensive about (see Chapter 4).

The Shibakawa family makes sure that their customers get a hands-on experience as well. A customer dropping in to say hello might find that, if the *okami-san* has time, she can give them some tips on how to tie obi or wear the kimono more easily – valuable information handed out for free. Halfway through my fieldwork, Shibakawa-san purchased a small handloom which visitors can try out. Shibakawa-san reasoned that many people were curious about weaving and what the process looked like but were not necessarily able to seek out workshops and try it out for themselves. Over the months, a cheerfully motley *hanhaba* (half-width) obi was woven on the loom by various hands, both steady and unsteady. My own wobbly weaving was added a number of times. The idea wasn't to get it right – the idea was to have a go.

Communication and connection: Internet TV broadcasts

Business owners in the kimono industry have been relatively slow to adopt an Internet presence and move into online retail (Hall 2020: 180). In part, this was due to the fact that established channels of distribution endured even though they were disrupted in the 1990s, and it was only later that patterns of selling kimono directly to customers online emerged. For business owners with a more entrepreneurial mind set, the rise of social media platforms represented an excellent opportunity. As I will explore further in the next chapter, social media, in particular Twitter, Facebook and Instagram, have become key means through which business owners with ideals and values similar to those of Shibakawa-san can communicate and forge friendships and business alliances. They also offer a way to reach audiences beyond the immediate circle of acquaintances, friends and customers.

Online platforms provide Shibakawa-san with another way to reach wider audiences. Every weekend, Shibakawa-san broadcasts a 'show' live from his shop on the Internet. Using a number of streaming platforms, Shibakawa-san discusses a range of subjects: features about particular weaving and dyeing techniques, *kitsuke* (kimono dressing tips for men, for women, on how to wear *hakama* [pleated trousers] and other special items), sizing and sewing, as well as the inner workings of the industry. He also explores kimono types and when to wear them and he offers perspectives on how kimono are changing with regards to style, colour and TPO (Time, Place and Occasion). He sees the channel as a way to disseminate knowledge for free about the kimono and also the industry, more generally speaking, but this knowledge is mediated by his worldview and his self-described 'passion' (*atsui omoi*). This sometimes involves challenging established rules of TPO for wearing the kimono and calling for the rules to be relaxed so as to encourage more people to wear the kimono, and for treating kimono 'beginners' with more kindness.

He advocates for people to understand that these rules are more flexible than they expect and are subject to significant regional and contextual variation. He also tries to explain how rigid rules can put people off wearing the kimono. 'Imagine someone who wants to wear kimono', he says in a broadcast dealing with TPO. 'But among her acquaintances, there is no one to ask about what to wear. So she buys a book, and finds out about TPO. But then when she tries wearing the kimono, someone says "oh you've got that wrong!" and she feels embarrassed, ashamed. Which means she stops wearing it. Why would you bother wearing something that's so expensive *and* ends up attracting criticism? That's the problem!'

The point of the broadcast is not just about listening passively to Shibakawa-san talking. All the platforms that support the broadcast enable viewers to leave comments. Viewers comment on each other's comments, and Shibakawa-san frequently takes up the comments, allowing the viewers a participatory role in the show.

In addition to using social media to keep in touch with customers and likeminded business owners, Shibakawa-san's broadcast platform allows him to share his views and grow the recognition of his business as widely as possible, thereby increasing interest in his business but also in his particular way of thinking about the kimono. Furthermore, Azumaya has an online shop which offers a wide variety of bolts and obi for customers who prefer to shop remotely. However, visiting Azumaya itself and meeting the Shibakawa family is often a goal in and of itself for customers interested in the kimono as fashion, which makes the physical space of Azumaya itself especially important.

A 'tasty' shop: place-making and Azumaya as home and community

In this section, I explore the way in which the place-making project of Azumaya reflects how the shop has become the 'home' of a fashion kimono lifestyle. Shibakawa-san told me that 'I want my shop to be a place where people hang out. Whether you've come to buy just one *koshihimo* ('kimono tie') or nothing at all, I want you to feel welcome.'

For many if not most retailers, making the right sense of space in a site of consumption is key to fostering positive consumer experiences. Charles McIntyre has noted that creating a sense of being immersed in a positive environment was a major part of the experience of going to a music shop (McIntyre 2009: 467). This state of immersion leads the customer to become so involved that they lose a sense of time and can set their worries and frustrations aside. Importantly, the shop also provides the basis for community-building in that it is a space to meet others, reinforce bonds and create pleasurable associations. In the case of Azumaya, this 'state of immersion' involves generating a sense of being at home and being relaxed, a space where customers feel that they can spend time regardless of whether they buy or not. This ensures an organic type of salesmanship in which customers have multiple chances to look at an item that has caught their eye, such as a bolt of cloth or an obi, and discuss the pros and cons with a member of the Shibakawa family. Often, the discussion will involve a debate around the 'sensible' nature of a purchase, such as whether or not the desired item would fit into an existing outfit. It is not uncommon for customers to bring in kimono or obi to match them with an item that has caught their eye. Shibakawa-san is careful not to place any pressure on the customer. He does not like the idea of using pressure, even accidentally, in order to encourage customers to buy. Not only does he find this personally distasteful, it is also antithetical to the kind of atmosphere he and his family have striven to create at Azumaya. This friendly atmosphere confers a home-like quality to Azumaya (see Figure 5.4).

Mass consumption, Sack argues, does not have the kind of personalised, familial environment that a 'home' has (Sack 1988: 199). Japanese shopping centres and chains are standardised according to managerial norms and practices. It has been extensively argued in anthropology that the commodities of mass consumption feed into the many projects of social and personal

Figure 5.4 Azumaya shop front viewed from inside the shop.

identity-building across the globe (see Douglas and Isherwood 1979, Miller 1987, 1995 and 2012, and Graeber 2011 among others).

I believe that it is fair to argue, however, that much of modern shopping has an impersonal nature, and the *sites* of consumption are by and large characterised by sameness. While there are always exceptions, most of us do not, typically, expect to build a rapport or relationship with the person handing us our order in a fast food chain, making our coffee in a coffee chain, or the person by the till at the supermarket. These retail spaces are familiar, but they are not, typically, 'homey'. Something of the alienability of these spaces, the fact that they are everywhere pretty much the same, stands in the way of feelings of homeliness or cosiness. As Uwe Spiekermann argues, this is partly due to the fact that 'the framework of retailing is normally determined by managers and executives, who reduce consumers and retailers to economic indicators in a battle for profitability and shareholder approval' (Trentmann 2006: 167).

The customers of Azumaya, in a sense, do have a home. Azumaya *is* a home. The Shibakawa family are often all present: Shibakawa-san and his mother, the *okami-san*, talking with customers, Shibakawa-san's wife, behind the desk taking care of accounts, his father moving from task to task and the children, whenever they are back from school (see Figure 5.5). Being

Figure 5.5 The Shibakawa family at work.

at Azumaya for any length of time means being witness to the life of the Shibakawa family, the rhythms of errands, school drop-off and pick up, grocery shopping and visits from neighbours and relatives. I was perhaps more often privy to the rhythms of the Shibakawa home life as I spent many days in Azumaya, but so were other visitors who would often visit on their days off to socialise and chat.

'Come with me, Julie,' the *okami-san* told me one day. Always bright-eyed and full of energy, she led me outside the shop. It was a warm day in late spring, and summer was just around the corner. She had just changed the display in the window, dressing the mannequins in *yukata* (light summer versions of the kimono) to reflect the change in the seasons. She had spent some time tying and retying the obi, then decorating them with lace. Lace is not usually part of the 'established' kimono aesthetic and its use often signals that the wearer is someone for whom the kimono is fashion rather than formal wear.

We stood together across the street from the window display.

'What do you think?' she asked me. 'Does it look right?'

'It does,' I replied. 'Eye-catching.'

She beamed at me. 'A display has got to look *oishii* ['tasty']. Customers need to look at it and think "oh, I want that!"'

Richard Wilk argues that the act of consuming, particularly shopping, evokes a desire that is akin to hunger, eating, and feelings of satiation (Ekström and Brembeck 2004: 17–18). The word *oishii* ('tasty') is often used in the context of the fashion kimono. Ima Kikuchi, a fashion kimono author and designer (see Chapter 6), supports the idea of a lifestyle in which wearing Western style clothes most of the time and kimono a few times as the most *oishii* clothing lifestyle.

Being at Azumaya often involves actual food as well – smells from the kitchen waft into the shop front and gifts brought for the Shibakawa family by visitors are shared amongst customers, and there is a bottomless supply of tea. The place-making of Azumaya involves eating and drinking, as well as consuming the kimono, whether that means buying them or simply being around them. A purchase means satiation but so, too, does the prospect of a future purchase. I knew of several customers at Azumaya who had planned their future purchases to coincide with a particular season, or to buy a kimono type that they didn't yet have. These purchases were often planned together, with Shibakawa-san doing his part by looking out for the right item for the customer if he didn't yet have it in stock. Future satiation of consumer desires was as much of a factor as present desires.

The place-making at Azumaya fosters a sense of community. Azumaya itself, and the identity of the Shibakawa family is grounded in the local region of Mikawa. Shibakawa-san is deeply rooted in his local community, with a strong regional Mikawa identity which is perceptible in his dialect and choice of food. The life of the Shibakawa family is at odds with that of much of Japan's population, who do not live in rooted communities and whose sense of community is far more fluid and diffuse. The dissolution of the geographically bounded local community in modern society, partially attributable to social and technological change (Sack 1988: 188), has meant that, for some, bounded, tight-knit communities have become places to aspire to and long for. Robert David Sack writes that 'we define our purposes and ourselves in terms of our relationships to others in communities. Behind the idea of community lies the question of geographical propinquity. A popular claim is that the real or authentic community is presumed to occur when the spatial manifestations of a particular system of production, consumption, and other social relations overlap and are enclosed within a single place' (Sack 1988: 188). Azumaya represents this overlap of production, consumption and sociability in the form of collaborative ventures, consumption in the form of purchases, window-shopping and planning to purchase, and socialising, all within the same space.

There is an argument in the literature on modernity in Japan that a particular kind of nostalgia for the past exists in Japanese society, encapsulated by the word *furusato* ('hometown') in Japanese. The word *furusato* carries a strong nuance of longing for a home, or a point of origin, lost in the past (see Robertson 1988, Ivy 1995 and Kelly 1986). It is this longing, perhaps, that goes some way to explaining why Azumaya's rootedness in the community of Nishio is so appealing, and why customers drive from far and wide to visit, but I would argue that this phenomenon is a widespread trend in developed, modern societies living in post-traditional communities. This nostalgia, throughout the industrialised world, is often articulated around the loss of the local community, the 'traditional sense of place as the basis of the moral order' (Sack 1988: 6–7). There is a profound wish to return to physical, local communities in which 'we can become rooted' (Sack 1988: 6–7).

The transformation of Azumaya runs parallel to Shibakawa-san's pursuit of self-reinvention and his desire to be a more authentic kind of salesman, occupying a role in the community beyond simply retail, as a presence to be relied on by the locals and consumer alike. This harkens back to a time when kimono shops, by virtue of their connections and social status, did occupy this role. Equally, Azumaya is very much a 21st century project, unafraid of entrepreneurship, risk-taking and online platforms. This combination of 21st century traits with a form of salesmanship that allows for a long-lasting personal connection between consumer and retailer makes for a very appealing combination, and explains in part Azumaya's high profile among customers specifically interested in the kimono as fashion wear.

The 21st century is characterised by an increasingly ambiguous relationship with mass consumption (Binkley and Littler 2008, Humphery 2010), and it is perhaps not surprising then that Azumaya and the fashion kimono provide an attractive alternative mode of consumption for a certain market of Japanese shoppers. The kimono itself, while not completely removed from mass production and mechanisation, also offers an alternative to Western clothing and mass production. This taps into a wider zeitgeist in which modern consumers long for 'authentic' shopping experiences that honour their values and lifestyles. Jenny Hall argues that parts of the kimono production process can be thought of as a kind of 'slow fashion' because kimono take time to make, and the scale of production is relatively small (Hall 2018). Terry Satsuki Milhaupt also notes that 'a growing interest in the kimono may have ties to a longing for a slower, more "traditional" way of life that was no longer sustainable in the high-growth, bubble economy of the 1980s' (Milhaupt 2014: 244).

Japan has long displayed ambivalence towards consumption, simultaneously spending and consuming in great quantities, particularly in the 1970s and 1980s, while maintaining a seemingly contradictory discourse of thrift, careful spending and moderation (Garon and Maclachlan 2006, Francks 2009: 208). Consumption across capitalist industrialised countries in the 21st century is also characterised by another dimension which is 'experience'. Joseph Pine and James Gilmore posited in their 1998 article 'Welcome to the Experience Economy' that the late 20th century was the stage for a shift from service-based economy to experience-based economy. Companies likely to succeed in the experience economy, they argued, were those that best knew how to engage 'customers in a personal, memorable way' (Pine and Gilmore 1998: 97).

Azumaya demonstrates how adaptable traditional businesses can be when led by owners who are entrepreneurial enough to align their business with consumer preferences and the wider, global consumer trends of the time, such as the hunger for experience. One of the problems now faced by the kimono industry is the difficulty in adapting to new business models and fostering a market of consumers that is not based on purchasing formal kimono. Shibakawa-san understood this problem, on both a business level and a personal level, and his model for adapting to the crisis has proven to be successful. Although he has selected a way of doing business that is undoubtedly demanding of him in terms of time and energy, his method of 'sticking out' has not only prevented him from being 'hammered down' but it has also helped his business thrive, in a way that feels true to him. While Azumaya reflects Shibakawa-san's wish to align his work more closely with his values, the transformation of Azumaya reflects shifts in broader consumer trends as well. Although Azumaya sells what might appear to be a very Japanese product, it does so in a way that appeals to Japanese people as modern consumers, who look for more personalised experiences, authentic products, and a lifestyle both personal and communal. The idea of 'authenticity', be it in products and in the relationship to retailers themselves, is valued by 21st century consumers. Charles Lindholm argues that modern consumers value the idea of authenticity so much that places and products considered to be authentic have the power to bring 'people together in collectives that are felt to be real, essential, and vital, providing participants with meaning, unity, and a surpassing sense of belonging' (Lindholm 2008: 1–2).

Azumaya is indicative of the much wider phenomenon of consumer ambivalence towards mass consumption and its sites. Shibakawa-san has aligned Azumaya with the values that 21st centuries consumers are sensitive to: personalised service with a genuine social bond, a sense of rootedness and community and, of course, authentic products with an identifiable point of origin whether made by hand or by mechanised loom. Azumaya offers the consumer an alternative world: removed from mass consumption and rooted in a community, while possessing all the structures of 21st century life, such as Internet broadcasts, online shopping and, of course, a narrative of fashion, style and self-expression which is more attuned to the customer than the kimono as formal wear.

In the following chapter I examine the wider network to which Shibakawa-san belongs. I call this network the kimono fashion network, which is comprised of a group of retailers, craftspeople, designers, writers and government officials who are proponents of wearing the kimono as fashion, and I delve deeper into the ways that this network represents a stage of adaptation to the crisis in the kimono industry but also an increasing alignment of contemporary kimono culture with 21st century modes of consumption, particularly those relating to the production of a 'lifestyle'.

Notes

1 *Yakuza* refers to organised crime groups in Japan.
2 A type of woven kimono which is particularly prized for its lengthy and labour-intensive production process.

References

Binkley, S. and Littler, J. 2008. 'Introduction: cultural studies and anti-consumerism: a critical encounter'. In *Cultural Studies* 22(5): 519–530

Bourdieu, P. 2013 [1977]. *Outline of a Theory of Practice*. Cambridge: Cambridge University Press

Douglas, M. and Isherwood, B. C. 1979. *The World of Goods: Towards an Anthropology of Consumption: with a new introduction*. London and New York: Routledge

Entwistle, J. 2000. 'Fashion and the fleshy body: dress as embodied practice'. In *Fashion Theory* 4(3): 323–347

Francks, P. 2009. *The Japanese Consumer: an Alternative Economic History of Modern Japan*. Cambridge: Cambridge University Press

Garon, S. M. and Maclachlan, P. L. 2006. *The Ambivalent Consumer: Questioning Consumption in East Asia and the West*. New York and London: Cornell University Press

Giddens, A. 1991. *Modernity and Self-Identity: Self and Society in the Late Modern Age*. Cambridge and Oxford: Polity Press

Graeber, D. 2011. 'Consumption'. In *Current Anthropology* 52(4): 489–511

Hall, J. 2018. 'Digital kimono: fast fashion, slow fashion?'. In *Fashion Theory* 22(3): 283–307

Hall, J. 2020. *Japan Beyond the Kimono: Innovation and Tradition in the Kyoto Textile Industry*. London and New York: Bloomsbury

Humphery, K. 2010. *Excess: Anti-Consumerism in the West*. Cambridge: Polity

Ivy, M. 1995. *Discourses of the Vanishing*. Chicago, IL and London: The University of Chicago Press,

Keane, W. 2005. 'Signs are not the garb of meaning: on the social analysis of material things'. In Küchler, S. and Miller, D., eds. *Clothing as Material Culture*. Oxford and New York: Berg

Kelly, W. 1986. 'Rationalization and nostalgia: cultural dynamics of new middle-class Japan'. In *American Ethnologist* 13(4): 603–618

Kikuchi, I. 2013. *Kikuchi Ima ga Tsutaetai! Katte ha Ikenai Kimono to Kimono Mawari* ('Kikuchi Ima Wants to Tell You! Kimono and Kimono Accessories That You Shouldn't Buy'; my translation of the title). Tokyo: Jitsugyo no Nihon Sha

Lindholm, C. 2008. *Culture and Authenticity*. Hoboken, NJ: Wiley-Blackwell Publishing

McIntyre, C. 2009. 'Diminishing varieties of active and creative retail experience: The end of the music shop?'. In *Journal of Retailing and Consumer Services* 16: 466–476

Milhaupt, T. S. 2014. *Kimono: A Modern History*. London: Reaktion Books

Miller, D. 1987. *Material Culture and Mass Consumption*. Oxford: Basil Blackwell

Miller, D. 1995. *Acknowledging Consumption*. Routledge: London and New York

Miller, D. 2012. *Consumption and its Consequences*. Cambridge: Polity

Pine, B. and Gilmore, J. 1998. 'Welcome to the experience economy'. In *Harvard Business Review* 76(4): 97–105

Roberston, J. 1988. 'Furusato Japan: the culture and politics of nostalgia'. In *International Journal of Politics, Culture, and Society*, 1(4): 494–518

Sack, R. D. 1988. *Place, Modernity and the Consumer's World: A Relational Framework for Geographical Analysis*. Baltimore and London: The Johns Hopkins University Press

Spiekermann, U. 2006. 'From neighbour to consumer: the transformation of retailer-consumer relationships in twentieth-century Germany' in Trentmann, F., ed. *The Making of the Consumer: Knowledge, Power and Identity in the Modern World*. Oxford and New York: Berg

Wilk, R. 2004. 'Morals and metaphors: the meaning of consumption'. In Ekström, K. M. and Brembeck, H., eds. *Elusive consumption*. Oxford: Berg

Woodward, S, 2007. *Why Women Wear What they Wear*. Oxford and New York: Berg

Wright, D. 2005. 'Commodifying respectability: distinctions at work in the bookshop'. In *Journal of Consumer Culture* 5(3): 295–314

Chapter 6

The kimono as fashion
Lifestyle, taste and individuated consumption

We leave early in the morning. The drive from Aichi prefecture to Tokyo would take around six hours. We move as a caravan, two cars, one with Kyoko, Takashi and me, and another with Yoshihide Shibakawa and two assistants. The cars are full of boxes and luggage, but above all, they are full of anticipation.

We are heading to one of the largest kimono sales event of its kind in Japan. The event is due to run in two parts: the first event, which is the one we are heading to, is a booth-type sales event taking place across two days, showcasing various goods and wares, with a central stage that will host fashion shows and talks relating to various aspects of kimono care and styling. The second, taking place a month later, is a fashion show.

This event has been long in the making, with months of negotiating, recruiting partners and planning how goods will be transported from shops and wholesalers from across Japan. Shibakawa-san has taken a key role in the planning and organisation of the event, together with a number of other retailers and producers who promote selling the kimono as fashion. The retailers, craftspeople, producers and, importantly, consumers converging on this event belong to a loosely bounded group that I have come to refer to as the 'kimono fashion network'. A varied group, they are united by their appreciation of a lifestyle in which the kimono is worn for fashion and style, rather than mostly for ceremonial or ritual occasions, or as Japan's national dress. There is respect for these latter usages among the network, but a strong commitment to the idea of kimono as fashion is a central uniting force.

It's September, and as we arrive in Tokyo, summer's lingering humidity is still heavy in the air. The venue is pure Tokyo: a construct of glass and steel, a far cry from the small town setting of Nishio, where we started out from. We have two whole large floors to set up. On the second floor, preparations are already underway. Booths are being prepared, and row upon row of mannequins are being dressed up in kimono, each featuring the styles put together by different shops and designers. During the event, visitors will get to choose which they think is the best style. We greet those who have already arrived, and then it's down to business – everyone moves with a sense of purpose and nerves are palpable. Azumaya is well-known among other retailers but also customers who wear the kimono as a fashion lifestyle, and my presence is legitimised through my connection to the Azumaya contingent. Like Kyoko, Takashi and the others, I will wear a kimono for the duration of the event – a simple, comfortable cotton kimono I had had made at Azumaya. I have brought Western clothes with me only in case of emergency.[1] My presence is further legitimised by my press badge, a clever idea from Shibakawa-san, who, aware of my role as an ethnographer, wanted to facilitate my interactions with booth owners. With the rest of the contingent caught up in preparations, I help with whatever I can – I buy refreshments, lay out pamphlets in strategic locations and ferry boxes between the car park and the booths. The work inevitably marks my kimono, and the practicality of the cotton kimono, both breathable and washable, quickly becomes apparent,

Key players in the extended network arrive, people with a high profile that I have heard of but not met in person. These are, as Shibakawa-san describes them, his allies, or *nakama*. This is not to say that everyone always agrees, of course, and differences of opinion exist within the network, but cohesion is important for friendships and business relationships. The broader sense of purpose in promoting the kimono as fashion tends to overcome differences in style or opinion.

The event unfolded with a certain amount of trepidation. The effort involved in bringing everyone together from different parts of Japan was considerable. Many participants were not based in Tokyo and had had to ship in their wares from different parts of Japan. In the hours running up to the opening of the event, activity reached a crescendo, with people hurrying back and forth setting up their booths.

When the doors open to customers, it's just a trickle at first. Curious twos and threes, wandering from booth to booth. Then there are more, many of them kimono-clad. Quite a few, using the maps we laid out for them, already know which booths to visit. As people flood in, so does the relief. At this rate, it seems, it may well have been worth it.

The hours pass, and scheduled events go off without a hitch. There are music recitals, fashion shows, and the highlight not to be missed: a talk given by Ima Kikuchi (Ima-san, as she is known to fans), the writer of books on the subject of kimono care and style. I've already referred a couple of times to her work in this volume and will discuss her wider role in the kimono fashion network later in this chapter. As well as being a writer, she is a captivating and entertaining speaker, and even before she begins to speak, the space in front of the stage is so packed that there is hardly room to stand. But it goes well; the running of the event is smooth, uneventful. Shibakawa-san patrols the venue, often too busy to stop and talk, but visibly pleased.

On the evening of the second and last day, a celebration dinner takes place, and the atmosphere is joyful. There is cause to be happy: around 10,000 people have come to the venue; and in subsequent years when the event runs again, the numbers will rise further.

What that first event in 2016 effectively showed is that the kimono as fashion, as fun and as a lifestyle choice, was on its way to becoming a full contender in the landscape of kimono retail. While uncertainty and anxieties about the future remained, the event proved to be a significant landmark: the kimono fashion network had officially arrived on the scene.

The making of the kimono fashion network: social media and a meeting of minds in a time of crisis

How did the kimono fashion network grow, and what were the factors that encouraged its creation? Looking at the event described above from an outsider's perspective, it's tempting to see the fashion network as an established and thriving community, but in fact it took time for a group whose aims and vision for their business, focused on fashion, to emerge. Gaining the kind of recognition and confidence that would enable them to take on a large-scale event was several years in the making. Part of the success of the event can be attributed to Shibakawa-san's enterprising nature and his appetite for a challenge, but the key ingredient was a group of people who shared similar ideas of what the future of the kimono, as a fashion lifestyle, could be. This event was the culmination of a long process of online and offline networking. It was also made possible by two features in particular: the Internet and the rise of social media, but also the dislocation of the chain of distribution since the crisis in the 1990s: the disruption of earlier, rigid business relationships enabled new, more flexible ones to be formed.

The first inkling I had that Azumaya was part of a larger network was when I first met one of Shibakawa-san's *nakama* ('friend' or 'ally') in January 2016. It was after a KdJ event, when the most loyal segment of KdJ had converged on Azumaya. Knowing that KdJ members would come to the shop, Shibakawa-san had invited Tetsuya Ueda from Kyoto. Ueda-san runs a company named Masugi, specialised in Ōshima *tsumugi*. Ueda-san is a self-possessed man with a steady, contemplative gaze to complement his lilting Kyoto accent. Ueda-san dresses in his own wares, and mostly wears kimono on a day-to-day basis (see Figure 6.1). He is on a mission to revamp the Ōshima *tsumugi*: once a favourite of well-to-do housewives in the Shōwa period (1926–1989), Ōshima is still a highly prized form of textile heritage in Japan. While requiring very specialised knowledge and expertise to be made, Ōshima *tsumugi* also occupies a difficult niche in that it is not usually worn for formal events, but equally it is still made of silk and, therefore, cannot be worn as casually as one of Azumaya's cotton kimono. Ōshima *tsumugi* are usually characterised by sober patterns and colours (such as navy or cream). Tetsuya Ueda's company Masugi's fashion-forward designs, with cats and musical instruments among others, are very different from the typical

Figure 6.1 Tetsuya Ueda in the headquarters of Masugi (Reproduced with kind permission from Tetsuya Ueda).

patterns of Ōshima *tsumugi*, which are usually quite staid, mostly geometric or floral patterns. The informal event was an occasion for Azumaya regulars to inspect Ueda-san's wares.

Shibakawa-san and Ueda-san put on a show for the visitors, sitting opposite each other and rolling out the bolts for everyone to see. The method was based on organic salesmanship, in that the customers could get a good look at the new items, have a think about them, and maybe ask for them later. Neither Shibakawa-san nor Ueda-san recommended any wares. Instead, they joked with each other and with customers, and they took note of the kimono that visitors particularly liked. For Ueda-san, this was especially important as it gave him a sense of what items would be worth making in the future. What stood out is that everyone seemed to be having a good time, enjoying the showmanship.

Intrigued by the camaraderie and the shared values between Shibakawa-san and Ueda-san, I arranged to visit Ueda-san in his company headquarters in Kyoto a couple of months later. The day of the appointment came, and having travelled from Toyota, where I was living, to Kyoto, I made my way into the back alleys of the old business district of Shijo in Kyoto, where I found Masugi tucked away in a narrow street with other manufacturers and companies. After greeting me courteously, Ueda-san told me the history of his company and I was able to get an insight into how he had, in many ways, followed a similar journey to Shibakawa-san:

> It was the beginning of the 2000s, I think, that sales over the Internet began to increase. Before that all took off, we had to sell our wares to the *tonya* [wholesaler], so we had no idea who was buying our products

in the end. The industry itself got smaller, and the chain of distribution got smaller too, and there were fewer *tonya* who would buy our products.

When you look at the Internet, you see lots of people talking about kimono. The Internet really helped us build a connection with our customers. We made ourselves a homepage and started using Twitter, which opened up our horizons. I'd always had doubts about being in this industry and not actually wearing kimono, but I let it slide, you know? I wore suits and occasionally I wore kimono too.

Then, one day, I asked someone I didn't know 'Do you wear kimono?'. They replied, 'I don't'. So I asked them why not and they said, 'Why are you asking *me* that? If *you* don't then why should *I*?!' I had to admit, I saw the point. From the next day on, I vowed not to wear Western clothes. I began wearing kimono. It was also round about that time that I started using Twitter. And I really started to understand what our customers who wear kimono think and feel about kimono. At the end of the day, when there are lots of wholesalers between the customers and us, it's hard to be sure what our customers would like.

So I set aside for a while the question of selling or not selling, making money or not making money, because I felt that we had to understand what was going on with our customers. We had to set up the kind of personal networks that we needed. People who make and sell kimono don't tend to wear kimono. In my mind, for us to wear kimono, it's like a weapon. It's an opportunity. We can make kimono that people actually wear. And for me the ideal situation is this: we pick up on our customers' wishes and because of that we can make something worthwhile.

There are many parallels with Shibakawa-san's journey. Like Shibakawa-san, it was only when Ueda-san started wearing kimono that he began to understand their appeal. Like Shibakawa-san, something clicked for Ueda-san because he could put himself in the shoes of his customers by wearing what they wanted to buy.

This generation of business owners in their late 30s and 40s reached the age where they were to shoulder serious responsibilities or take over from the older generation. Many owners had experienced frustration within the industry for some years but had not been able to find ways to change their business until the crisis of the 1990s altered the industry from within. The rigid chain of production and distribution up until the 1990s kept every section of the chain separate with only limited possibilities for innovation or collaboration across sectors of the industry. These barriers between craftspeople, producers, wholesalers and retailers started to become more porous after the economic crisis. Ueda-san recalls the effect of the economic crisis as follows:

What really changed for us was when a particular *tonya* [wholesaler] went bankrupt. Whenever we asked the people with the skills to help out, they would refuse because they worked for the big *tonya*. Other places refused too. But after that particular *tonya* went bankrupt, they finally started to agree. It was then that we got an exclusivity agreement with the people whose skills we needed. After that, the place that made the kimono also closed down. They said the going was just too tough. So then we began doing our own manufacturing as well. There were so many changes at that time.

The recession closed down businesses and brought down overall sales, but it also removed barriers for businesses such as Ueda-san's, who could now redefine themselves across the previously fixed categories of wholesaler, manufacturer, retailer and craft workshop. For Ueda-san, this proved to be an opportunity to bring his family business into line with fashion and design, something he himself felt passionately about. He also believed that this change would enable him to make products guided by the wishes of the market and his customers.

Ueda-san's is one of the many individual stories of change and innovation that I encountered in the kimono industry. In the wake of crisis, many business owners who could only occupy certain roles began to experiment with other aspects of the industry. Internet and social media, in particular, enabled people with similar hopes for the future of the industry to find each other and establish regular, easy communication. In the late 2000s, with the rise of social media, Shibakawa-san told me that he began to reach out to other shop owners, as well as craftspeople, designers and wholesalers. Ueda-san, meanwhile, was also doing the same. What united them was a shared sense of urgency about how to stay in business, but also a budding wish to wear the kimono as fashion. The lack of agency in deciding on fashion trends and ideas was prevalent for retailers, and on the production and wholesale side there was a concern with not meeting customers or being able to pinpoint customer wishes and needs. Social media proved to be a way to communicate their frustrations and aspirations that was impossible before. By subsequently meeting in person, alliances, friendships and business deals evolved over meals and pints of beer. During the period between the late 2000s and 2014, this informal network grew around a single, simple idea: market the kimono as fashion wear. This idea was both a business model, but also a personal conviction for many.

What makes the network rather striking is that it offers a different model of sociality than the vertical stratification that is taken to be characteristic of Japanese society more broadly speaking. Chie Nakane famously presented Japan as a 'vertical society' divided into seniors, people of similar rank and juniors (Nakane 1970). Though critiqued for its essentialising statements on the supposed uniqueness of this seniority system and for a certain lack of academic rigour (see Hata and Smith 1986), Nakane's work is certainly useful in the sense that senior/junior relationships are a key social dynamic in Japanese society. What is interesting in the case of the kimono fashion network is that senior/junior stratification, but also gendered, class, income and age-based hierarchies, appear more muted. This is consistent with the kinds of horizontal sociality present in subcultures. Sarah Thornton, in her work on club cultures, used Pierre Bourdieu's notion of 'capital' (see Bourdieu 1986a), coining the term 'subcultural capital'. This is the means through which members of a culture establish their hierarchies through assessing how well each member has met the criteria for membership. In Thornton's work, this was through being 'hip' and being recognised as 'hip' by your peers (Thornton 1995). In the case of the kimono fashion network, as with many fashion subcultures, hierarchical relationships were achieved through style, taste, and passion for the kimono as much as through broader social hierarchies prevalent in the general population.

Members of the network are often friends as well as business partners, socialising in the form of visits to each other's shops, workshops or headquarters, as well as nights out on the town. Equally frequent are co-organised events, promoting each other's products, as Shibakawa-san does for other members of the network on his regular weekend Internet live broadcast, and commenting and liking their posts on Facebook and Instagram, and re-tweeting tweets.

Crucially, social media allowed the members of the kimono fashion network to begin chipping away at arguably the most significant hierarchical barrier of all: the one between producers and their customers. This created opportunities for a different kind of salesmanship. Social media enabled members of the industry who were interested in Internet-based forms of marketing and sales, towards which the kimono industry as a whole had been rather inimical, to actually get a sense of what the customers wanted.

The advocates of kimono as fashion rather than formal wear tend to be savvy Internet users and masters of social media, regardless of whether they are retailers, craftspeople, *kitsuke* (kimono dressing) professionals or customers. In Shibakawa-san's view, both customers and fellow business owners could be considered a *nakama* ('friend' or 'ally'). This also marks them as distinct from the 'mainstream' kimono industry, which typically does not have a strong Internet presence and is not very active on social media, and would maintain distinct roles as retailer on one side and customer on the other. The Internet also offers a venue for competition in the sense that clever use of the Internet can provide a measure of how well-known or popular a shop or business can become.

The network members' use of social media, but also their informality and willingness to get to know their customers, create a sense of community in which customers can feel involved and implicated in the industry. This is especially powerful both because customers are then emotionally involved and invested in the kimono as a lifestyle, but all the more so because the kimono industry, typically speaking, is quite secretive and little known to outsiders. Here are two profiles of well-known members of the kimono fashion network.

Ima Kikuchi

Familiar to her fans as Ima-san, Ima Kikuchi (see Figure 6.2) occupies an important position at the heart of the network. Although primarily a writer, she has widespread partnerships across wholesalers, manufacturers, craftspeople and shop owners, including a brand of kimono created in collaboration with craftspeople and wholesalers in her hometown of Yonezawa in Northern Japan. Yonezawa is historically a production centre for woven textiles and *benibana* flowers (safflower), which are used in the dyeing process to produce a delicate range of oranges, pinks and reds. Ima-san co-owns the kimono brand Skala[2] together with a local manufacturer. Ima-san is in a unique position because of her role as a popular writer of books about the kimono and about kimono lifestyle, peppered with the humorous illustrations which she draws herself. Many of her publications are in the style of advice books: *40 dai kara no shin-kimono seikatsu* (Kikuchi 2015) ('Kikuchi Ima Wants to Tell You! New kimono lifestyle as from 40 years old'; my translation of the

Figure 6.2 Writer, designer and stylist Ima Kikuchi (Reproduced with kind permission from Ima Kikuchi).

title) gives women advice on how to start building a kimono outfit, what sorts of kimono to buy and what will make good investments as opposed to bad ones. Ima-san's choices in terms of kimono, as well as her conviction that people should try and enjoy the kimono without becoming too afraid of the rules, are something of a breath of fresh air for people interested in wearing the kimono but who worry about the rules or what other people will think. Ima-san spreads these messages through her books and at her well-attended speaking events, such as the one at the Tokyo sales event I described above. In addition to being a writer, she is a charismatic and entertaining speaker who is very active in terms of public engagement. As well as her charisma and her fashion, a key to her popularity is her frankness and her humour. One of her books in particular, *Katte ha ikenai kimono to kimono-mawari* (Kikuchi 2013) ('Kimono and accessories that you shouldn't buy'; my translation) called into question some of the sales methods and approaches in the industry. This means that Ima-san also occupies the role of an advocate for consumers. Her role is, therefore, a unique one, as she is a writer, advocate, fashion influencer and entrepreneur all in one.

Kōichi Fujii

Another high-profile figure in the network is Kōichi Fujii who runs a tie-dye business in Kyoto called Fujii Shibori.[3] The word 'tie-dye' in English might evoke the bright psychedelic patterns of the 1960s in the West, but this resist-dye technique, known as *shibori*, has a longer history in Japan and there are several regional centres of production, most notably Arimatsu and Narumi in Aichi prefecture. A number of different ways of binding the cloth before dyeing produce a wide variety of patterns and styles. Shibori techniques have often been used in making *furisode* ('swinging sleeve' kimono). The final effect is that of a large number of small knots densely packed to produce a sweeping, textured effect. This was so popular with *furisode* that this effect is now often emulated through straightforward dyeing, rather than fully tie-dyeing the cloth, which is time-consuming and technical.

Fujii-san's wares produce an altogether different aesthetic. In contrast with the small tie-dye designs on *furisode*, the patterns are large and bold, strikingly symmetrical and regular (see Figure 6.3). The signature dye is a deep marine blue, but the workshop produces many different colours. The uniqueness of the techniques allows for good branding and makes the wares especially memorable. These qualities, the refined and unusual nature of the techniques combined with the striking design, make Fujii-san's fabrics well-suited to customers who buy the kimono for fashion, as these shoppers are likely to want to make a statement through their clothes. The complexity and time-consuming nature of the technique means that the products tend to lean towards a higher price tag, but that being said, kimono accessories, bags and umbrellas are also on offer, which are less expensive. The tie-dye wares of Fujii

Figure 6.3 Fujii Shibori wares (Reproduced with kind permission from Kōichi Fujii and Fujii Shibori).

Shibori are renowned for the difficult techniques used in their making and the meticulousness required, such as the *sekka-shibori* or snowflake tie-dye, which is among the most well-known designs that they produce. Because the tie-dye is so distinctive, it is immediately recognisable by the members of the network and thus carries significant cultural capital within the community.

Individuated consumption and generational change in Japan: putting the innovators of the kimono fashion network into context

So far, I have addressed the transformation of the kimono, in some areas of the market, from formal wear to fashion wear, from an internal perspective, documenting the changes that business owners made in the face of the crisis and turmoil their industry was undergoing and how they found each other and connected over shared values. It is helpful here to zoom out further and place the kimono fashion network within broad trends in consumption and consumer culture in Japanese society. This will contextualise why, in the wake of the 1990s, a more individualised, fashion-based and personalised version of the kimono has emerged and started to gain popularity, enabling the creation of a fluid kimono fashion network comprised of producers and retailers, but also customers. Certainly the weakened status of wholesalers after the crisis of the 1990s had a considerable effect, as did the creative ventures of individual business owners such as Shibakawa-san and Ueda-san. Socio-cultural changes in the usage of the kimono have contributed to a more diverse understanding of what the kimono is for and how it should be worn, although an established canon of rules related to appropriateness in terms of age, seasonality, formality and ways of dressing remains strongly entrenched. Zooming out to a macro perspective on consumption within Japanese society enables us to understand where to place the innovators in the kimono fashion network within broader generational shifts in consumption practices in Japan, revealing how the development of the kimono fashion network parallels the increasing individualisation of consumption practices in Japan.

A growing body of literature has characterised Japanese society as increasingly individualised (Yoda 2000: 650). Japan, along with other Asian countries, has widely been described both inside Japan and outside as a 'collectivist' society in which individuals give preference to the interests of the group over their own, so a shift towards a more 'individualistic' societal model is a noteworthy trend. This characterisation of Japan as 'socio-centric' or relational can be found across disciplines, in psychology literature, such as Hazel Rose Markus and Shinobu Kitayama's influential article (1991), as well as in the social sciences. This concept is firmly anchored in foundational sociological and anthropological literature about Japan, such as Ruth Benedict's *The Chrysanthemum and the Sword* (1977 [1947]) and Nakane Chie's *Japan Vertical society* (1970). The Japanese self has been characterised extensively as 'interdependent', 'sociocentric' or 'relational' and defined by group identity: within the company or the family household (*ie*). This is often cast in direct opposition to Western 'selves' which are conceived as being primarily individualistic in nature and less strongly defined by roles within a company or family. This sometimes stark opposition has been widely circulated in Japanese society, especially through a body of texts known as *Nihonjinron*, or theories of 'Japaneseness' which aim to explain the key features of the Japanese national character. A mainstay of this literature is the notion that Japan is 'unique' and the particular features of social cohesion and group identity are diametrically opposed to Western society in particular. *Nihonjinron* has been widely critiqued and has been the subject of much debate (see Dale 1986, Yoshino 1992, Goodman and Refsing 1999 and Befu 2001 among others), and so has the idea that it is possible to draw a sharp distinction between 'purely' sociocentric societies on the one hand, and purely 'individualistic' societies on the other. In the debates that ensued, Charles Lindholm critiqued the characterisation of Japan on the grounds that the distinction between individualistic and sociocentric societies is too simplistic, with both Western and Japanese societies demonstrating both traits (Lindholm 1997). Other academics, such as John Clammer and John Dower, have argued that while Japan recognises individuality (*kosei*), by and large Japanese society is less comfortable with individualism as a concept (*kojinshugi*), which can be associated negatively with self-centredness and the inability to function properly within a group – an ability which is highly prized in Japanese society (see Clammer 1997: 47; Hardacre 1998: 10).

In consumer trends, we can see an increasing tendency towards consumption which expresses the tastes and preferences of the individual – in other words expressing *kosei*. While this might not be the same as stating that Japan as a society has become increasingly characterised by Western-style 'individualism', it is possible to argue that consumption in Japan is increasingly individuated. Robert Dunn uses the term 'individuated mode' to 'convey the capacity of individual consumers to exercise degrees of sovereignty and autonomy, creating their own definitions of commodities' meanings and values' (Dunn 2008: 182). These trends are important to map in the context of the kimono industry, particularly as the members of the fashion network have consciously observed these changes and partaken in individuated consumption themselves.

As already noted, in the post-war period, Japan became a mass consumer society. Consumption in the post-war period has been intimately tied to class – the growth of the middle-class was linked to material milestones in the acquisition of certain items, such as the 'three treasures' of the 1950s: washing machine, refrigerator and television. In the 1960s, this evolved into a culture of home decoration, furnishing and personalisation (*mai-hōmu*), and car ownership (*mai-kā*) (Francks 2009: 201–202). Rising salaries permitted these purchases, and consumption milestones were celebrated as the hallmark of a more equal, prosperous and increasingly 'middle-class' society (Francks 2009).

By the 1970s, consumption choices had increased and diversified, enabling a new generation to participate in both large-scale fads and trends, such as Hello Kitty, which spread far beyond Japan and has enjoyed global popularity in subsequent decades (Yano 2013: 9). Other niche, or subcultural, forms of consumption also appeared. A new generation of consumers began to emerge, with more individuated and differentiated consumer tastes, making purchases that were for personal enjoyment and to build a self-image or a lifestyle. This generation, characterised by increasingly individuated consumption, is often referred to as the *shinjinrui* or 'new breed' because their patterns of behaviour and life choices appeared outlandish in comparison with those of their baby boomer parents. Referencing the work of Thomas Havens, Kataryna Cwiertka and Ewa Machotka indicate that it was the consumption choices and lifestyles of the *shinjinrui* and their focus on their personal fulfilment through consumption that marked them as different from the older generation (Havens 1994: 151–157 in Cwiertka and Machotka 2018: 136).

It is important to note here that it is difficult to draw a hard and fast line between what counts as 'purely' individuated consumption, in other words a consumption choice which is self-expressive, creative and centred around the subjectivity of the consumer, a consumption choice that reflects a concern with pure practicality, or a choice which is primarily influenced by class values and group identity, among others. Because both the concepts of identity and consumption are so complex, Dunn notes that 'generally speaking, it remains unclear the *extent* to which consumption shapes or conditions identity formation and *how* this occurs' (Dunn 2008: 158; italics in original). For instance, customers who like to wear the kimono for fashion might buy a fashion kimono as a way to build a fashion lifestyle and as a means of self-expression, but they may well also be conscious of, and influenced by, the shared tastes and aesthetics of a peer group also interested in kimono fashion. The determining factor might not be class in this case, since clothing purchases in particular lie at the complex interface between internal subjectivities and the wider social constructs related to taste, class, ethnicity, gender, age, aesthetics and appropriateness, to name but a handful.

Having acknowledged this complexity, we can establish that, broadly speaking, Japan experienced a shift from mass consumption towards individuated consumption in which self-expression and lifestyle play a key role. As Tomiko Yoda has argued,

> Japan's transformation into one of the most affluent societies in the world was accompanied by the palpable weakening of its postwar values and norms, particularly on matters such as work ethics, respect for hierarchy and authority, sexual mores expected of women and youths, and the strong sense of collective identification, while the pursuit of individual identity and individuated lifestyles has become a powerful trend.
>
> Yoda 2000: 650

Japanese lifestyle choices, though individuated, are characterised by a diffuse sense of sociality in which others with like-minded pursuits and interests are joined. This is reminiscent of Marcel Maffesoli's notion of 'tribal' associations in which people gather in loosely defined groups whose temporary cohesion is predicated on emotional connection (Maffesoli 1996). This understanding of social grouping is a post-modern understanding that 'traditional' forms of sociality, rooted in fixed communities and stable social structures, have dissipated in post-modern societies characterised by flux and change. Maffesoli's concept has a particular resonance in Japan where the word 'tribes' (*zoku*) has often been used to characterise subculture, especially youth subcultures that were perceived to be socially deviant. It also resonates with the ways in which the stabilising forces of work and family became increasingly unstable in the 1990s following the economic crisis. Munenori Suzuki et al. argue that the structures linked to group-oriented identities were fundamentally destabilised. Companies became less able to offer life-time employment, thus reducing the likelihood that employees would stay with one company for their entire lives (Suzuki et al. 2010). Families, too, are increasingly in flux, with a growing number of single-person households, and family structure moving away from multi-generational households (Hirayama 2017).

So, how do members of the kimono fashion network fit into this landscape of individuated consumption, economic crisis and social change? Kimono retailers undoubtedly move in circles that many Japanese people are unfamiliar with, dealing with items and a business model that may seem removed from the usual or typical experience of consumption that Japanese people have. Certainly, this has been the case for some decades in the post-war period. Although the kimono industry has been integrated into the market, the experience of selling and consuming the kimono remained different from the consumption landscape that had become the norm in the rest of society. Having the purchasing power to buy the kimono demonstrated economic capital and being able to wear it and master the aesthetic and seasonal codes encoded within the kimono demonstrated cultural capital (Richardson 1986). Both of these facets served to reinforce the status of the purchasing family. However, this kimono type did not easily adapt to the changing landscape of consumption in which individuated preferences began to dominate and demonstrating economic and cultural capital through kimono purchases became less and less salient in the late 20th and early 21st century.

Business owners in the kimono industry were not blind to these changes. Change, however, was delayed. Initially, business owners did not particularly innovate because the existing model of selling the formal kimono was profitable, so they felt no urgent need for change even though the model of selling the kimono was largely out of sync with the rest of Japan as a consumer society. Further, there was internal pressure to keep the shape of their business unchanged and to preserve existing business contacts inherited from their parents. The retailers and business owners (in their late 30s, or 40s and 50s) among my participants were often the children of the *shinjinrui* (the 'new breed') generation, and had become *shakaijin* ('full members of society')[4] just before or around the time of the economic crisis of the 1990s and the recession. Among some members of this generation, the desire for change was strong. This narrative was clearly reflected in Ueda-san's journey and desire for change in the way he did business, and the ways in which he wanted to make sure that his business reflected customer preferences and tastes. A desire for change and for a closer match with customer preferences was often magnified by the strong personal preferences that these retailers had in terms of what they bought in their own lives as consumers, their own tastes and lifestyles, and the ways in which they could express themselves through what they consumed. For many in my research, their wish was to try and bring into harmony their business of making and selling the kimono on the one hand, and the modes of consumption that they themselves were most accustomed to. Yoshihide Shibakawa, owner of the kimono shop Azumaya, (see Chapter 5) had thought a great deal about what niche the kimono should occupy for the consumer. If it is not being worn for ceremonial wear, then, he reasoned, it could be branded differently. 'I want people to think of kimono the same way that they think of iPads,' he once said to me. 'Sure, they're expensive, but they're fun and it's not a huge stretch to buy one.' Shibakawa-san's kimono are indeed typically less expensive than a formal kimono in an average kimono shop and would fall within the price range of an iPad. This also draws a direct parallel with the forms of consumption that modern Japanese customers are most used to, such as buying iPads, itself representative of a particular consumption choice in selecting Apple products.

This newer generation, Shibakawa-san also reasoned, was better equipped to make changes because they had these kinds of new ideas, particularly related to branding. This generation had also been members of a consumer society that was in flux, and increasingly tribal in its association with particular lifestyles. Shibakawa-san told me:

> Our generation is at a crossroads, in all areas of the industry. People in their 40s are rare in the industry, but we're in a good position. We know all the traditional stuff *and* we have new ideas, too. With the kimono, if people aren't there to explain how it works and why it's special, customers won't always understand. In the past, customers were loyal to a shop because they liked the people there. Now, people are loyal to a shop because they like the brand as well as the people.

What retailers in the kimono fashion network have attempted to do is to bring their wares into line with a type of consumption that their customers are more familiar with, such as iPads. In doing so, they bring the discourse of identity-building through consumption and lifestyle into the world of kimono retail, which had previously followed the model of selling formal wear that was patterned on aesthetics and codes that were largely (though perhaps not completely) distinct from the typical consumption experience in Japan. They are aligning the kimono with global discourses on lifestyle and fashion, while at the same time retaining the particularities of the kimono (such as shape, ways of dressing, obi, shoes, accessories, seasonal codes). In other words, they are able to offer customers a view of the kimono, which had become alien to them, through the lens of modern lifestyle consumption. This is a potent combination: the kimono combines elements of nostalgia and an appeal to the past with a style of consumption that customers recognise more easily: fashion, lifestyle and self-expression.

Our kimono 'laifu': consumption, taste and sociality in the kimono fashion network

Members of the kimono fashion network belong to many walks of life: they are members of the kimono industry, in other words, retailers, wholesalers, producers and craftspeople, but also designers, independent artists and creators, writers, bloggers, customers, aficionados and generally speaking people with an interest in the kimono as fashion. They form a diffuse community which is reminiscent, as mentioned previously, of the emotional tribal associations described by Maffesoli (1996). Their lifestyle revolves around integrating the kimono, usually as fashion wear, or everyday wear, into their lives. For some, this involves wearing the kimono on special days out, such as Kimono de Jack gatherings (see Chapters 1 and 6), and for others, this involves wearing the kimono every day. Stakes are of course different for different members: on the retail side, livelihoods are involved, and items must be sold. But members of the fashion network on the retail side often take pride in participating in the same lifestyle as their customers; they aren't just purveyors, but participants as well. For this reason, socialising within the community often takes place across retailer/customer boundaries, and customers often enjoy being seen with or socialising with particular retailers or figures who have gained a reputation within the community. Socialising across these boundaries reinforces the sense of a shared kimono lifestyle in which sociality and a shared sense of taste play a crucial role.

The concept of lifestyle is especially illuminating here. Perhaps because of its association with the media and social media, lifestyle seems 'light' as a concept, perhaps trivial. Mikael Jensen points out that the term eludes easy definition because of its sheer ubiquitousness in popular discourse (Jensen 2007: 63–64). In many parts of the world, we speak of lifestyle in terms of food, hobbies, what we wear, the places we choose to live and the people we choose to associate with. In a review of the literature on the concept of lifestyle, Robert Stebbins gives a straightforward definition: 'a distinctive set of shared patterns of tangible behavior that is organized around a set of coherent interests or social conditions or both, that is explained and justified by a set of related values, attitudes, and orientations and that, under certain conditions, becomes the basis for a separate, common social identity for its participants' (Stebbins 1997: 357). Stebbins cites Robert Bellah et al. to note that the expression 'lifestyle enclave' may be used to described people who have 'shared patterns of appearance, consumption, and leisure activities' without other unifying features, such as sharing a history or political views (Bellah et al. 1985: 335 in Stebbins 1997: 349).

Lifestyle, and the medium of consumption through which lifestyle often operates, is intimately tied with the project of self-creation and the generation of identity and belonging. Anthony Giddens proposed that lifestyle is intimately linked to the project of self-narrative, which lies at the core of identity itself (Giddens 1991: 81). Giddens posited that the more traditional forms of identity-building based around bounded communities lost their hold, the more 'daily life is reconstituted in terms of the dialectical interplay of the local and the global, the more individuals are forced to negotiate lifestyle choices among the diversity of options' (Giddens 1991: 5). The importance of lifestyle in the generation of identity has, if anything, grown even more complex since Giddens wrote his book on identity in the early 1990s, with the further spread of globalisation and the growth of social media both contributing to the time-space compression that is characteristic of modern life, as proposed by David Harvey (1989). Giddens further argues that lifestyle is more than just a choice – it is, rather, an inevitability:

> The notion of lifestyle sounds somewhat trivial because it is so often thought of solely in terms of a superficial consumerism: lifestyles as suggested by glossy magazines and advertising images. But there is something much more fundamental going on than such a conception suggests: in conditions of high modernity, we all not only follow lifestyles, but in an important sense we are forced to do so – *we have no choice but to choose*. A lifestyle can be defined as a more or less integrated set of practices which an individual embraces, not only because such practices fulfil utilitarian needs, but because they give material form to a particular narrative of self-identity.
>
> Giddens 1991: 81 (my emphasis)

A large component of our lifestyle revolves around the way we choose and what we consume from what is on offer around us and, in turn, what we make of the things we consume. Many lifestyles tend to focus on items or objects: cars, motorbikes, clothes, etc. Mike Featherstone argues that mass production has enabled such a multitude of lifestyles (Featherstone 2007: 96). Daniel Miller has similarly argued that consumption is the key that enables projects of selfhood and expressions of the self but also expressions of belonging to wider social groups (see Miller 1987, 1995 and 1998).

As mentioned in the previous section, Japan is very much a consumer society. With regards to leisure activities and pursuits, Japan has been referred to as the 'consumer society *par excellence*' (Manzenreiter and Horne 2006: 412) due to the extent to which leisure goods and services are commercialised in Japan. Wolfram Manzenreiter and John Horne argue that since markets are differentiated to a great extent in Japan, based on gender, lifestyle, taste and other factors, this has enabled a particularly powerful connection between certain consumer goods and identity, especially with regards to group belonging and a sense of community (Manzenreiter and Horne 2006: 413). A further characteristic of the interlocking of consumption and identity in Japan is located in what Mike Featherstone calls the 'aestheticization of modern life', which he takes to be a 'preoccupation with customizing a lifestyle and stylistic self-consciousness' (Featherstone 2007: 98–99). He further argues that the word lifestyle 'connotes individuality, self-expression, and a stylistic self-consciousness. One's body, clothes, speech, leisure pastimes, eating and drinking preferences, home, car, choice of holidays, etc. are to be regarded as indicators of the individuality of taste and sense of style of the owner/consumer' (Featherstone 2007: 96). The aesthetic dimension of lifestyle, in other words the attention paid to what the outfits look like, is especially relevant for the kimono fashion lifestyle in which the 'look' of the kimono is key.

So far, I have used the terms 'network', 'community' and 'lifestyle' to describe the kimono fashion network, because I consider all of these terms to be salient: it is a community in the sense that there is a clear defining boundary between those who are in the 'kimono lifestyle' and those who are not, but it is also a group characterised by various criss-crossing internal networks: networks between retailers and consumers, but also amongst retailers, in which consumers can become implicated to a certain extent. Some networks are stronger, such as those between members of the inner circle, or more diffuse, such as those between 'outer' members – for instance, interested fans who only occasionally buy kimono. Neither 'network' nor 'community' completely captures the essence of the kimono fashion network, as the group is characterised by both concepts.

Lifestyle, and its narrative of self- and community-building, is at the heart of the kimono fashion network yet, for most of the 20th century, the kimono lay somewhat outside of the realm of lifestyle: it was considered as something that *had* to be worn at particular times, such as weddings, coming of age ceremonies, school entrance and graduation ceremonies or for cultural pursuits such as tea ceremony or flower arranging (Valk 2018). It has even been said that the kimono was not subject to fashion, or that if it was, it was a much slower moving and altogether different fashion than the frenzied, ever-changing world of fashion for Western clothes. What the kimono fashion network has achieved is to align the kimono with a modern lifestyle choice, belonging to a globalised discourse on fashion and self-expression.

Members of the network speak of having a 'kimono *laifu*' ('kimono life') and together with their customers, they engage in lively debate about what the best kind of 'kimono *laifu*' is. At times, the English word 'life' is used, as indeed is the word 'lifestyle'. Passion for the kimono is a key element, as is the sense that members of the kimono fashion network know that their lifestyle differs from the established rules and aesthetic codes governing the kimono. This is evidence of a particular type of taste, which is almost subcultural in the sense that, to a varying extent, the styling of fashion kimono differs from the established set of rules. The formalisation of the kimono, as discussed in Chapters 3 and 4, led to aesthetic tastes becoming rigid in the post-war period. Kimono types were to be matched with particular kinds of obi, depending on the time of year, on age and on the occasion. Failure to meet these aesthetic codes and rules was taken as a sign that, at best, the wearer was ignorant of the codes or, at worst, that they had no taste. The taste of the kimono fashion network is altogether more playful and less rigid. It isn't so much the case that the network completely breaks the established canon – indeed, they have considerable respect for the upper echelons of formality. But the network encourages greater flexibility with rules and aesthetics when it comes to wearing the kimono as fashion, rather than to attend a particular event. The quintessential example of the kimono fashion network's taste is the *hanhaba* obi (half-width), which, according to the established canon, is an informal obi, mostly worn with light summer *yukata* or polyester kimono. Kimono fashion network members, however, use this obi much more widely, often with elaborate knots and ties that do not follow established rules or patterns, and with silk or formal kimono as well as informal polyester kimono or *yukata*. Such distinctions might, from an outside perspective, seem small, but in fact these are bold statements of taste and preference.

Pierre Bourdieu famously argued that taste was a key part of the way social classes distinguished themselves from one another (Bourdieu 1986b). This taste is one in which members of the kimono fashion network have to position themselves with regards to the established aesthetics: how much do they deviate from the canon, and where in the outfit will this deviation express itself? Learning taste also involves learning about the types of fabric and what makes them special, and how those material properties will aid (or hinder) projects of lifestyle and image-building. Members of the community, retailers and customers alike, extol the virtues of particular fabrics that chime with their sense of taste, such as *kōtaku-kan* ('shine'), softness, warmth or resistance to creasing. Members learn to appreciate the look of the fabric and its feel, as well as the overall look when combined with other elements of the outfit, alongside other members who reinforce the value of the fabrics. Of course, disagreements over style occur, and not all members feel the same way about a given style. The network leaves room for preferences and differences of opinion among members.

The intensity of the feelings that members of the network, both customers and retailers, have towards certain fabrics bears a similarity to the feelings that aficionados of branded goods have. As Robert Foster argues, the value creation process in brands functions by generating a 'relationship of trust with consumers, of empathy, of positive emotional response bordering on passion' (Foster 2008: 16). It is not surprising then, that the concepts of passion and love are mainstays of the kimono fashion network, and the words *suki* or *daisuki* ('love/like' and 'really love/like') are frequently used by its members. Shibakawa-san and Ueda-san, among others, speak of the benefits of 'branding' kimono. Branding not only encourages consumers to form strong emotional attachments to branded products (Foster 2008), it also encourages widespread recognition. Previously, kimono were distinguished by the techniques that went into making them, which in turn were associated with places, such as Kaga Yūzen (see Chapter 3). Many retailers were convinced that this type of branding, based on regional techniques, was difficult for many Japanese to understand and was very different from the type of branding that Japanese customers typically encountered when shopping. This latter type of branding was seen as the better option because it was more familiar. And, indeed, the production and retail side of the kimono fashion network are establishing themselves through products branded in a particular way, such as the *zori* shoemaker Calen Blosso, known for its comfortable and stylish *zori*, rather than through a particular regional method.

An amusing exchange that I witnessed between Kyoko and her husband Takashi illustrates the link between fashion kimono and lifestyle perfectly. In May 2016 I visited the Toyota Automobile Museum during a Kimono de Jack gathering with Kyoko and Takashi. Together with a large group of kimono-clad visitors, we had toured the entire museum and we were taking a rest in the café. The café overlooked a large car park filled with period Toyota Celicas (a kind of sports car manufactured by Toyota since the 1970s). Kyoko was observing the drivers who had driven their period cars and seemingly left them in the car park to talk. Kyoko remarked, 'I don't get it. They are just standing around, not doing anything. Why?' Her husband Takashi replied, 'that's exactly the point. They're scoping out each other's cars, looking at what other people have. It's just like KdJ and our kimono. We hang out to compare ourselves, to see what other people have got.' Kyoko laughed. 'Ok, I get it now! That makes perfect sense.'

In fact, *kimono laifu* has much in common with other consumer object-based lifestyles, such as cars or motorbikes. John Schouten and James McAlexander explored the Harley-Davidson biker lifestyle in America, which they call a 'subculture of consumption' (Schouten and McAlexander 1995). They define this as 'a distinctive subgroup of society that self-selects on the basis of a shared commitment to a particular product class, brand, or consumption activity' with 'an identifiable, hierarchical social structure' and 'a unique ethos, or set of shared beliefs and values; and unique jargons, rituals, and modes of symbolic expression' (Schouten and McAlexander 1995: 43). This comparison between the kimono and the motorbike is not entirely innocent: Takashi himself is a car and motorbike enthusiast. My fieldwork happened to coincide with his long-anticipated acquisition of a Harley-Davidson motorbike. Takashi was intensely committed to all of his hobbies: photography (he is KdJ and Shibakawa-san's pro bono photographer, including for the event described at the beginning of this chapter), kimono, cars and motorbikes. It may seem unusual for kimono to be part of the same lifestyle-building project as motorbikes or photography, but for Takashi this is a cohesive lifestyle. His investments in objects treasured for their material qualities are planned, executed and savoured, often over a length of time. For Takashi, these projects offer both a source of enjoyment but also a way to craft an image and a sense of himself in the world (see Figure 6.4).

As with many other lifestyles, there is a feeling of reward that comes with participation in the lifestyle – it helps people 'feel good', and this brings about a wish to participate again or commit further to the lifestyle. Ethnographers interested in lifestyle who were initially 'outsiders' in the lifestyle, such as myself in relation to the kimono fashion network, often find themselves subject to the rewarding and pleasurable qualities of the lifestyles that they study, and wanting to experience the feelings of enjoyment that they bring. Schouten and McAlexander in their exploration of the Harley biker lifestyle also noted how easily they became sucked into the biker lifestyle:

Figure 6.4 Takashi dressed in a kimono with a long *haori* (kimono overcoat) (Reproduced with kind permission from Takashi).

> The more we integrated motorcycling and related activities into our daily consumption patterns the better we understood the nuances of the biker's lifestyle and identity. An unanticipated outcome of our increased ethnographic involvement was that we became motorcycle enthusiasts. Two or three days without riding a motorcycle brings on a yearning to ride.
>
> Schouten and McAlexander 1995: 46

Although consumption is not entirely free from negative emotions, feelings of reward and pleasure can be tied to the act of consuming and spending. These positive emotions also derive from the inherent sociality present in belonging to a lifestyle.

Kimono fashion demonstrates the ways in which retailers have benefited from the crisis of the 1990s by finding opportunities to re-shape their businesses as they see fit, particularly in aligning the kimono as a fashion and lifestyle choice. In doing so, they have been able to use the changing landscape of consumption practices, which has itself been integral to their own lives, to revitalise their businesses and produce strategies to negotiate the post-1990s crisis in the kimono industry. They may at times be perceived as breaking the rules of kimono-wearing and kimono aesthetics, but the network has nevertheless gained traction in the past years, as demonstrated by the sales event I described at the opening of this chapter, which has also taken place in subsequent years. Their momentum is aided by their careful use of innovative aesthetics, a varied price range, online platforms, social media, and a horizontal sociality based around a shared lifestyle, all of which are ingredients which can appeal to 21st century customers. Individuated consumption and the appeal of the kimono as fashion is one aspect of the way in which kimono retail is changing and adapting to new markets; the following chapter will showcase a changing kimono retail scene which caters to increasingly diverse markets.

Notes

1 Advice which was given to me by Kyoko – in case I was to fall ill, for instance, it would be more comfortable to be in Western clothes.
2 https://kiorien.jp/skala/ (accessed 06/11/2019).
3 http://fujiishibori.jp/ (accessed 16/06/2020).
4 *Shakaijin* typically refers to someone who has entered the work force and is therefore thought of as a mature, contributing member of society.

References

Befu, H. 2001. *Hegemony of Homogeneity: An Anthropological Analysis of 'Nihonjinron'*. Melbourne: Trans Pacific Press

Bellah, R. N. 1985. *Habits of the Heart: Individualism and Commitment in American life*. Berkeley, CA: University of California Press. Cited in Stebbins, R. 1997. 'Lifestyle as a generic concept in ethnographic research'. In *Quality and Quantity* 31(4): 347–360

Benedict, R. 1977 [1947]. *The Chrysanthemum and the Sword: Patterns of Japanese Culture*. London: Routledge and Kegan Paul

Bourdieu, P. 1986a. 'The forms of capital'. In Richardson, J. G., ed. *Handbook of Theory and Research for the Sociology of Education*. New York: Greenwood Press.

Bourdieu, P. 1986b. *Distinction: a Social Critique of the Judgement of Taste*. Trans., Nice, R. Florence, SC: Routledge

Clammer, J. 1997. *Contemporary Urban Japan: a Sociology of Consumption*. Oxford and Malden: Blackwell

Cwiertka, K. J. and Machotka, E. 2018. *Consuming Life in Post-Bubble Japan: a Transdisciplinary Perspective*. Amsterdam: Amsterdam University Press

Dale, P. N. 1986. *The Myth of Japanese Uniqueness*. London and Sydney: Croom Helm and Nissan Institute for Japanese Studies

Dower, J. W. 1998. 'Sizing up (and breaking down) Japan'. In Hardacre, H., ed. *The Postwar Development of Japanese Studies in the United States*. Leiden, Boston and Köln: Brill

Dunn, R. G. 2008. *Identifying Consumption: Subjects and Objects in Consumer Society*. Philadelphia: Temple University Press

Hata, H. and Smith, W. A. 1986. 'The vertical structure of Japanese society as a utopia'. In *Review of Japanese Culture and Society* 1(1): 92–109

Havens, T. 1994. *Architects of Affluence: The Tsutsumi Family and the Seibu Enterprises in Twentieth-Century Japan*, 1st ed. Cambridge, MA: Harvard University Asia Center. Cited in Cwiertka, K. J. and Machotka, E. 2018. *Consuming Life in Post-Bubble Japan: a Transdisciplinary Perspective*. Amsterdam: Amsterdam University Press

Harvey, D. 1989. *The Condition of Postmodernity: an Enquiry into the Origins of Cultural Change*. Oxford: Basil Blackwell

Hirayama, Y. 2017. 'Individualisation and familisation in Japan's home-owning democracy'. In *International Journal of Housing Policy* 17(2): 296–313

Kikuchi, I. 2013. *Kikuchi Ima ga Tsutaetai! Katte ha Ikenai Kimono to Kimono Mawari* ('Kikuchi Ima Wants to Tell You! Kimono and Kimono Accessories That You Shouldn't Buy'; my translation of the title). Tokyo: Jitsugyo no Nihon Sha

Kikuchi, I. 2015. *Kikuchi Ima ga Tsutaetai! 40 dai kara no shin-kimono seikatsu* ('Kikuchi Ima Wants to Tell You! New kimono lifestyle as from 40 years old'; my translation of the title). Tokyo: Jitsugyo no Nihon Sha

Lindholm, C. 1997. 'Does the sociocentric self exist? Reflections on Markus and Kitayama's "Culture and the self"'. In *Journal of Anthropological Research* 54(4): 405–422

Featherstone, M. 2007. *Consumer Culture and Postmodernism*. Los Angeles, London, New Delhi and Singapore: SAGE Publications

Foster, R. J. 2008. 'Commodities, brands, love and kula: comparative notes on value creation'. In *Anthropological Theory* 8(1): 9–25

Francks, P. 2009. *The Japanese Consumer: An Alternative Economic History of Modern Japan*. Cambridge University Press

Giddens, A. 1991. *Modernity and Self-Identity: Self and Society in the Late Modern Age*. Cambridge and Oxford: Polity Press

Goodman, Roger and Refsing, Kirsten., eds. 1999. *Ideology and Practice in Modern Japan*. London and New York: Routledge

Jensen, M. 2007. 'Defining lifestyle'. In *Environmental Sciences* 4(2): 63–73

Maffesoli, M. 1996. *The Time of the Tribes: the Decline of Individualism in Mass Society*. Los Angeles, London, New Delhi and Singapore: SAGE Publications

Manzenreiter, W. and Horne, J. 2006. 'Leisure and consumer culture in Japan'. In *Leisure Studies* 25(4): 411–415

Markus, H. R. and Kitayama, S. 1991. 'Culture and the self: implications for cognition, emotion, and motivation' in *Psychological Review* 98(2): 224–253

Miller, D. 1987. *Material Culture and Mass Consumption*. Oxford: Basil Blackwell

Miller, D. 1995. *Acknowledging Consumption*. Routledge: London and New York

Miller, D. 1998. *A Theory of Shopping*. Cambridge: Polity

Nakane, C. 1970. *Japanese Society*. Berkeley, CA: University of California Press.

Schouten, J. W. and McAlexander, J. H. 1995. 'Subcultures of consumption: an ethnography of the new bikers'. In *Journal of Consumer Research* 22(1): 43–61

Stebbins, R. 1997. 'Lifestyle as a generic concept in ethnographic research'. In *Quality and Quantity* 31(4): 347–360

Suzuki, M., Ito, M., Ishida, M., Nihei, N. and Maruyama, M. 2010. 'Individualizing Japan: searching for its origin in first modernity'. In *British Journal of Sociology* 61(3): 513–538

Thornton, S. 1995. *Club Cultures: Music, Media, and Subcultural Capital*. Cambridge: Polity Press

Valk, J. 2018. 'From duty to fashion: the changing role of the kimono in the twenty-first century'. In *Fashion Theory* 22(3): 309–340

Yano, R. C. 2013. *Pink Globalisation: Hello Kitty's trek across the Pacific*. Durham, NC: Duke University Press

Yoda, T. 2000. 'A roadmap to millennial Japan'. In *The South Atlantic Quarterly* 99(4): 629–668

Yoshino, K. 1992. *Cultural Nationalism in Contemporary Japan: A Sociological Enquiry*. London and New York: Routledge

Chapter 7

New directions
Second-hand retail and new business models

The sight is now a common one. In the courtyards of temple precincts are vast quantities of second-hand kimono sold in pop-up stalls and flea markets. The dates for these markets are often fixed. In the courtyards of the Ōsu Kannon temple in Nagoya, for instance, the flea markets are on every 18th and 28th day of the month. Second-hand kimono have become an increasingly large part of these flea markets in Japan since the 1990s. Here, you can purchase silk kimono and obi very cheaply, and for a fraction of the price at which they were originally sold.

There has been a saturation of kimono in Japanese homes, kimono accumulated from purchases in the post-war period, especially purchases destined for women's bridal trousseau, as I've described in Chapter 3 and elsewhere (Valk 2020b). This has in turn both discouraged customers from purchasing more and encouraged people to dispose of those that they already have. This is especially the case when a relative passes away, and the family are not sure what to do about her kimono collection.

The accumulation of kimono in the home brought about a business opportunity for those in the kimono industry who were able, or adventurous enough, to spot it. The flea markets are, of course, one example, but a number of established kimono retailers have also moved into the second-hand business. The Gotō family (featured in Chapter 1 and subsequent chapters), are an example of a family-owned business who shifted their business model from made-to-order to second-hand. However, there are others who made this shift on a larger scale.

One such business owner is Kenichi Nakamura, the managing director of Tansu-ya. Tansu-ya is one of the largest second-hand kimono retail businesses, with shops across the whole of Japan (see, for example, Figure 7.1. The visibility of second-hand shops has increased since the start of the 21st century and Tansu-ya is among the most prominent. I had been intrigued by Tansu-ya for some months during my fieldwork. Towards the end of my research in Japan, once I had got to know the writer, fashion guru and designer Ima Kikuchi, she introduced me formally to the managing director of Tansu-ya, Nakamura Kenichi, who agreed to an interview with me.

Figure 7.1 A Tansu-ya shop front (Photo courtesy of Kenichi Nakamura, reproduced with kind permission).

It's swelteringly hot in July when I find my way to the headquarters of Tansu-ya in the business district of Rinkai-cho in Tokyo and the cool office building of the company comes as a welcome relief. After office workers show me into a small conference room, Nakamura-san arrives to greet me. He is wearing a kimono, and does so with the comfort and ease of someone who wears one often. As with members of the kimono fashion network in the previous chapter, wearing the kimono demonstrates an appreciation as well as dedication to the kimono as a lifestyle and as fashion. For customers interested in wearing the kimono as fashion, seeing business owners wearing kimono represents a confirmation that the retailers enjoy the style as much as they do.

Nakamura-san has a confident cadence of speech and an ease with the language of business and economics. Unlike some of my other participants, he is used to telling his story. In addition to running his large second-hand business, he has also written two books: one on the path he followed to change the family business from wholesaling to second-hand retail (Nakamura 2006), and the other a manifesto for wearing the kimono as a means to be happy (Nakamura 2008). I ask him, first, when he thinks that second-hand kimono started to appear in Japanese society.

'By the early 1990s, I think. We opened our first second-hand shop in 1999, but at least six or seven years before that there were already other shops.'

Nakamura-san comes from a family with roots in the kimono industry. His grandfather, the second son of a farming family, set up a wholesaling business in 1924 in Kyoto (Nakamura 2006: 144; my translation). Under Nakamura-san's father, the company came to specialise in Tokyo Yūzen: formal, hand-painted kimono.

'One *hōmongi*[1] could cost 600,000, 800,000, one million, sometimes two million yen.[2] They sold well before the bubble burst in the 1990s, but not after. I became head of the company in 1993, right after the bubble burst. The first thing I did was to move our base of production abroad. After that, we shifted our business away from wholesaling to manufacturing.'

For Nakamura-san, the crisis of the 1990s represented a watershed moment.

'It was as though the arteries of the industry had seized up,' he told me. 'Money, goods, information – none of it flowed properly. So even if we did our best, money wasn't coming in. It seemed clear to me that if we carried on as we had, we would eventually disappear, along with the industry itself. We thought it was important to sell things directly to the customer, so we did a 180-degree shift, and we became retailers.'

Many of my other participants had observed the way in which customers had tended to stop buying kimono, at least the expensive formal kind, and had noted the way in which the kimono seemed to have dropped out of favour for ceremonial, ritual occasions. Nakamura-san had a different observation to make, however.

'I consider that the reason we've seen such a drop in sales is not because Japanese people hate the kimono. Rather, it's because our industry was no longer able to deliver the kinds of services and kimono that suited our customer's changing values. That's why I think the market declined.'

The phrase 'changing values' caught my attention, and I asked Nakamura-san what he meant, and how he thought that these values had changed.

'Back in the day, it used to be the family, the *ie*,[3] buying the kimono. The biggest change since then is that we have gone from family demand to individual demand.'

In the past, as I have explored in previous chapters, the kimono could be said to represent the whole family's cultural and economic capital. Further, kimono were bought usually with more than one generation in mind and the idea that descendants would also wear the same kimono. Nakamura-san had sensed what members of the fashion network had also grasped, which was that they needed to change the way they marketed the kimono, and in doing so, carve out new markets for themselves. Nakamura-san suggests that Japanese people, for the most part, like the kimono, even if they might not have many occasions to wear it. A small but not insignificant number are interested in wearing the kimono as fashion and a form of self-expression, rather than as formal wear. Encouraging this market to grow is one of the ways in which retailers have become creative in the face of the crisis affecting their industry.

'We estimated that being a wholesaler and selling goods on to shops had no future. We became retailers in order to tap into latent markets.'

From Nakamura-san's perspective, staying in his company's traditional line of business would not be sustainable. Latent markets and latent potential consisted of two things: on the one hand, the potential market of people who like the kimono and want to wear it, but also the sheer number of kimono and obi lying unused in *tansu* (the dedicated kimono chest) throughout Japan. He had estimated that about 400 million obi and 400 million kimono were stored in homes throughout Japan.

'Think of this,' he explained, 'the kimono industry's total sale of kimono between 1950 to 2015 was 56 trillion yen. Of those sales, 45 trillion was silk kimono. Everything else was goods not made of silk. Wool, polyester, cotton… hardly any of that makes it into our shops. So we don't count that 11 trillion. I estimated that with the remaining 45 trillion yen, about 90 per cent still remains inside people's *tansu*. Why did I estimate that 90 per cent remains? Because Japanese people feel that silk kimono are very special. They look after them. That's why I estimate that 90 per cent remains, which means 40 trillion yen's worth of kimono. So converting that into numbers of kimono, I estimated that there would be roughly 400 million kimono and 400 million obi sleeping in people's *tansu*. A rough number, but an amazing quantity, isn't it?'

Setting up a second-hand chain required a certain amount of nerve and a willingness to try the unknown and leave familiarity behind. But for Nakamura-san, the crisis faced by the industry was in fact an opportunity for change. In one of his books, in which he describes his business philosophy, Nakamura-san writes,

> There's a world of difference between living your life thinking that a crisis is an ordeal and thinking that a crisis is an opportunity. Of course, a crisis causes problems, it's an emergency situation, after all. But in that moment, if you can move forward with aspirations, if you make things evolve and develop, then that crisis itself becomes the best hint showing you which direction you should turn in next, and how best to change. If you think of things in this way, it's actually much worse to never go through a crisis at all.
>
> Nakamura 2006: 142 (my translation)

Nakamura-san had chosen the option to reshape the family business model. About changing business models, Nakamura-san is also sanguine. In his book, he writes that it is part of the nature of the times that business models have to change:

> From now on, a single business model won't last for 30 years, I believe. So, it doesn't matter how successful a business is, in an instant you can

become out of tune with the times, and you will end up part of a declining industry. But if you see everything in a negative light because our industry is declining, there's no end to it. After that, the game is to see where you need to go in order to be able to discover the next successful model.

Nakamura 2006: 12 (my translation)

What Nakamura-san is suggesting here is that, at the time he was writing in 2006, market conditions had become so characterised by flux and change that expecting business models to last was no longer realistic. Crisis, in others words, was to be expected.

In 2020, a crisis of a different nature spread across the world. The Covid-19 pandemic has affected a large number of businesses in Japan, including Tansu-ya, which now faces difficulties following the closure of some shops during the pandemic. At the time of completing this book in mid-2020, the full extent of the long-term effects of the pandemic on the retail industry in Japan are as yet unknown, but perhaps the creativity with which Nakamura-san had changed the course of his family business once before will serve the company once again.

Something for everyone: the appeal of second-hand kimono

There are figures suggesting that second-hand retail has become increasingly popular among a market of Japanese customers interested in kimono, particularly among those looking for affordable kimono and customers keen on vintage aesthetics. In the yearly reports on the kimono market conducted by the Yano Research Institute, the market share of second-hand kimono is reported to have grown from 9.5 per cent in 2011[4] to 12.9 per cent of the total market in 2019.[5] Why is it that the second-hand retail industry has emerged, and how has its popularity increased?

The first reason is, as Nakamura-san indicated, the sheer volume of kimono in Japanese homes. These are often referred to, in the words of my participants, as 'sleeping' in their *tansu*. They are also sometimes referred to as *tansu no koyashi*, or 'tansu fertiliser'. Both expressions refer to the kimono's dormancy in the *tansu*, and the hope that they may one day be 'woken up' from their sleep (Valk 2020b).

As I have explored in earlier chapters, the bridal trousseau was a steady and reliable market for the kimono industry for many years in the post-war period, as it enabled the emerging middle-class to use the kimono to establish their economic and cultural capital. However, the importance of the family household and its status has considerably waned in the 21st century. This is not to say that the characteristics of the *ie* (household) have vanished and no longer have a hold on Japanese understanding of family, but certainly the significance of upholding the household's image through the kimono by providing a bridal trousseau as an expression both of *oyagokoro* ('parental affection') and status, has weakened. Nakamura-san explained to me in his interview that silk kimono stay in the home because people value silk and are therefore not keen to dispose of them. Certainly the importance of silk, together with rice, is well-documented in work on Japanese cosmology (see Creighton 2001 for silk, Ohnuki-Tierney 1993 for rice), but the kimono also has intense symbolic significance within the family as a repository of female histories and identities, and these links are not easily denied or broken (Valk 2020b). For many of my participants, caring for kimono inside their homes, even when they take up space and when it is not clear how and to whom the kimono will be passed on, was preferable to disposing of them. Nakamura-san estimates that only about 10 per cent of kimono and obi out of his approximate figure of 800 million kimono and obi are used from time to time.

That being said, the generation of 'kimono caretakers' in their 50s, 60s and 70s, sometimes in their 80s, are often involved in practices of *shūkatsu* ('end of life activities') which involve tidying, disposing of objects, and preparing the house and the items within ahead of the person's death, in part to make things easier for the family once the person has passed. In the course of these preparations, a selection of kimono may be sold to second-hand shops. It is sometimes the case, too, that when the primary 'caretaker' of a kimono collection passes away, the family decides to sell the kimono to second-hand shops. I have argued in a related article that kimono within the home can be considered as inalienable wealth, intended to be passed down from mother to daughter, or at least between female relatives (Valk 2020a). Annette Weiner famously developed the concept of inalienable wealth in her work on Oceania, in which objects were removed from circulation in order for their value to increase (Weiner 1994: 394). The wider context of Japanese society, in particular the role of the formal silk kimono, has changed, meaning that these inalienable objects are now not so easily passed between women and between different generations of women. As Nakamura-san estimated, there is an enormous repository of 'sleeping' kimono in Japan, and even if just a small proportion of this number makes it into second-hand retail, it is still more than enough for second-hand retailers to set up a business. Indeed, a not inconsiderable number of these kimono are being sold to second-hand shops. At the time of our interview in 2016, Nakamura-san told me that the most frequent type of kimono his company bought was over 40 years old – kimono that would have been purchased in the mid-1970s. This was also the time when formal kimono sold very well.

The sale of kimono to second-hand shops may seem paradoxical given that the silk kimono is treasured both for its association with female family history and the high esteem in which silk is held in Japan. Inge Daniels has noted that a particular relationship of duty exists between people and things: 'the duty people felt towards objects is grounded in an awareness of the interrelatedness of human and nonhuman entities. In other words, things offer their service to people who, in return, should be thankful and treat objects respectfully' (Daniels 2009: 396). This means that, if they have exhausted their use in the home and there is no greater value to be found in creating space in the home by disposing of them, then selling the kimono to a second-hand shop is sometimes considered a good option because there is the hope that someone, even an unrelated stranger, might take care of the kimono and use it once more. I noticed this idea at work several times when I spent time at the Gotō family's second-hand shop. Customers and people interested in browsing, especially older women, would comment to the Gotō family that they thought it was so much better for kimono to be sold second-hand than to be destroyed, which was considered a sad fate.

The second reason behind the growth of the second-hand kimono market is that it offered precisely the opposite of the standard kimono industry: affordable kimono. I have argued elsewhere that kimono decrease dramatically in value when they enter the second-hand kimono market (Valk 2020a). This is because kimono, particularly expensive silk kimono, were sold in the post-war period as items which would belong, as Nakamura-san suggested, not just to an individual, but to a household: the kimono was ideally to have a long life-span and be passed down several generations of women. This is what customers had in mind buying silk kimono in particular in the post-war period, and retailers encouraged this trend, building the potential for inalienability into the sale of the kimono. This means that, when kimono are sold into second-hand channels, they lose their status within a particular family narrative, and a loss of value as the family heirloom translates into lower economic value. This does vary tremendously according to how the second-hand kimono is priced, however. Each shop or chain has its own particular rules, and will assess the quality of the kimono and price it accordingly. This means that prices vary wildly but are generally much more affordable than a standard made-to-order kimono. Prices generally ranged between 500 yen (for older or slightly damaged items) and 5000 yen.[6] Some obi were priced higher, and kimono that had originally been quite expensive, particularly those made using regional techniques or by hand, were usually not on display and had higher price tags. In the vast majority of cases, the price is a far cry from the range of 80,000 to 600,000 yen[7] which is standard for made-to-order kimono, depending on the fabric, the mode of production and the regional technique.

The affordability of second-hand kimono is often combined with a very different shopping experience. While standard kimono shops and chains can be daunting places to enter, shopping in a second-hand kimono shop is quite similar to shopping for Western clothes. The shops are often browsable, customers can look at the wares in their own time, and because the kimono are usually already sewn up and do not need to be made to order, customers can try on the kimono then and there as they would with Western clothes. The flip side is that, because many of the kimono in second-hand shops are several decades old, they tend to fit women of shorter stature and slighter builds, which was characteristic of most women's physique at the time. Many second-hand shoppers confirmed to me that you could find very good kimono at a bargain price in second-hand shops, but that these kimono tended to be quite small and would not fit a taller woman.

Some second-hand shops combine their browsability with services similar to those of a standard kimono shop, offering customers the opportunity to re-dye, re-stitch or re-sew their kimono. As a result, the shopping experience is easier and more familiar to a typical Japanese consumer.

There is another major reason why second-hand kimono have become popular, beyond their affordable price tag and the browsability of their shops. In the first decades of the post-war period Japan's 'economic miracle' ushered in an era of consumption characterised by a preference for the new household items and electronic goods that epitomised the new middle-class lifestyle of a modernised Japan (Francks 2009: 158). However, towards the end of the century there was a rising interest in vintage aesthetics and second-hand fashion, expressed in a variety of ways in Japan. One of these is an interest in vintage jeans, for example, as evidenced by Philomena Keet's research on vintage jeans and authenticity (Keet 2011). This was not unique to Japan: a global interest in second-hand and vintage aesthetics was developing at the end of the 20th century, and vintage fashion became desirable and fashionable. Vintage is characterised by nostalgia for a particular time period, and valuing clothes that come from this particular era. An example of iconic eras in a Western context include the 1920s flapper styles and the hippie and punk aesthetics of the 1970s among, of course, many others. Aleit Veenstra and Giselinde Kuipers argue that the enjoyment of vintage aesthetics is underpinned by an 'aesthetic preference for authenticity' which has made its way into the mainstream (Veenstra and Kuipers 2013: 357).

Alexandra Palmer and Hazel Clark note that, while vintage fashion has become mainstream, the exact place of second-hand clothing within local fashion systems differs across the world (Palmer and Clark 2005: 4). This raises an important question about the distinction between 'second-hand' and 'vintage' clothes, and what this might mean in the Japanese context. A variety of words are used in Japanese to describe second-hand kimono, mostly English loanwords such as *recycle*, *antique*, *re-use*, and occasionally *vintage* as well, all rendered in Japanese *katakana* script.[8] There is also a word in *kanji* (Chinese characters) used for second-hand kimono, which is *furugi*. This simply means 'old clothes' and can apply to Western clothes as well. *Recycle* and *re-use* both have fairly practical connotations, and *antique* and *vintage* express a connection with specific time periods, as indeed they do in English. My interpretation of the use of English is that it has a veneer of 'coolness', as many English words tend to do in Japanese marketing and sales. It also introduces more distance from the reality of the clothing as having been pre-owned, as conveyed by the expression *furugi* ('old clothes').

As Nakamura-san suggested, the kimono market has increasingly become one in which individuals, rather than households, buy kimono. As we saw in Chapter 6, self-expression, taste and personal preference all dictated the choices made by members of the kimono fashion network, be they retailers or customers. This is not to say that women buying kimono in the 1960s, 70s and 80s were not preoccupied with aesthetics and taste but a key motivation for purchase was a concern with the way the kimono would represent them and their household unit during ritual and ceremonial occasions. They also wanted to make sure that the kimono could be worn by their daughters and even granddaughters. The market now has a much more sizeable number of people who, when buying kimono, second-hand or not, tend to be more concerned with whether the kimono suits them and fits their tastes – the 'individuated' consumption discussed in Chapter 6.

For second-hand shoppers, the attractions of second-hand kimono are many. They tend to be affordable, and so they are an 'easier' entrance into the world of kimono, which tends to be rather alien for most of the Japanese population. Buying a second-hand kimono that ends up not fitting you properly is a less costly mistake than buying an expensive made-to-order kimono that proved not to be a good fit, or turned out to be difficult to find the right obi for. Buying kimono requires understanding how to coordinate an outfit made out of parts that differ significantly from Western clothes and this understanding takes time to build. One of my participants would wryly refer to the money spent on kimono that failed to be easily coordinated with accessories or obi as *benkyō-dai*: the fee spent on learning a lesson.

But there is a further, key part of second-hand kimono retail that presents an advantage compared to new, made-to-order kimono, and that is the role of the aforementioned vintage aesthetics. This is where the age range of second-hand customers tends to come into play: Manami Okazaki notes that women in their 20s and 30s with an interest in kimono tend to be drawn to the aesthetics of a particular era, especially Taishō (1912–1926) aesthetics (Okazaki 2015: 12). Kimono from the Taishō period are characterised by colourful, playful patterns, which are often promoted by specialist kimono magazines such as *Kimono Hime* ('Kimono Princess'), a magazine renowned for showcasing alternative kimono styles which are often based around a particular theme, such as vintage clothing from the Taishō period, styled in 'edgy, unconventional combinations' (Milhaupt 2014: 8). A number of social media profiles, websites and blogs are also dedicated to the Taishō vintage aesthetic and the coordination of vintage styles for kimono.

I spent an afternoon with a group of young people in their 20s and 30s living in Nagoya who had become interested in vintage kimono. Many of these young people had started looking inside the *tansu* belonging to their mothers and grandmothers, and this is where their interest in kimono came from. They took me to visit their favourite second-hand kimono shops, in search of different aesthetics and styles. One of them was particularly fond of the woollen 'ensembles'[9] that became popular in the immediate post-war period and that women tended to wear over New Year, and enjoyed both the scratchiness of the woollen fabrics and the bright chemical dyes that had been used to render it sharp shades of green, red and black. Other shoppers with an eye on vintage aesthetics associated with a particular era similarly look for particular types of fabric, and are keenly attuned not just to how they look, but how they feel and smell as well (Valk 2020a). Thus, shopping in second-hand kimono shops is exciting because you can never be sure what you might find. Marilyn DeLong, Barbara Heinemann and Kathryn Reiley argue that this type of shopping and hunting is a skill, requiring 'aesthetics, taste, clever dressing, historical curiosity, and an ability to discriminate the authentic product, and revalue it in a new setting' (DeLong et al 2005: 24).

Japan's scene of subcultural fashions is prolific (Narumi 2010: 416), particularly those originating in the Tokyo districts of Harajuku and Akihabara. Among the most famous are Lolita fashions (though not to be confused with Vladimir Nabokov's novel *Lolita*). This fashion is based on a hyper-feminine and childlike aesthetic, with modest, frilly dresses loosely inspired from historical European fashions. Lolita subculture is itself sub-divided into different aesthetic strands, each with their own sartorial rules (Kawamura 2012), and has become so popular that Lolita trends have appeared outside of Japan as well (see Monden 2008 and Rahman et al. 2011). There are also a number of other styles, such as *dekora*, which involves using as many brightly coloured accessories, clothes and stickers as possible, as well as fashions based on hip-hop music and on Goth aesthetics (see Condry 2007, Kawamura 2012, Skutlin 2016 for various examples). An overview of these many different subcultures is beyond the scope of this chapter, but the context of subcultural fashion, and its associated 'tribes', is relevant to the popularity of second-hand kimono. Hiroshi Narumi questions the usefulness of the term 'subculture' in the Japanese context, but is equally critical of the term 'tribe' (*zoku*) that has often been used in the Japanese media. Narumi considers that the term implies a 'fabricated presentation of youth' (Narumi 2010: 417). For lack of a completely accurate and neutral word, I use the term 'subculture' here, while acknowledging that there is no such thing as a completely homogenous and internally consistent set of tastes, clothing choices and ideas within a given subculture (see Baxter and Marina 2008 for a nuanced discussion on this topic). Some clothing subcultures in Japan are intensely social, with group members bonding over shared aesthetics and tastes, and perhaps also bonding over a shared sense that wider society with more 'mainstream' tastes does not fully understand them (Gelder and Thornton 1997, Muggleton 2000). This is the case to a certain extent with the kimono fashion network (Chapter 6), whose choices relating to the kimono occasionally cross over the line of what is typically considered 'acceptable' by wider society. The people interested in second-hand kimono are often influenced by the idea of kimono-as-fashion and the kimono fashion network contains a number of second-hand and vintage fashion enthusiasts. Further, vintage kimono enthusiasts also tend to have the loose, free-form type of sociality characteristic of Michel Maffesoli's notion of 'tribes' (Maffesoli 1996). Their taste and aesthetics are also fluid and less regimented than in other subcultural styles which commit strongly to one particular 'look'.

The age range of customers varies widely, and is not limited to shoppers in their 20s and 30s. Nakamura-san noted there was a varied age range among his Tansu-ya customers, ranging from teenagers to women in their 70s and 80s. There were some foreign customers – Nakamura-san estimated that about 8 per cent of sales came from foreign customers. I likewise observed second-hand kimono shoppers in their 60s and 70s. For them, the second-hand shopping experience was also about the thrill of what you might find, but this was often focused on finding a particular type of kimono in the mix, something which was valuable in terms of its method of production, such as an Ōshima *tsumugi* kimono whose delicate and understated aesthetics tend to be prized by older research participants. A second-hand Ōshima *tsumugi*, and kimono which are similar to this type but perhaps machine-woven rather than woven by hand, will cost significantly less than a new Ōshima but, as one of my participants in her 60s put it, 'who would know that you bought it second-hand?'. This thought was especially pleasing to her. She loved the idea that she could obtain something that was highly valued by people around her without having to pay a high price for it. For her, the value of the techniques involved in making the kimono and its attractive price trumped the value of having a kimono made to order for her specifically. This fits in with the narratives about women's role in managing household finances that women in their 60s and 70s would have been familiar with when growing up. In the post-war period, dominant ideals of gender revolved around the bread-winning salaryman for men, and the *sengyō shufu* ('professional, full-time housewife') for women (Dasgupta 2000: 192). In this scenario, the housewife was not only in charge of looking after her husband and her children, but she was also often in control of household finances (Vogel and Vogel 2013: 9). This position of responsibility vis-à-vis money, in which the husband frequently handed over his salary to his wife, was characterised by a strong 'propensity for saving and frugality' (Iwao 1993: 85). Encouraging frugality and good management of household finances was in fact part of wider political and economic narratives in the 1950s aimed at the recovery of the Japanese economy (Garon 1997: 186). Thus, although women now in their 50s and 60s witnessed an era of prosperity characterised by preferences for new items, the competing ideal of frugality also makes second-hand kimono an attractive option.

This market of shoppers, covering a broad range of ages and with a variety of shopping motivations, is, then, the latent market that Nakamura-san was envisioning when he first transitioned his wholesaling and manufacturing trade to second-hand retail. Certainly, courage was needed to make the leap, and others have also made the change, albeit not on quite such a large scale.

The format of second-hand shopping appears to reflect a more diverse and individualised market in which customers are drawn both by the affordable prices and the aesthetics of the kimono, and points towards a kimono market which is increasingly differentiated and diverse in terms of distribution channels and customer choices.

However, the second-hand market is only one of the ways in which the kimono industry has diversified and changed in the wake of the crisis and reduced sales of formal kimono.

Doing it all at Some Kōbō Yu

Nestled in a side street in the shadow of the sprawling Higashi Honganji temple complex is a typical Kyoto townhouse. The latticed sliding doors and wooden façade appear, at first, to be simply a traditional Kyoto house, but a discreet sign reads 'Some Kōbō Yu' – literally 'Fun Workshop' or 'Play Workshop'. The word *yu* is the Chinese reading of the word *asobu* which, loosely translated, means to play or have fun. Peek through the door, and you will see an inviting display of purses, scarves and handkerchiefs with Yūzen (hand-painted) designs on display in the narrow entranceway.

I came across Some Kōbō Yu through a happy coincidence. I had travelled to Kyoto for a series of interview appointments with wholesalers, and I was staying in a *ryokan* (Japanese inn) near Higashi Honganji. I was chatting with one of the *ryokan* staff about my research, and her face lit up.

'There are people who make kimono nearby, you know! They are very friendly, I'm sure that they would talk to you.'

She fetched a map from the check-in desk to show me where exactly the workshop was. My first visit ended in disappointment, as I had picked a Tuesday and the workshop is always closed on Tuesdays. On my second visit, the workshop was open. Inside the small shop interior is a raised platform with *tatami* mats, *tansu* and a mannequin with a kimono on display. One thing catches my eye, and keeps it.

At the back of the *tatami* room, elaborate wheels are built into the walls and the ceiling. Between the wheels, kimono fabric is stretched out a foot or so above the floor, enabling the craftsperson, kneeling on the floor in traditional Japanese style, to paint designs onto the cloth. There is a small workspace between the two sets of wheels, allowing three craftspeople to work at any given time (see Figure 7.2). On the ground between the wheels are piles of little plates holding different types of dye and a large number of paintbrushes. The radio plays cheerfully in the background.

When they are done painting a section of the design directly onto the silk, the craftspeople simply turn the wheels. The entire system rattles, pulling the cloth up the wall and the craftspeople move on to a different section of the bolt without ever having to move. The device is simple, ingenious, and mesmerising.

Figure 7.2 Craftspeople at work in Some Kōbō Yu.

The craftspeople at work when I visit are part of the Yamada family. Some Kōbō Yu, I later find out, is a family business in which workloads are distributed between two brothers, Kiyoshi and Tetsuo Yamada, Tetsuo Yamada's wife and their son. At the time of my first visit, Kiyoshi Yamada and Tetsuo Yamada's wife are working on the bolts.

Amused by my hypnotised expression, they invite me up into their workspace to take a closer look at the designs they are currently painting. The family has made the choice to keep their shop and workspace open, allowing casual visitors and customers alike to see them at work. This approach is quite unusual – craft workshops, as discussed in Chapters 2 and 3, are not usually retail spaces. It is possible to visit kimono craft workshops, but in most cases this happens at specific times or on designated open days.

I knew quite quickly, then, that Some Kōbō Yu took a different approach than many of the shops and craft workshops that I had been to. As the Yamada family allowed me to stay, cup of warm tea in hand, to watch them work, they told me that they work closely with their clients to make custom designs. The Yamada family specialises in Yūzen techniques: hand-painting elaborate designs directly onto the silk bolt. This style differs in terms of aesthetics from the Kaga Yūzen craft depicted in Chapter 3. Some Kōbō Yu offer both conventional Yūzen patterns, such as floral designs, but they also make unconventional design choices, often in collaboration with their customers, that differ from classic Yūzen styles and patterns.

The workshop has a website with a wealth of sample patterns, base colours for the bolts and suggestions for coordinating particular patterns and colours. I had encountered scenarios in which customers commissioned custom-made items directly from craft workshops, but these tended to be because the customer had a particular relationship with the craftspeople that meant they were able to do this. For the Yamada family, however, this had become a successful business model.

I developed a relationship with the Yamada family over the months that followed, returning to the workshop whenever I visited Kyoto. On following occasions, I met the older Yamada brother, Tetsuo, with whom I have continued to correspond over the years. Like many kimono-related businesses, Some Kōbō Yu is a family business, founded in the 1950s by the Yamada brothers' father. The older brother, Tetsuo, went on to undertake an apprenticeship with a wholesaler. The younger brother, Kiyoshi, also spent some time working for a wholesaler but subsequently became apprenticed to a Yūzen dye craftsperson. They took over the family business in the late 1970s. For a time, business went well, but the market became increasingly unstable as consistent sales of kimono declined, and the brothers closed the business. Later, Kiyoshi set up their current business, Some Kōbō Yu, in the townhouse near Higashi Honganji.

In 2006, the workshop had started to think about selling directly to customers, rather than working exclusively with wholesalers. This was because demand for goods from wholesalers kept dropping. Now the workshop supplies newer, online kimono businesses as well. The family had a balance of skills that they could bring to the table. Tetsuo had his experience of wholesaling while his wife, son and his brother Kiyoshi have a broad range of skills in making kimono. Tetsuo speaks warmly of his brother Kiyoshi's creativity and mastery of a variety of techniques and crafts.

Tetsuo told me that in order to build a business such as Some Kōbō Yu, it was necessary to have a range of attributes, especially salesmanship, marketing and connections with other parts of the industry. I surmised that, without these, it would be difficult for craftspeople to set up a business in which they sell directly to customers. This is unsurprising – as I discussed in Chapters 2 and 3, the chain of distribution had relied on a separation of labour that disconnected craftspeople from the wholesaling and retailing segments of the industry.

I had become interested in commissioning an obi for myself with a custom pattern, and Some Kōbō Yu seemed like an ideal option. We spent some time in person and online discussing patterns, colours and fabrics. I had decided on a floral pattern, but I also wanted to include birds. I also wanted to have a Western aesthetic to my obi, which would match a dark blue kimono with a decidedly Western aesthetic that I already owned. I forwarded a great many pictures of the styles and patterns that I liked, including pictures of flowers and birds. These, to my mind, represented my parents – my father, who had passed away in 2014, had always loved birds, and my mother is a keen gardener. I settled on honeysuckle, a plant that grows in the garden of the house where I grew up and for which both my mother and I had always had great fondness. The plant is not typically included in the canon of flowers that normally populate kimono designs, such as plum blossom, cherry blossom, peonies, wisteria and chrysanthemums (among others), but the Yamada family was not daunted. Because the family often collaborates directly with customers to co-create their designs, they were used to fulfilling unusual wishes for design, and they enjoyed the challenge of something new and different.

Our discussions culminated in a final visit to Kyoto. This happened to be while my mother and brother were visiting. Both brothers and Tetsuo Yamada's wife were present at the time, and they worked as a team to help us decide what pattern to use.

The Yamada family joked that they had seen plenty of mother-daughter pairs come to discuss custom kimono and obi, but they had never had a brother come along too. We debated back and forth about the merits of where to place the pattern, what colours to use and if the pattern should include a bird. I initially wanted it to, but Tetsuo Yamada tactfully replied that a bird was unlikely to perch on the fragile tendrils of a honeysuckle plant. I had to admit that this was true. I liked falcons, always drawn to their beautiful silhouettes and their link to the meaning of my last name. But the Yamada family didn't like the idea – birds of prey are almost always used in men's kimono, mostly on the inside lining of a *haori* (kimono overcoat). They were never condescending in their refusal to depict certain patterns – we were negotiating, together, the boundaries and grey areas of an accepted canon of patterns and designs. This meant finding the line between innovation that felt aesthetically 'right' from their perspective as Japanese craftspeople, and a design that could slip too far beyond kimono aesthetics and into the bizarre. I sensed from the Yamada family a feeling of responsibility – they wanted me to wear something that would not, in Japanese eyes, cause me to be judged.

We decided on the pink honeysuckle flower (see Figure 7.3), and debated the final placement of the flower with enthusiasm. Off-centre was best – in Japanese aesthetics, asymmetrical patterns are deemed pleasing to the eye . I had also wanted to include a design that featured Arctic terns – a favourite bird of my father. But the garden theme of the honeysuckle and the maritime theme of the Arctic tern did not go together, as the Yamada family pointed out. I had to concede the point, but I could not decide which I wanted most. I loved the flower theme, but at the same time I wanted to build in the tribute to my father. Half-joking, I wondered aloud if I shouldn't have two obi made in order to have both patterns.

The family surprised me with their reaction – they were adamant that I shouldn't spend more than was necessary. This, too, formed part of their sense of responsibility towards me. It was something that I had encountered

Figure 7.3 The central pink honeysuckle pattern on the obi made for me by Some Kōbō Yu.

before, especially with Shibakawa-san at the shop Azumaya (Chapter 5) who felt the need to ensure that customers spent their money sensibly, especially if he sensed that they were at risk of overspending.

The Yamada family found an ingenious solution. Some obi have an 'inner' pattern on the side of the obi that lies against the body. It is possible to also show this side of the obi on the outside, but this involves a mirrored process for tying the obi.[10] This meant that I could, essentially, have two obi in one. We also agreed on extra details – adding bumblebees to orbit the flowers. These were to be *kumabachi* (literally 'bear bee'), a Japanese species of bee – a subtle Japanese touch on an obi that was otherwise characterised by Western aesthetics. The waves above which the terns were to fly, too, were Japanese in their design.

Our collaborative effort resulted in a unique obi that I treasure to this day – a one-of-a-kind obi that reflects a joint creative process. In making this kind of creative link with their customers and enabling people to customise their kimono and obi, the Yamada family have created an unusual and desirable business model. The skill set possessed by the Yamada family, with craft, wholesaling and retailing experience, has allowed them to manage all the aspects of the kimono industry on their own. Further, their model has enabled them to keep relationships with other wholesalers and craftspeople, meaning that not only can they make kimono and obi beyond the skill set of their in-house craftspeople, but they have access to a pool of craft skills.

The Yamada family's innovative strategy was made possible through their possession of a range of skills. Their business shows one of the ways in which the industry has become increasingly diverse. Although different from the second-hand industry, the Yamada family's choices as a result of adversity had highlighted a similar conclusion to Nakamura-san's: the kimono market was now increasingly one in which individuals like to make personal choices for their own kimono that reflect their own aesthetic preferences, rather than buying for family members and relying on the retailer to pick appropriate kimono or obi from a set of established styles and patterns.

Nakamura-san and the Yamada family are just two examples of the ways in which business owners who, in the past, belonged to the clearly delineated domains of craftsmanship, wholesale, manufacturing or retail, have responded to the economic recession and unfavourable sales, and changed the ways in which their businesses are run. The rise of independent businesses, independent craftspeople and new business models has been particularly marked since the start of the 21st century, especially in the 2010s. This is because the economic crisis of the 1990s affected wholesalers and closed down a number of wholesaling businesses, thereby reducing their control over the system of distribution and business relationships. Jenny Hall reaches the same conclusions about the power of wholesalers over the system of distribution in the context of her fieldwork in the Nishijin textile-producing district of Kyoto, and the importance of specialised knowledge as a pre-requisite for tackling distribution (Hall 2020: 180). Hall points to the importance of the Internet in allowing workshops to explore new avenues to sell their goods. Kimono producers have been under pressure to find new ways to sell their goods since relationships with established distribution channels were significantly disrupted in the wake of the 1990s crisis. This disruption was, for many, an opportunity to establish new businesses, both online and offline. The owner of a shop in Aichi prefecture told me that since the wholesalers had lost their hold over the industry as a whole, they had become free to choose their own wholesalers to do business with. Although sales were not as good as they had been, they felt now that they had more control: 'before, wholesalers could just turn me away if I asked to do business with them. Some of them wouldn't give me the time of day. Now, wholesalers ask *me* to sell their items in my shop.'

The shaking up of the chain of distribution has rocked the foundations and the established 'common sense' of who does what in the kimono industry. In the wake of this crisis, new approaches are now possible, and a number of independent businesses are being set up. During my fieldwork I met several independent craftspeople and business owners who were either self-taught artists or had training through art schools or courses. In previous decades, this would have been a difficult route to break into the kimono industry, in which craft skills were usually passed down within families. An outsider would normally have to go through an apprenticeship before being recognised as a craftsperson, and in some cases they still do. Following the apprenticeship, their work would have been marketed and sold through the usual channels of producers and wholesalers. Nowadays, craft workshops often struggle to find successors and apprentices, but independent artists and craftspeople are making inroads into the industry thanks to a more fluid and flexible distribution system.

Through the kimono shop Azumaya, I encountered Akiko Matsui, an independent *rōketsu* (batik) dye artist. She had studied a variety of dye techniques during her course at university, but became especially fascinated with *rōketsu*. After working for a time in a workshop, she then made her own business under the brand name of Chiesu. She sells a number of goods using her craft, including obi, but also purses, bags and business card holders, thus straddling both the kimono and non-kimono world (see Figures 7.4 and 7.5). She distributed her goods in a number of ways: in craft fairs but also through kimono shops such as Azumaya (Chapter 5 and 6) who are open to selling wares from both wholesalers and independent craftspeople. Matsui-san's craft, with its silver threading and whimsical designs featuring cats and peacock feathers inspired by fairy tales and patterns beyond the canon of traditional Japanese kimono patterns, is particularly well-loved by members of the kimono fashion network. In part as a result of the loosening of established chains of distribution, it is easier for the wares of independent artists such as Matsui-san to reach customers both online and in kimono shops themselves, especially those that cater to customers who wear the kimono as fashion.

Figure 7.4 Chiesu brand *hanhaba* (half-width) obi (Reproduced with kind permission from Akiko Matsui).

Figure 7.5 Chiesu brand kimono and obi (Reproduced with kind permission from Akiko Matsui).

As discussed in Chapter 5, Azumaya was perhaps unusual in that the Shibakawa family had established many collaborative relationships with craftspeople, both 'traditional' and independent, as well as producers of various types. This involves a considerable amount of work, and is a more complex approach than simply working through three or four wholesalers for the goods. Channels quickly become complex if a retailer is dealing with multiple independent designers and craftspeople as well as established workshops and wholesalers. But in an individuated market, this is a sensible approach: variety and the ability of the item to express *kosei* ('individuality') are particularly valuable traits. Independent craftspeople often bring a freshness to their designs that catches the eye of customers.

Across the board, fluidity in terms of distribution is on the rise, and so are the different types of kimono, obi and accessories available. The increasing importance of customer wishes for a personalised, customised aesthetic encourages retailers and craftspeople to invent new items with brand recognition, which often dovetails quite comfortably with established and esteemed techniques – such as Chiesu's *rōketsu* goods or, to give another example, the modernised Ōshima *tsumugi* designs pioneered by Tetsuya Ueda (see Chapter 6). In her book *Japan Beyond the Kimono*, Jenny Hall gives a number of case studies of Kyoto-based craft workshops that have opted for innovative methods of production, often using the 'traditional' element of craft practices as a selling point for their wares. She gives the example of Pagong, the retail side of a Kyoto-based company named Kamedatomi, whose roots lie in dyeing and printing, especially stencil-printing, kimono fabrics since 1919 (Hall 2020: 92). In 2001, the company launched the brand Pagong, which sells Western clothes featuring stencil-dyed Japanese patterns using the range of stencils owned by the company. I visited Pagong myself in 2016, and was graciously given a tour of the stencil-dyeing facilities in their headquarters, including a very large number of archived stencils used by the company for decades. As Hall notes, Pagong is unusual in that most of the production is done in-house, rather than outsourced to another craft workshop or abroad. Hall explains that it was the shrinking of the kimono market that caused the company to both reduce their staff and use their skills on Western clothes such as T-shirts and dresses rather than kimono (Hall 2020: 92). Although they switched from kimono to Western clothes, the selling point for Pagong is the techniques and the original nature of the patterns that they use.

While the focus of Hall's work is on the tension between tradition and innovation as well as the sensory properties of the material the craft workshops produce, I would argue that behind the innovative practices and choices of members of the industry, be they craftspeople, retailers or wholesalers, are complex factors relating to the economic recession since the 1990s and the changing market for kimono and kimono-related goods in the 21st century. The theme of adaptation and creativity in the face of adversity is clear in Hall's case study of Pagong, and demonstrates how some craft workshops and businesses have decided to expand their business beyond the kimono. As a result, there is an increasingly blurred line between the worlds of *wafuku* ('Japanese clothes') and *yōfuku* ('Western clothes'). These industries were, until relatively recently, kept very much distinct. The Western clothing business and *gofuku* ('kimono industry') did not overlap in terms of production, wholesaling or retail. But increasingly this distinction is becoming blurred as members of the industry look for alternatives to just selling the kimono and kimono-related goods. It might seem as though craftspeople are in the easiest position to adapt and diversify, as textile seems suitable for innovation and to be used for other products such as Western clothing, but this is not always the case, as the craftspeople need to be able to adapt their wares to a new product and business model, and then decide whether or not to go independent and how to distribute their wares. Some have taken the leap, faced with the uncertainty of the kimono market and declining sales of formal kimono in the 21st century, but not all are able to learn the business and marketing skills that would enable them to tackle new business models in which they do not rely solely on wholesalers.

What does seem clear is that, as the kimono loses its hold as the go-to item of clothing for formal wear, and as the market for kimono becomes more fluid, diverse and individualised, there is a growing tolerance and acceptance of mixed *wafuku* and *yōfuku* styles. Among the kimono fashion network, in particular, are a number of people, inspired by kimono fashion magazines such as *Kimono Hime*, who wear kimono with boots instead of *zori* (special kimono shoes), or both women and men who wear shirts beneath their kimono. I encountered a number of people who experimented with blending these styles, and they often faced opposition, even criticism, from members of the public for doing so. This is because, for much of the Japanese public and especially older generations of women who have strong views about the aesthetics of the kimono and what should and should not be used in a kimono outfit, blending Western and Japanese dress is viewed, at best, as ignorant, and at worst as poor taste, tacky, and disrespectful of what older generations understand to be 'traditional'. The kimono's symbolic weight and its ability to so powerfully evoke Japanese femininity means that many people feel it is important to wear it correctly. As I've described in Chapter 2, this means, in effect, following a set of rules.

These (mostly) older women, who offer usually unsolicited comments or advice in public, were often referred to by members of the kimono fashion network as the 'kimono police' (*kimono keisatsu*) and were frequently the subject of exasperated amusement. Those who used these blended styles are usually equipped with the perfect comeback to the critique that combining shirts and kimono is untraditional: there are historical precedents for the combination of different elements from Western and Japanese wardrobes. In the early 20th century, with the foundation of women's colleges, women increasingly adopted the male *hakama* (pleated trousers) (Slade 2009: 108), which has ever since remained a symbol of education for women and is still used today primarily in graduation ceremonies. This adoption overlapped with the rise of the *moga* (from *modan gāru* – 'modern girl'), the Japanese equivalent of the flapper who adopted Western dress codes and fashions (Slade 2009: 105–7). In an era where sartorial cross-pollination was the norm, heeled Western boots became associated with the *hakama*, and still remain an option today for university graduation ceremony outfits for Japanese women. People seeking to wear the kimono in innovative ways, flirting with gender, mixing Western styles in with Japanese styles, and challenging established aesthetics and rules, appear to be on the rise, but they nonetheless have to be willing to confront a conventional idea of what the kimono is and should look like.

The kimono industry has become increasingly diverse. Second-hand businesses now occupy a growing proportion of the market. Independent business owners are finding toeholds and new business models are becoming more common. While the second-hand industry has its own chain of distribution separate from the 'standard' kimono industry, the independent business owners are able to use more flexible methods to distribute their products than before: some use wholesalers, but also deal directly with retailers and customers. This reflects two key features: adaptation in the face of a chain of distribution that has become increasingly fragile and in which wholesalers have less sway than they used to, but also a market that has become increasingly individualised, in which customers look for and explore self-expression.

Notes

1. A *hōmongi* is a formal kimono often used to attend events of a formal, ceremonial nature, such as weddings or a child's school entrance or graduation ceremonies.
2. Approximately £4398, £5882, £7357 and £14,714 respectively.
3. The *ie* refers to the household unit, characterised by a hierarchy with a household head, and the inclusion of deceased ancestors and descendants yet to be born. Passing on the family name to the next generation is also considered to be an important part of the *ie*.
4. www.yanoresearch.com/press/pdf/1061.pdf (accessed 20/01/2020)
5. www.yanoresearch.com/en/press-release/show/press_id/2441 (accessed 22/07/2020)
6. Approximately £3.50 and £35.
7. Approximately £570 to £4398.
8. The Japanese language is comprised of three scripts: *kanji* (Chinese characters) and two syllabaries, *hiragana* and *katakana*, the latter of which is often used for loan words from foreign languages.
9. The word 'ensemble' in Japanese (*ansanburu*) refers to a kimono and a *haori* (kimono overcoat) cut from the same fabric. This style is typical of the post-war period and is now rarely in demand for made-to-order kimono.
10. Obi sashes have two sides. In most cases, the obi sash is tied in such a way that it is wrapped anti-clockwise around the midriff. This means that there is one side with a pattern and one side without. Reverse tying the obi means tying it clockwise. The Yamada family's idea meant that the obi became 'reversible' as it had a pattern on both sides, which obi typically do not have.

References

Baxter, V. K. and Marina, P. 2008. 'Cultural meaning and hip-hop fashion in the African-American male youth subculture of New Orleans'. In *Journal of Youth Studies* 11(2): 93–113

Condry, I. 2007. 'Yellow B-Boys, black culture, and hip-hop in Japan: toward a transnational cultural politics of race'. In *Positions: East Asia Cultures Critique* 15(3): 637–671

Creighton, M. 2001. 'Spinning silk, weaving selves: nostalgia, gender, and identity in Japanese craft vacations'. In *Japanese Studies* 21(1): 5–29

Daniels, I. 2009. 11. 'Seasonal and commercial rhythms of domestic consumption: a Japanese case study'. In Shove, E., Trentmann, F. and Wilk, R., eds. *Time, Consumption and Everyday Life: Practice, Materiality and Culture*. New York and London: Bloomsbury Academic

Dasgupta, R. 2000. 'Performing masculinities? The "salaryman" at work and play'. In *Japanese Studies* 20(2): 189–200

DeLong, M., Heinemann, B. and Reiley, K. 2005. 'Hooked on vintage!'. In *Fashion Theory* 9(1): 23–42

Francks, P. 2009. *The Japanese Consumer. An Alternative Economic History of Modern Japan*. Cambridge: Cambridge University Press
Garon, S. M. 1997. *Molding Japanese Minds: the State in Everyday Life*. Princeton, NJ: Princeton University Press
Gelder, K. and Thornton, S. 1997. *The Subcultures Reader*. London: Routledge
Hall, J. 2020. *Japan Beyond the Kimono: Innovation and Tradition in the Kyoto Textile Industry*. London and New York: Bloomsbury
Iwao, S. 1993. *The Japanese Woman: Traditional Image and Changing Reality*. Cambridge, Mass.: Harvard University Press
Kawamura, Y. 2012. *Fashioning Japanese Subcultures*. London and New York: Berg
Keet, P. 2011. 'Making new vintage jeans in Japan: relocating authenticity'. In *Textile* 9:1: 44–61
Maffesoli, M. 1996. *The Time of the Tribes: the Decline of Individualism in Mass Society*. Trans., Smith, D. London: Sage
Milhaupt, T. S. 2014. *Kimono: A Modern History*. London: Reaktion Books
Monden, M. 2008. 'Transcultural flow of demure aesthetics: examining cultural globalisation through Gothic & Lolita fashion'. In *New Voices* (2): 21:40
Muggleton, D. 2000. *Inside Subculture: The Postmodern Meaning of Style*. Oxford: Berg
Nakamura, K. 2006. *Tansu-ya de Gozaru* ('Tansu-ya at your Service'; my translation of the title). Tokyo: Shōgyōkai
Nakamura, K. 2008. *Kiru dake de Shiawase ni Naru* ('Just wearing it will make you happy'; my translation of the title). Tokyo: Zennichi Shuppan
Narumi, H. 2010. 'Street style and its meaning in postwar Japan'. In *Fashion Theory* 14(4): 415–438
Ohnuki-Tierney, E. (1993). *Rice as Self: Japanese Identities through Time*. Princeton, NJ: Princeton University Press.
Okazaki, M. 2015. *Kimono Now*. Munich, London, New York: Prestel
Palmer, A. and Clark, H. 2005. *Old clothes, New Looks: Second Hand Fashion*. Oxford: Berg
Rahman, O., Wing-Sun, L., Lam, E. and Mong-Tai, C. 2011. ' "Lolita": imaginative self and elusive consumption'. In *Fashion Theory* 15(1): 7–27
Skutlin, J. M. 2016. 'Goth in Japan: finding identity in a spectacular subculture'. In *Asian Anthropology* 15(1): 36–51
Slade, T. 2009. *Japanese Fashion: A Cultural History*. Oxford and New York: Berg
Valk, J. 2020a. 'The smell of Shōwa: time, materiality and regimes of value in Japan's second-hand kimono industry'. In *Journal of Material Culture* 25 (2): 240–256
Valk, J. 2020b. 'The Alienating Inalienable: rethinking Annette Weiner's concept of inalienable wealth through Japan's 'sleeping kimono''. In *HAU: Journal of Ethnographic Theory* 10 (1): 147–165
Veenstra, A. and Kuipers, G. 2013. 'It is not old-fashioned, it is vintage, vintage fashion and the complexities of 21st century consumption practices'. In *Sociology Compass* 7(5): 355–365
Vogel, S. H. and Vogel, S. K. 2013. *The Japanese Family in Transition: From the Professional Housewife Ideal to the Dilemmas of Choice*. Lanham, MD: Rowman & Littlefield Publishers Inc
Weiner, A. 1994. 'Cultural difference and the density of objects'. In *American Ethnologist* 21(2): 391–403

Chapter 8

Crisis and hope interwoven
The future of the kimono industry

Japan today offers a chequered image of kimono culture. In early January, you may well catch a glimpse of young women decked out in (mostly rented) colourful, formal *furisode* ('swinging sleeve' kimono) for their coming of age ceremony at the age of 20. In November, should you visit a Shinto shrine, you might well see families bringing their children aged three, five and seven, clad in kimono, to the shrine to pray for their growth and good health. In July and August, teenagers and young adults gather at summer festivals and fireworks wearing light summer *yukata* (a casual cotton version of the kimono). At any time of year, in the streets of Kyoto, you will see flocks of tourists, both domestic and international, decked out in polyester rented kimono, taking pictures against the background of Kyoto's many World Heritage Sites. If your luck is just right, you might spot a gathering of kimono-clad people, maybe headed to a tea ceremony event or, just possibly, members of the kimono fashion network on their way to a Kimono de Jack event.

In the streets of Kyoto, and any other town or city in Japan for that matter, you will come across kimono shops, both standard and second-hand. If you find your way into a department store and make your way up through the floors, one of them will probably be home to a kimono shop. If you venture inside and check the price tags, you will most likely find luxury items costing well into the hundreds of thousands of yen. In the courtyards of Buddhist temples on specific days in the month, however, there are piles of second-hand kimono and obi which have spilled out of women's overly full *tansu* (kimono closet) and into the second-hand market.

If the fancy takes you, and you know where to look, you will still hear the rhythmic clattering of power looms in the weaving district of Nishijin, though many are now silent. Scattered across Japan are myriads of craft workshops, still working against the odds, producing, dyeing, weaving, embroidering and sewing kimono. Although Japan as a society appears to be moving ever further away from the kimono, the industry soldiers on through the crisis, aided by its resilience and driven by the twin forces of hope and creativity.

This book has, hopefully, come close to taking you on the journey described above and presented you with images of crisis, transformation and change in the industry that produces one of the world's most iconic and recognisable forms of dress. The image is one of complexity: on the one hand, the kimono continues to enjoy its status as quintessential Japanese dress, the unparalleled ambassador of Japanese femininity, Japan's aesthetic sensibilities and traditional culture. In parallel, casualised ways of enjoying the kimono for both Japanese and non-Japanese people have become more widespread in recent years, as evidenced by the booming rental industry. Yet when it comes to sales of made-to-order kimono in traditional channels, the figures speak for themselves and decline is clear: from a market size of 1800 billion yen in 1981 (Donzé and Fujioka 2018: 258) to 260.5 billion yen in 2019, and an estimated 238 billion yen in 2020 (taking into account the projected effects of the Covid-19 pandemic), according to research conducted by the Yano Research Institute.[1]

This book has demonstrated that traditional industries are not simply the passive recipients of economic, social and cultural change and can prove to be surprisingly resilient – even adaptable. In an ever-changing landscape in which the next sale is never guaranteed, and with the meaning of traditional clothing called into question by the acceptability of Western clothes as formal wear, what do business owners in the kimono industry hope for? How do they mobilise creativity to adapt and stay in business? Within times of uncertainty and through the process of adapting, creating and hoping, what narratives of self and the 'right' way to do business emerge? In exploring these questions, this book has aimed to contribute to the way we think about crisis by looking at an area of society and cultural production that research on crisis has tended to ignore, and has aimed to draw together disparate strands of social theory and social thought on crisis, to show how crisis can produce generative and creative processes. In doing so, we can question not only the role of the 'traditional' in modern societies, but also the idea of crisis itself.

Questioning crisis

Crisis is often associated with abnormality and disjuncture, in particular with large-scale catastrophic events such as war, environmental disasters, revolution, financial breakdown or health pandemic. We speak of crises in multiple forms but their nature can vary tremendously in intensity and severity, depending on a multitude of social, political and economic factors. It is safe to say, however, that there is no such thing as a human life lived without the experience of crisis in some form, such as bereavement, illness, financial difficulty, loss or the experience of persecution, displacement or violence. Large-scale crises, such as an economic crisis, may also become deeply intertwined with personal crisis if it leads to job loss or financial insecurity, or the decline of an entire industry such as the kimono industry. We speak of individuals going through crisis when difficult and traumatic events occur.

While crises of various forms take place in every human life, we are also affected by a broader sense that society is in crisis. Nauja Kleist and Stef Jansen point to the way that information about political, economic and environmental crises is a constant presence in day-to-day life through television, the Internet and social media, a situation which can easily create a sense of permanent crisis: 'the production of anxiety through circulating images of crisis and uncertainty might thus be a self-fuelling process' (Kleist and Jansen 2016: 375). In the Japanese context this sense of crisis is particularly prevalent. As Iza Kavedžija notes, 'amid a faltering economic climate, Japanese people have witnessed a proliferation of narratives of decline and diminishing hope' (Kavedžija 2016: 1).

Beyond the normalisation of crisis narratives through mass media and social media in both Western cultural spheres and Japan, Kleist and Jansen note that 'surges and wanings of the register of hope should also be cast against the diminishing resonance of modernist metanarratives of progress that provided models for political intervention and social change for much of the twentieth century' (Kleist and Jansen 2016: 377). They identify that, by the 1970s, there was a disillusionment with the failures of the grand projects and ideologies of the 20th century. From then onwards, a distrust of political and economic systems, which repeatedly showed their weaknesses in various forms across the globe, has been emerging as the norm. We have, in other words, become used to the feeling that our societies are in crisis and it is not always easy to draw a hard and fast line between what counts as a society-wide crisis and a personal crisis on the scale of the individual.

In anthropological and sociological approaches to crisis, analyses tend to be split along thematic lines. Themes range from environmental crisis (Hamilton, Bonneuil, and Gemenne 2015), political crisis (Greenhouse, Mertz and Warren 2002), and studies of war, violence, displacement and migration (Kleist and Thorsen 2017). Explorations of economic crisis tend to be distinct from this body of literature, with a greater focus on the mechanisms through which economic collapse occurs (Knight and Stewart 2016: 3). Many empirical studies of economic crisis have taken place in the financial sector (Ho 2009 and Miyazaki 2013). However, a key aim of this book has been to provide an empirical investigation of the effects of crisis beyond financial centres and to focus on the ways in which economic crisis affects a traditional industry, including the examination of the narratives of hope and the processes of creativity that emerge as a result.

The objective was, firstly, to understand the place of a traditional industry in the capitalist market economy of Japan but also to highlight the effects, on the ground, that the financial collapse of the 1990s and the ensuing recession has had on the lives of people who make and sell the kimono. This approach weaves together the effects of economic crisis on the sustainability of the post-war model of kimono marketing and retail with an examination of how crisis in the industry has pushed retailers and producers to consider broader changes in the fabric of Japanese society, such as consumer priorities, shifting definitions of family and obligation, but also shifting definitions of fashion, lifestyle and self-expression. Within these changes, economic crisis pressures the producers and retailers of traditional culture to find different avenues and markets for their wares.

The purpose of this book has also been to demonstrate that while the nature of the kimono itself is currently in flux and its long-term future remains uncertain, in fact its modern history, and since the late 19th century in particular, has been one of constant change and adaptation, inextricably interwoven with broader social, cultural and economic changes. Placing the kimono, which carries immense symbolic and cultural weight in national discourse, firmly in the context of its creation and production, allows us to highlight how exactly economic conditions contribute towards the shaping of what we consider to be 'traditional Japanese culture'. The kimono, with its highly dense symbolic and cultural value, in particular its ability to convey an image of refined and essentially Japanese femininity, is often viewed as a purely cultural artefact, outside of time in terms of its aesthetics and fashion, not subject to either the whims of the market or to external factors such as socio-cultural change. This book argues that this is very much not the case: economic conditions have profoundly shaped the Japanese – and indeed, the world's – understanding of what a kimono is. The booming economy of the 1960s, 70s and 80s and the growth and establishment of a middle class encouraged the development of a kimono best suited to embody propriety and highly detailed aesthetic codes designed to show status and cultural capital. The kimono industry capitalised on this strategy, but the financial collapse of the 1990s and the subsequent recession pushed retailers to make radical changes in their business models. In parallel, social mores surrounding the acceptability of Western clothing for ritual events and ceremonies have increasingly distanced the average Japanese woman from the kimono. As a result, socio-cultural change, combined with a recession impacting Japanese spending habits, have severely decreased the overall sales of kimono but also compelled retailers to diversify the types of kimono available. The crisis has coincided with a growing acceptance across Japanese society of different kimono styles and types and an increasing tolerance for experimentation with kimono fashion. For retailers attuned to these changes, these changes have offered up venues for creative marketing and sourcing of goods, as well as new models for interacting with customers.

The two forms of crisis, society-wide and personal, were often intertwined in the case of my participants. The crisis of their business was also a personal crisis which affected their professional life, their sense of themselves in society and often the nature of their family life and the continuity of family business. Thus the wider crisis of the kimono industry was, for many, a personal crisis as well. The experience of crisis in their industry, especially the realisation that the formal kimono no longer sold well and was unlikely to help them support their families, pushed them to reflect on strategies to stay in business, pressuring them to find the different creative solutions outlined throughout this book. Crisis also brought to the fore a questioning of their roles as business owners, generating profound soul-searching and self-questioning: what is my role in society? What kind of retailer do I want to be? How should I change? How much do I want to change? Their economic pursuits were intimately linked with value, both in terms of the generation of profit but also their value in terms of their esteem for their profession and of themselves. My investigation of these narratives of self and economic life is aligned with the concern economic anthropology has with what, as Susana Narotzky and Niko Besnier put it, 'ordinary people understand by "a life worth living" and what they do to strive toward that goal, particularly under conditions of radical uncertainty' (Narotzky and Besnier 2014: S5). These 'conditions of radical uncertainty' raise interesting questions about the processes of change, accommodation and adaptation that people undergo in economically unfavourable times (Knight and Stewart 2016: 3). The ongoing wish to generate value, both financial and personal, and in the case of kimono producers and retailers, cultural value as well, becomes an arduous task under conditions of crisis.

Crisis and time, crisis over time

We tend to think of crisis as an event which possesses a particular temporality. Crisis, for most of us, represents a highly disruptive or damaging event, followed by a period of fallout from the event, and possibly, recovery. As Henrik Vigh puts it, 'We experience crisis when a traumatic event fragments the coherence or unity of our lives, which we otherwise take for granted, leaving us to reconfigure the pieces before we normalise our social being and once again go about our lives' (Vigh 2008: 7). The common understanding, then, is that crisis represents a momentary disjuncture with a clear 'before' and 'after' that disrupts the course of normal life. But in some cases, there may not be a clear event, the line between before and after is not clear, and there may be no recovery period afterwards.

Vigh argues that in many parts of the world, crisis is experienced not as a moment in time that violently rips apart the fabric of normality, but rather as a constant state of affairs: 'not a short-term explosive situation but a much more durable and persistent circumstance. Not a moment of decisive change but a condition' (Vigh 2008: 9). This understanding of crisis as a condition, 'crisis as context' as Vigh puts it (Vigh 2008: 9), is especially well-suited to analyses, both epistemological and empirical, of economic crisis. Economic crisis, as with the banking crisis of 2008, can take the shape of a sharp and violent disruption, but the fallout of economic crisis generally tends to be longer-lasting, leaving an enduring impact on people's ability to support themselves and their families, secure medical treatment and pursue life projects among many other things. Thus, crisis may take the shape of a condition, rather than a single event. In the introduction to a special issue of *History and Anthropology* dealing with crisis and austerity measures in Southern Europe, Daniel Knight and Charles Stewart point out this temporal dimension to economic crisis: while their interlocutors in Southern Europe live in times characterised by ongoing economic uncertainty, the relationship to the past becomes of increasing importance in narrating the present and negotiating the future (Knight and Stewart 2016).

Crisis, then, is a shape-shifting, time-eliding entity: in some cases a one-off event that causes individuals and groups to negotiate the past, pre- and post-crisis, and in other cases a continuous state of affairs. I would argue that any one crisis can take both forms: a moment of sharp, intense disruption but also a chronic state in which people are forced to adapt, over time, to a variety of unfavourable conditions that constrain their ability to lead their lives as they would choose. In the case of the kimono industry, crisis has taken both forms. The bursting of the economic bubble in the early 1990s caused wide-scale damage to wholesalers and retailers, with many businesses closing during this time. This event represents crisis in the way that we most typically understand it. But the effects of this crisis have continued well into the 21st century, producing a narrative of 'Japan-in-crisis' both in Japanese society and reflected in the scholarship about Japan.

The nature of protracted crises, as Kleist and Jansen argue, causes people caught up in them to reflect on and negotiate their relationship with time, both past and future, as they navigate a difficult present. For some in the kimono industry, the sharpness of the initial financial crisis brought bankruptcy, forcing them to close their businesses and lay off employees. For many this effectively spelled the end of the road. This was a very difficult time, especially for wholesalers (see Chapter 3). For others, in particular retailers, the crisis was a more protracted affair, with custom declining steadily over the years. In some cases, with some shops, it has been possible to stay afloat with a small number of loyal customers, or thanks to savings accumulated over the years and, possibly, a side business or separate source of income, but the decline of custom brings about fear and doubts for the future. If it is difficult now, won't it simply keep getting more difficult in the future? In particular with family-owned shops, there is a pressure to continue the family business at all costs because it is so deeply tied to family identity and family life. If the family business struggles, then difficult choices line up on the horizon, such as changing the family business or potentially closing it down. Protracted economic decline, combined with changing attitudes towards the relevance of formal silk kimono in Japan for ritual and ceremonial occasions, and the meaning of this kimono type within the family, have brought about a very particular type of crisis within the industry itself, which is not strictly speaking limited to economic factors alone. These changes are social, cultural and demographic.

Protracted crisis could be said to be psychologically quite insidious, placing pressure and worry on the shoulders of those affected by the crisis.

Relationships to time, both past and future, are thrown into focus, as Knight and Stewart also indicate was the case with their interlocutors in Southern Europe (Knight and Stewart 2016). In the kimono industry, while anxiety about the future was almost universal, with the exception of those with particularly optimistic views or those whose efforts had secured them long-term financial stability, members of the industry had ambiguous relationships with the past. Some members idealised the times when the formal kimono sold well and looked back with nostalgia to the post-war decades in which the kimono held great importance as a tool for women to represent their families and themselves in the best light and secure social status. These were times when selling kimono was much easier than it is now, and for some this represents a golden age in which sales were reliable and bonds with customers, if carefully negotiated and trust successfully obtained, ensured that retailer-customer relations could last for years, if not decades. In the case of some shops, such as the Gotō family business (see Chapter 1 and subsequent chapters), these relationships could span generations. It was a time in which many retailers could feel comfortable in their roles not just as salespeople but as the purveyors of expert knowledge.

Others, however, look back on these times less favourably. For some retailers, these decades represent a complacency that established the parameters of kimono retail too narrowly within the framework of formal, expensive kimono. They see it as a period of constraint in which innovation was not possible or, at least, not easily accepted. Almost every one of my participants had been pushed by the crisis in the kimono industry to reflect on the post-war past of the industry and what parameters had brought them to the current situation of falling sales and demand. This led to self-reflective narratives about the industry, its past and current state, and their current position within the industry. Some criticised the distribution system that favoured wholesalers and prevented cross-pollination and collaboration, while others claimed the problem lay with the industry's image, in particular the idea that kimono shops were forbidding places to enter and the concern felt by some customers that they might end up buying something that they didn't want or something that exceeded their budget.

For some, the position adopted was one of resilience – a determination to keep going and persevere against the odds. For others, the narrative was one of change – something had to give, and they would rather jump than be pushed. These attitudes could be combined, and at times my participants exhibited both traits. It is this aspect of crisis which has led to some strikingly creative results. We tend to think of crisis, unsurprisingly, as negative. This is because crisis has disruptive, damaging, even traumatic potential. This has also been the case in the kimono industry, but the process of disruption shattered common sense ideas of how the industry *should* be run, and shook to the core existing business relations and modes of retail that had previously appeared to be set in stone. In short, disruption brought about new potentialities. It is this sudden availability of possibilities or, to put it differently, the pressure to find alternatives and new markets, that led business owners such as Kenichi Nakamura (see Chapter 7) to develop a positive attitude towards crisis, even developing the mantra 'crisis is opportunity' (my translation). As he writes in his book, and as I have already quoted in Chapter 7, 'it's actually much worse to never go through a crisis at all' (Nakamura 2006: 142; my translation). Seemingly paradoxically, as a result of the crisis, some retailers began to develop a different, more optimistic relationship to the future. To a certain extent, those involved in the industry *have* to think about the future because the nature of economic activity is to plan ahead. The future was uncertain, but precisely because it was uncertain, it also offered hopeful, creative visions of a different way to do business.

Crisis, hope and creativity

Hope is, in many ways, the counterpart to crisis, and it is perhaps no surprise that just as studies of crisis in the social sciences have become increasingly common, so too have studies of hope (Webb 2016 (2007): 66, Kleist and Jansen 2016). Lorena Gibson traces the origins of studies on hope to the early 1990s, 'when the entrenchment of global capitalism and neoliberalism (which, it should be noted, was viewed by many as a project of hope) following the collapse of the Soviet Union led to a worldwide shrinking of hopes for political and economic alternatives, and a corresponding crisis of confidence in theories of social and political transformation' (Gibson 2019: 577). Hirokazu Miyazaki further underscores that studies in hope increased with neoliberalism and its associated penetration of the market into multiple spheres in life (Miyazaki and Swedberg 2017: 5–6). Because crisis shakes up the status quo and produces situations of uncertainty, but also possibility, it can also draw on human capacities for hope. Exploring hope allows us as social scientists, as Gibson puts it, to investigate 'how people experience the spaces between probability and possibility' (Gibson 2019: 574).

As a voice adding to these reflections on hope and the ability to hope in times of uncertainty, I argue that it is important to understand the crisis, not just in the kimono industry itself, namely the effects of the recession in the 1990s and the socio-cultural and economic changes that damaged sales of formal kimono but, beyond that, which retailers have *reacted* to the crisis and the creative ways in which they envisage a better future. Crisis has indeed claimed its victims in the industry and continues to do so. But for those who are still in business, the fundamental job remains the same: keep selling kimono. And because conditions are more adverse and previous forms of marketing and salesmanship are no longer successful, crisis is breeding two things in those who remain: resilience, in other words the willingness and disposition to endure, keep going and adapt to unfavourable conditions. But also creativity: the ability to alter existing forms of retail, stimulate or create new markets. Inspired by Victor Turner, Renato Rosaldo, Smadar Lavie and Kirin

Narayan 'define creativity as human activities that transform existing cultural practices in a manner that a community or certain of its members find of value' (Rosaldo, Lavie and Narayan 1993: 5). This is exactly what some members of the kimono industry have undertaken under conditions of crisis: a transformation of the kimono that can be of value to new and different customers.

Because a present characterised by crisis is filled with challenges, the future represents both a source of anxiety ('what if the situation stays the same or gets worse?') but also a source of hope ('things might get better'). As Kleist and Jansen write, 'uncertainty and precariousness, namely, can be read by the social actors in them and by analysts both as disorienting and as full of potential' (Kleist and Jansen 2016: 388). The potential to be creative and different comes from the removal of normality and the status quo: 'crisis contrasts with forms of stability that enable the design of projects and that support the trust that existing configurations will enable the realization of those projects. Against this idea of normality, crisis signals a rupture that emerges as a menace at the same time that it forces ingenuity and creativity' (Narotzky and Besnier 2014: S7). The idea of forced creativity is important here. In much the same way as 'crisis' evokes negative associations, 'hope' and 'creativity' evoke positive associations. Kleist and Jansen warn against a tendency in the social sciences to 'speak unquestioningly positively of hope and indeterminacy as vibrant, if ill-defined, sources of potential for the future' (Kleist and Jansen 2016: 372). This is especially the case when people may have no choice other than to be creative: the pressures imposed upon them by crisis bring to the fore resilience and resourcefulness.

People in the kimono industry had, in a sense, little choice other than to be creative, but for some this was embraced as a real opportunity to be different. Crisis facilitated difference because established power dynamics, particularly those that favoured wholesalers and secured their hold over the rest of the industry, had been destabilised. In an already unstable situation, the penalties for standing out from a conservative industry, and trying something different and something new, were also diminished. Practical obstacles, such as pre-existing business relationships between certain wholesalers, retailers and producers that could preclude new business deals, were shaken, and in some cases removed, making the entire chain of distribution more fluid than it had been before. It became easier for independent craftspeople to establish themselves and find channels of distribution by working directly with retailers and bypassing wholesalers. It also became easier for retailers to sell items that were no longer entirely governed by the aesthetics of formal kimono and to experiment with different types of aesthetics to see what their customers would like. In this way, the disruptions caused by the crisis removed barriers, enabling a greater diversity of kimono types and also a greater variety of ways for customers to obtain kimono.

Jenny Hall's recently published book, *Japan beyond the Kimono: Innovation and Tradition in the Kyoto Textile Industry*, showcases a wealth of case studies of craft workshops, entrepreneurs and retailers in Kyoto who are using kimono-related techniques and craft to make products that are not kimono or obi (Hall 2020). Others, such as wholesaler-turned producer-turned second-hand retailer Kenichi Nakamura (Chapter 7), shifted their business model from made-to-order kimono to second-hand kimono. The Gotō family, on a smaller scale, also moved their main business away from bespoke kimono and towards second-hand retail.

For others, the process of altering their business model was a profoundly transformational experience that shifted their sense of self and their role in the industry. The owner of Azumaya, Yoshihide Shibakawa (Chapters 5 and 6), and Tetsuya Ueda who runs a business making and selling fashion-oriented kimono (Chapter 6) saw the destabilisation of the industry after the economic crisis of the 1990s as an opportunity for change and a chance to redesign their business according to their own values. As Ueda-san recalled (see Chapter 6), this involved a time of reflection for him in which he set aside the question of making profit, and really focused instead on what customers wanted. For him and other members of the kimono fashion network, this meant closing the gap that they perceived existed between the members of the industry and their customers, and it involved changing their relationship to the kimono. For quite a few members of the network, this meant growing to like the kimono more than they had before and integrating it much more closely into their own lives. More than one retailer recalled being challenged on not wearing the kimono, which led to a period of reflection on what the garment meant in their own lives. Especially for male retailers, the reintroduction of the kimono into day-to-day life is an especially strong statement, as the kimono is still to this day associated with women. The decision to wear the kimono often, or even every day, enabled male retailers to unequivocally demonstrate their passion for the kimono. This act also encourages other men to become interested in the kimono as fashion, and places male retailers who choose this option as fashion icons for other men. In the circles I mixed with, especially with the kimono fashion networks, men wearing kimono were particularly well-viewed by women, who would often praise men wearing the kimono as *kakkoii* ('cool'). Many participants in the community would speak of the kimono for men as being more aptly suited to a Japanese physique, and therefore more flattering than Western clothes.

Showing passion for the kimono has proven to be a much-needed trait with a new target market of customers who relate to the kimono as fashion rather than just as clothing for ceremonies or rituals. In other words, the retailers began to demonstrate to their customers that the kimono was more than just a product to sell, and that they were personally invested in the kimono as a fashion and as a lifestyle. The use of Internet and social media in the mid-2000s was a key moment for business owners with new ideas about how and what to sell, to find each other, but also to relate to customers more closely than before, when these tools had not been available. In this way, the crisis followed by the introduction of social media and social networks enabled a new form of sociality to emerge between retailers but also between retailers and customers. The emergence of this sociality, particularly among members of the kimono fashion network, has generated a feeling of solidarity, togetherness and hopefulness about the future of the business and the kimono itself, firmly located within the ideal of kimono as fashion and self-expression.

Hope and creativity, it should be said, are not evenly distributed, which raises interesting questions about why hope and creativity manifest in some members of the industry and not others. This is not an easy question to answer, and to me the answer seems to lie in individual and sub-group responses to the crisis. Some retailers, for instance, have changed little about their business methods and accept the idea that eventually they will no longer be in business. They embrace the idea that they will continue for as long as they can and not beyond. Others, on the other hand, have radically changed their business and, indeed, themselves. Hope, and the ability to hope, is conditioned by a number of factors, including macro-level financial and economic factors and political (in)stability, but also micro-level factors relating to the individual. Hope, then, cannot be said to be equally distributed, and the ability to hope is conditioned. Within the kimono industry, hope and creativity appeared to vary on an individual basis, perhaps linked to the level of entrepreneurial ambition that the business owner possesses, their willingness to take risks and design projects for the future. Hirokazu Miyazaki notes that 'hope suggests a willingness to embrace uncertainty and also serves as a concrete method for keeping knowledge moving in conditions of uncertainty' (Miyazaki and Swedberg 2017: 8). Acceptance of uncertainty certainly seems to be a condition for hope and creativity in the kimono industry but the question remains of why the ability to hope for different futures and enact change varies so much. This might be due to the nature of hope itself and the different ways that it manifests in individuals. As Darren Webb notes, 'a clear and consistent grasp of what it is to hope will always elude us' (Webb 2016 [2007]: 80). Further, 'our hopes may be active or passive, patient or critical, private or collective, grounded in the evidence or resolute in spite of it, socially conservative or socially transformative' (Webb 2016 [2007]: 80). This variety in types of hope, and, of course, the variation between individuals, to some extent explains the difference in hope between retailers. This also goes some way to explaining the discrepancies in ability to externalise that hope into new forms of retail that in turn transform the nature of kimono culture and re-frame the 'traditional'.

Studies of hope raise philosophical questions around what hope is but also around the origins of hope and creativity. In paying close attention to where hope originates, the easy answer would be to point to the agency of the retailers and other members of the industry, in other words their ability to act. But this, to me, only answers part of the question. I was invariably struck by the depth and complexity of the narratives of crisis and hope that my participants had created. For some, these were relatively private musings that they shared with me. These were nonetheless intricately complex observations about the limitative structure of the industry prior to the crisis of the 1990s, as well as reflections on stagnating markets, changing customer demands and rapidly shifting demographics. For others, these were reflections to be broadcast to a wide audience and shared with the world, such as Kenichi Nakamura, who disseminated his reflections in print form, and Yoshihide Shibakawa, who uses live-streaming as a platform to showcase goods and other retailers and designers, but also as a means to connect with other people and share his views on the industry. While communicating in this way does necessary profile-raising work for businesses, I was struck by the prevalence of these narratives about both the place of the kimono industry in Japan today and its future, and the ways in which business owners used platforms to broadcast ideas of change, hope and creativity. This suggests a highly self-reflective process in which retailers continually re-evaluate their role as kimono providers in a society in which demand for the traditional is decreasing. As a result, their role is by necessity bigger than simply selling to keep their business going – they are in dialogue with something larger than themselves, namely the ebb and flow of what the role of the 'traditional' is in Japanese society.

A fit for the future? The role of the kimono in 21st century Japan

Business owners in the kimono industry have increasingly been confronted with the idea that the very meaning of their work is called into question. In the post-war years and up until the end of the 20th century, the role of the kimono was very clear: it was, firstly, a way to represent status, wealth and cultural capital within the family. Secondly, it was intended to be a family heirloom, passed between women in the family to encode and perpetuate female family history. Finally, it was to act as an ambassador, conveying a globally understood message of quintessentially Japanese aesthetics and femininity. Of these three factors, only the latter remains unshaken by the economic crisis and changing domestic attitudes towards the kimono. Changing familial norms linked to what is often described as a crisis of the family in Japan, such as the increasing nuclearisation of the family and isolation of the individual, have had an effect on the importance attached to wearing a kimono for key life events such as attending weddings or graduation ceremonies. This does not mean that the kimono no longer effectively conveys social status and an understanding of kimono-related aesthetics and cultural codes, but that the importance of wearing the kimono in order to demonstrate status and cultural capital is no longer as highly prized as it used to be.

Because the kimono is such a powerful representative of Japanese culture and Japanese womanhood, business owners are called upon to reflect on their role as the providers of this very particular item in the canon of Japanese 'tradition'. They are called upon to reflect on their role especially as the function of the kimono in Japan itself is changing, and old models of business suited to a booming post-war economy and a middle class with disposable income are no longer reliable. The striking theme in the many narratives that I heard in Japan among kimono business owners was this awareness of a change in the meaning of the kimono itself in Japanese society. For others, this crisis was the first step in the change towards providing a kimono that could mean something other than women's formal wear for ceremonial occasions – not so much erasing or replacing this function as providing alternatives to it, alternatives that could grow new markets and stimulate kimono sales.

The effect of the crisis on the kimono industry itself has of course meant a decline in sales but it has also brought about a greater diversity in types of kimono available, and generated a corresponding diversity in markets, with the appearance of customers who buy the kimono as part of a fashion lifestyle rather than for formal or ceremonial occasions. The emergence of male customers in this lifestyle is especially interesting and a relatively recent phenomenon. With male kimono shop owners such as Yoshihide Shibakawa (see Chapter 5) and business owners such as Tetsuya Ueda (see Chapter 6) or Kenichi Nakamura (see Chapter 7) actively promoting the kimono by wearing it themselves, the interest of male customers in it has grown. Shops and kimono-related services such as *kitsuke* (kimono dressing) catering specifically to men have become increasingly visible in recent years, suggesting an uptick in interest on the part of men. In addition to the outreach efforts of business owners in the industry, this interest is also possibly partially supported by the popularity of the summer '*yukata*' for both women and men (especially younger generations), as well as the generally positive portrayal of kimono-clad men in media and films.

The loosening of rules around how to wear the kimono has led to increasing sartorial experimentation, with wearers combining Western clothes and kimono, and others mixing womenswear and menswear. The kimono has inspired fashion designers across the world but in terms of its usage in Japan the general pattern appears to be towards a decline in wear. However, within this decline, a diversification has emerged, and with each stylistic innovation a new meaning of wearing traditional clothing is being forged. While the formal kimono remains associated with older women, younger age groups are experimenting with different fashions and styles. Bold statements of taste and individuality are now increasingly made through the kimono, enabled by business owners who were able to read trends and shifts in an increasingly individuated consumer market. The crisis of the 1990s, the ensuing recession and Japan's 'separation from the kimono' set the scene for both the creative adaptation to and stimulation of new markets, as well as a more diverse range of entrepreneurial activities enabled by the disruption of the pre-existing chain of distribution. These are the important insights gained when we locate 'traditional' culture within the parameters of its production and distribution and pay careful attention to the economic parameters that define its creation.

Kimono retail and consumption are increasingly characterised by change, diversification and catering to a market of individuals. Within these shifts, business owners are exploring creative avenues to ensure that they survive the crisis facing their industry, which in turn affects the possibilities for new kinds of kimono culture in Japan. The future, however, remains uncertain. While crisis has damaged the industry, it has also provided a space for hope and creativity. Crisis is characterised by a high potential for change. The future promises that there will continue to be kimono for many years to come, but also that the meaning of the kimono in Japan, and across the globe, will continue to evolve in conjunction with economic, social and cultural change.

Note

1 From research conducted by the Yano Research Institute, available here: www.yanoresearch.com/en/press-release/show/press_id/2441 (accessed 25/09/2020).

References

Donzé, P.-Y. and Fujioka, R., eds. 2018. *Global Luxury: Organizational Change and Emerging Markets Since the 1970s*. Basingstoke: Palgrave Macmillan

Gibson, L. 2019. 'Anthropology as respair: anthropological engagements with hope and its others'. In *Anthropological Quarterly* 92(2): 575–585

Greenhouse, C. J., Mertz, E. and Warren, K.B. 2002. *Ethnography in Unstable Places: Everyday Lives in Contexts of Dramatic Political Change*. Durham, NC and London: Duke University Press

Hall, J. 2020. *Japan Beyond the Kimono: Innovation and Tradition in the Kyoto Textile Industry*. London and New York: Bloomsbury Visual Arts

Hamilton, C., Bonneuil, C. and Gemenne, F. 2015. *The Anthropocene and the Global Environmental Crisis: Rethinking Modernity in a New Epoch*. London: Routledge

Ho, K. Z. 2009. *Liquidated: an Ethnography of Wall Street*. Durham, NC and London: Duke University Press

Kavedžija, I. 2016. 'Introduction: reorienting hopes'. In *Contemporary Japan* 28(1): 1–11

Kleist, N. and Jansen, S. 2016. 'Introduction: hope over time—crisis, immobility and future-making'. In *History and Anthropology* 27(4): 373–392

Kleist, N. and Thorsen, D. 2017. *Hope and Uncertainty in Contemporary African Migration*. London: Routledge

Knight, D. M. and Stewart, C. 2016. 'Ethnographies of austerity: temporality, crisis and affect in Southern Europe'. In *History and Anthropology* 27(1): 1–18

Miyazaki, H. 2013. *Arbitraging Japan: Dreams of Capitalism at the End of Finance*. Berkeley, CA: University of California Press.

Miyazaki, H. and Swedberg, R. 2017. *The Economy of Hope*. Philadelphia, PA: University of Pennsylvania Press

Nakamura, K. 2006. *Tansu-ya de Gozaru* ('Tansu-ya at your Service'; my translation of the title). Tokyo: Shōgyōkai

Narotzky, S. and Besnier, N. 2014. 'Crisis, value, and hope: rethinking the economy: an introduction to supplement 9'. In *Current Anthropology* 55(S9): S4–S16

Rosaldo, R., Lavie, S., and Narayan, K. 1993. *Creativity/Anthropology*. Ithaca, NY: Cornell University Press

Vigh, H. 2008. 'Crisis and chronicity: anthropological perspectives on continuous conflict and decline'. In *Ethnos* 73(1): 5–24

Webb, D. 2016 (2007). 'Modes of hoping'. In *History of the Human Sciences*. 20(3): 65–83

Glossary of Japanese terms

Ansanburu	from the French 'ensemble', meaning a matching kimono and *haori*
Anshin	reassurance, relief, peace of mind
Awase	lined kimono
Benkyō-dai	a fee for a lesson
Dekora	a subcultural fashion which involves using as many brightly coloured accessories, clothes and stickers as possible
Dentō	tradition
Dentō kōgeishi	masters of traditional craft
Fudangi	ordinary, everyday clothing
Fukuro-obi	a formal obi type, often made using brocade
Furisode	'swinging sleeve' kimono; a kimono with long sleeves, usually worn by young and/or unmarried women
Furugi	old clothes, second-hand clothes
Furusato	place or town of origin; sometimes used metaphorically
Gofukuya or gofukuten	kimono shop
Hakama	pleated trousers with a stiff board at the back; historically worn by men, but worn by women for certain sports and graduation ceremonies
Hanao	the band or strap on the *zori* shoes that goes between the toes
Haneri	a plain or decorative piece of cloth sewn over the collar of the underkimono
Hanhaba	an obi which is half the width of the standard obi; usually worn for casual occasions and with the summer yukata
Haori	a kimono overcoat (can be short or long)
Hiragana	Japanese syllabary
Hitoe	unlined kimono

Hōmongi	a formal kimono often worn to attend events such as weddings or graduation ceremonies
Gyōkai	industry or business
Ie	a word meaning 'family' but also 'household' – this word also refers to the traditional Japanese household system
Izakaya	Japanese-style pub or bar
Irotomesode	a very formal kimono, a colour version of the *kurotomesode*
Jūsan-mairi	a ceremonial visit to a Shintō shrine for children aged 13
Kaga Yūzen	a traditional style of kimono-making in and around Kanazawa (see Chapter 3)
Kanji	Chinese characters
Katakana	Japanese syllabary (often used for foreign loanwords)
Kimono	literally 'things to wear': a word that has come to describe the dominant form of Japanese dress that emerged in the 20th century based on the pre-existing *kosode*
Kimono-banare	'separation from the kimono': a phrase describing the way in which the kimono has become unfamiliar to most Japanese people
Kimono de Jack (KdJ)	an informal group of kimono aficionados who gather in different locations and 'highjack' them by wearing kimono. There are multiple chapters throughout Japan
Kimono keisatsu	literally 'kimono police': people who correct someone wearing a kimono or say something about a kimono outfit
Kinarete iru	to be 'used to wearing' (something)
Kitsuke	the act of putting on a kimono and, in some circumstances, the body of knowledge about how to put on and wear a kimono
Kōdineto (kōde)	from the English 'coordinate': meaning a coordinated outfit in which all the elements have been thought through
Kōgei	craft or artisanat
Kojinshugi	individualism
Komon	an informal kimono, often with a pattern all over the kimono
Kosei	individuality, sometimes distinctiveness
Koshihimo	thin ties used at multiple points in the process of putting on a kimono (usually between three and five are used, depending on the style)

Glossary of Japanese terms 175

Kowaii	scary
Kurotomesode	a black kimono with an elaborate pattern on the lower half, usually worn by the mother of the bride or groom at a wedding
Kosode	literally 'short sleeves': a garment which is the ancestor of the modern kimono
Laifu	from the English 'life'
Maeita	a piece of stiff plastic or card wrapped around the waist that helps the obi sit comfortably
Maniakku	obsessive (especially of interests, hobbies or passions)
Nagajuban	underkimono
Nagoya-obi	an obi with a characteristic pre-folded and stitched section
Nakama	friend or ally
Natsukashii	feelings of nostalgia, reminiscent of something in the past (often positive)
Netsuke	decorations that can be slipped into the obi
Noren	a divided curtain hung in doorways (common with certain businesses)
Obi	the sash worn around the kimono: comes in a variety of styles and multiple tying methods are possible
Obiage	a small sash that usually covers the *obimakura* (a padded cushion used to create the most common form of obi tie, known as *otaikomusubi*)
Obidome	a decorative piece for the *obijime*
Obijime	a tie used to keep the obi in place with many styles of obi tying
Obimakura	a padded cushion used to create one of the most common forms of obi tie, known as *otaiko-musubi*
Ohashori	fabric folded at the waist underneath the obi (women only – women's kimono are purposely tailored longer than the woman's actual height to create this fold)
Oishii	tasty
Okami-san	the female manager of a kimono shop, or the mother/wife of the male owner. The word is also used in other traditional establishments, like *ryokan*
Okeiko	a lesson
Omiyamairi	the first visit of a newborn to a Shintō shrine
Oshare	to have style, be stylish or be dressed up
Ōshima tsumugi	a complex weaving kimono-making technique using pre-dyed threads. The technique is

	associated with the Amami Islands and Kagoshima
Otaiko-musubi	a very common method of tying an obi: it enables the pattern of the obi to be displayed aesthetically
Oyagokoro	literally, 'parents' heart': the sense of love and obligation parents feel towards their child
Oyomeiri-dōgu	literally, 'items for brides': a bridal trousseau
Reisō	formal wear
Ryokan	a traditional Japanese inn
Ryōsai kenbo	an influential Meiji period (1868–1912) adage meaning 'good wife, wise mother'
Sanchidonya	a regional wholesaler
Seikatsu	life, livelihood or lifestyle
Shakaijin	a full, adult, responsible member of society
Shakkanhō	traditional system of measurement
Shibori	tie-dye
Shichi-go-san	'seven-five-three': a festival for three- and seven-year-old girls and five-year-old boys
Shikohin	non-essential or luxury item
Shinise	an established, old shop
Shinjinrui	a term meaning 'new breed', used to describe the generation growing up in the 1970s. The term evokes the alien nature of this generation's priorities and consumer habits
Shūkatsu	'end of life' activities (such as putting a house in order)
Tabi	kimono socks, splitting the big toe from the other toes, worn with *zori*
Tanmono	a bolt of kimono cloth
Tansu	traditional Japanese furniture, often used for kimono; a kimono chest
Tatami	traditional Japanese flooring made of rushes and straw
Tonya	wholesaler
TPO	Japan-made English acronym: Time, Place and Occasion
Tsukesage	a slightly plainer version of the *hōmongi* kimono
Ubugi	a type of kimono draped over a baby when the baby is first presented to a Shintō shrine (see *omiyamairi*)
Wafuku	a category word meaning 'Japanese clothing'
Wassai	a method of sewing for Japanese clothes
Yakuza	a term referring to organised crime groups
Yōfuku	Western-style clothing

Yosoiki	formal wear
Yukata	a light kimono-like garment. Some types are worn in the summer (especially during summer festivals), and others traditionally worn after bathing
Yuki tsumugi	an elaborate weaving kimono-making technique associated with Ibaraki prefecture
Zoku	tribe
Zori	shoes that resemble flip-flops in structure, but are ornate and decorated

Index

Accessories 23–25, 95–96, 100–101
Adaptability 8, 108
Aesthetics 34, 123, 132, 139, 142–146, 149–150, 155; Aestheticisation of modern life 127
Age 25, 27–28, 60, 64, 145
Authenticity 41, 58, 82–83, 96, 108
Azumaya 4–5, 16–18, 23, 30, 70, 74, 82, 88–109, 112–114, 124, 150, 152–153, 167 *see also* Shibakawa, Yoshihide

Body 22–25, 27–28, 30–32; Body techniques 17, 32
Bourdieu, Pierre 25, 55, 93, 117, 129, 142
Bridal trousseau 9, 15, 18, 22, 61–66, 84, 135, 139–140
Business model 32, 61, 77, 94, 108, 138–139, 150–151, 154–155, 167

Class 33, 38, 57, 60, 68, 117, 123; Edo period (1603–1868) social classes 28, 56; Merchant class 28, 37–38; Middle class 15, 28, 31, 40, 55, 57, 63, 67, 74, 110, 122, 139, 142, 161, 170
Clothing 27; Anthropology of 12–13; As communication 27–28; As embodied practice 25–27; And identity 13; Industry 12; Notion of traditional clothing 7–8, 128
Coming of age 35, 41, 56, 64, 66, 77, 84, 128, 158
Consumption 11, 13, 15, 33, 40, 54, 66–67, 73, 103–105, 107–109, 120–127, 130–132, 142–143
Cotton 5, 18, 54, 57–58, 91, 97–99, 112; Industry of 36, 97–99
Craft 37, 42–44, 76–77, 99, 147–148, 150–152, 154, 156, 167; Definition of 40–41; Global craft markets 13; Miyazaki Yūzen 48; Techniques 2, 33, 48–49, 53, 58
Craftspeople 8–9, 18, 36–37, 41–44, 50, 52–53, 70, 76–77, 84, 95, 99, 146–156
Creativity 8, 11, 12, 18, 19, 33, 45, 75, 76, 77, 78, 84, 85, 94, 98, 100, 110, 121, 122, 137, 139, 148, 150, 154, 158–171
Crisis 10, 75, 85, 123–124; 1990s financial crisis in Japan 8–10, 12, 18, 43–45, 64, 66, 70, 73–76, 90, 99, 113, 115, 125, 137, 151, 163, 165, 167, 170; And creativity 85, 94, 108, 137, 159, 165–166; Definitions of 10–11, 159–163; And hope 11–12, 165–166, 171; In the kimono industry 4, 6–7, 12, 18, 85, 131–132, 137, 151, 158, 164–166; As opportunity 75, 115–116, 120–121, 138, 146, 151, 165–167, 170–171; Narratives of 6, 9–10, 74, 159–160, 168–169; And resilience 78, 85, 165–166 *see also* resilience

Dalby, Liza 8–9, 28, 34–35, 39, 55–56
Dentō kōgeishi ('masters of traditional craft') 2, 53
Department stores 30, 37, 40, 70, 79
Distribution system 12, 42–44, 152, 164

Family business 42, 76–78, 95, 116, 136, 139, 147–148, 161, 163–164
Fashion 7, 13, 16, 18, 92, 94, 97, 109, 111–112, 116–117, 128, 131, 142, 161, 167–168; Edo period (1603–1868) trends 37–38; Fast fashion 59; Influence of Western fashion 12;

Lolita fashion 144; Slow fashion 108; Subcultural fashions 144
Francks, Penelope 7, 37–38, 63, 66, 73, 108, 122, 142
Furisode ('swinging sleeve' kimono) 35, 41, 59, 66, 77, 84, 119, 158

Geisha 7
Gender 27–28, 29, 35, 127, 145, 155; Femininity 6, 34–35, 56–57, 79, 155
Giddens, Anthony 101, 126–127
Goldstein-Gidoni, Ofra 9, 34–35
Gotō family 1–6, 16, 42, 75, 77, 141, 164, 167

Habitus 25–26, 93–94
Hakama 58, 102, 108, 155
Hall, Jenny 38, 102, 108, 151, 153–154, 166–167
Hōmongi 39, 50, 58–59, 97, 137
Hope 8, 10–12, 159–160, 165–166, 168–169; *Kibō kakusa shakai* ('hope/ expectation differential society') – Masahiro Yamada 10
Housewife 15, 65–66, 69, 113; Ideal of 65, 145

Identity 13, 28, 41, 78, 91, 105–106, 121, 123, 125–127, 131, 163
Ie (household) 64–65, 78, 137–138

Japaneseness 34–35, 56, 121

Kaga Yūzen 48–54, 57, 58, 67, 77, 96, 129, 147
Kanamaru family 49–53, 75, 77
Kikuchi, Ima 83–84, 96, 106, 112, 118–119, 135
Kimono: Academies 32, 59, 78; Accessories 4, 23–24, 96; As communication 28; Declining sales of 7, 9, 44, 73, 94, 159; As an expression of Japanese aesthetics 6, 34–35, 56–57, 67, 79, 169; As fashion 7, 16, 18, 23, 39, 92, 94–97, 103–104, 106–107, 109, 111–113, 116–117, 119–120, 123, 125–126, 130, 132, 136–137, 144, 152, 170; Formalisation of 6, 17, 39–40, 59, 128; Gender differences in tailoring and wear 29–30; Historical transformation of 28–29; As lifestyle 6, 16, 18, 22, 88, 90, 94–96, 106, 111–118, 123, 126–130, 132; Mutability of 30; Peak sales of 9, 58, 65, 159, 161; Prices of 30, 44, 52, 79, 81–82, 84, 97–98, 137, 141–142; Seasonal rules 33; 'Sleeping' 6, 138–140; Tailoring 2, 24, 30; Types of 33, 58–59, 97; *Wassai* (Japanese sewing) 80, 97–98; Wearing skill 4, 22–23
Kimono de Jack 4–6, 88–89, 113, 126, 130, 159
Kimono Fashion Network 117, 120–122, 124–126, 128–130, 136, 143–144, 152, 155, 167–168
Kitsuke (kimono dressing) 22, 59, 62, 65, 77–78, 80, 102, 170
Kosode 28–30
Kurotomesode 51, 58, 97

Lifestyle 7, 39, 94, 108–109, 125–131, 142
Linen 36, 54, 58, 63, 98
Luxury 31–32, 34, 36–37, 40, 43, 53–57
Irotomesode 58–59

Maffesoli, Michel 145
Magazines 32, 143, 155
Marketing 16, 19, 40, 43, 54, 58, 82, 94, 96, 117, 142, 148, 154, 160–161, 165
Meisen 38–39, 57
METI (Ministry of Economy, Trade and Industry) 2, 16–17, 58, 79, 84
Milhaupt, Terry Satsuki 28, 30, 36–37, 39–40, 54, 80, 108, 143
Miyazaki, Hirokazu 168
Miyazaki, Yūzen 48

Nakamura, Kenichi 6, 56, 84, 136–141, 143, 145, 151, 165 *see also* Tansu-ya
Nihonjinron 121
Nishijin 9, 37, 72, 151, 158

Polyester 58, 80, 83, 129, 138

Obi 1, 4, 6, 15, 23–27, 30, 62, 66, 72, 78, 148–150, 152; Coordination with kimono 2, 60; Different types of 9, 33, 45, 52, 58–59; *Hanhaba* obi 102, 128–129; Prices of 61; Styling and accessories 23, 96
Ōshima 81–82, 92, 96, 113–114, 145, 153

Oyagokoro (literally 'parent's heart'- parental obligation) 64, 140
Oyomeiri-dōgu 63 *see also* bridal trousseau

Resilience 8, 11–12, 73, 77–78, 85, 158, 164–166; Definitions of 75–76
Ritual 6, 8–9, 17, 35, 84, 161, 163; Expertise in 60–61; Role of women in 55–57, 78, 143

Samurai 28, 38, 56
Seasonality 33 *see also* kimono, seasonal types
Second-hand 1, 3, 13, 56, 77, 82, 84, 135–146, 155, 158, 167; Price of second-hand kimono 141–142, 145
Seken 34
Self-expression 16, 27, 109, 123–128, 137, 161, 168
Sewing 1, 8, 35–37, 52, 79, 102, 142, 159 *see also wassai*; Sewing machines 39, 54
Shibakawa, Yoshihide 5, 16, 18, 74, 88–109, 111–117, 121, 124–125, 129
Shintoism 8
Shopping 77, 79, 80, 105–106, 108–109, 141–142, 145–146
Silk 2–7, 9, 13, 18, 24, 39, 41, 71, 80, 83; Silk and craft 37; Silk and bridal trousseau 65; Silk kimono, luxury and wealth 31–32, 38, 53–57, 64, 67
Social media 16, 97, 102–103, 113, 116–117, 126, 132, 143, 160, 167–168; Facebook 102, 117; Instagram 2, 102, 117

Tabi (kimono socks) 4–5, 24, 96
Tanmono (bolt of cloth) 2, 30, 80–81
Tansu 2, 22, 39, 63–65, 139, 158; Definition of 63
Tansu-ya 6, 56, 84, 135–139, 145 *see also* Nakamura, Kenichi
Tea ceremony 8, 62, 65, 78–80, 82, 128
Textile 38, 78, 99, 113, 151, 154; Textile mixes 98
Tonya 9, 44, 114–116 *see also* wholesaler
TPO (Time, Place, Occasion) 32–33, 57, 59, 102–103
Tradition 7–8, 35; Traditional arts 62, 65–66, 78
Tsukesage 58–59

Ueda, Tetsuya 81, 113–116, 121, 124, 129, 153, 167, 170

Vintage 139, 142–145

Wafuku 154–155
Westernisation 8, 29, 54–55
Wholesaler 8, 12, 16, 18, 42–44, 52, 70–76, 84–85, 95, 99, 115–116, 148, 151–156, 163–164, 166 *see also tonya*
Wool 39, 54, 57–58, 98; Introduction of 36

Yōfuku 154–155
Yukata 33, 72, 88, 106, 129, 158, 170

Zori 5, 24, 52, 70, 96, 100–101, 129, 155